The Russian Symbolists

An Anthology of Critical and Theoretical Writings

Edited and Translated by
Ronald E. Peterson

Ardis, Ann Arbor

Copyright © 1986 by Ardis Publishers
All rights reserved under International and Pan-American
Copyright Conventions.
Printed in the United States of America

Translated from the original Russian

Ardis Publishers
2901 Heatherway
Ann Arbor, Michigan 48104

Library of Congress Cataloging in Publication Data

Main entry under title:

The Russian symbolists.

Bibliography: p.
1. Russian poetry—20th century—History and
criticism—Addresses, essays, lectures. 2. Symbolism
(Literary movement)—Soviet Union—Addresses, essays,
lectures. 3. Russian poetry—Theory, etc.—Addresses,
essays, lectures. I. Peterson, Ronald E. II. Title.
PG3065.S8R87 1986   891.7'09'15   86-1105
ISBN 0-88233-796-3 (alk. paper)

46187

CONTENTS

PREFACE

This book attempts to fill a gap in scholarship about Russian literature by offering a collection of statements by Russian Symbolists about Symbolism. The essays selected are generally the best known and most representative pieces by these authors on the topic of symbolism; in some cases, the essays are also the best produced by individual authors, but they were all chosen because they deal in some way with Symbolism. The editorial statements from four journals that follow the essays provide general views about Symbolism, as formulated by different groups and under differing circumstances.

Unlike other literary and critical movements in Russia, and later the Soviet Union, Russian Symbolism has no official platform or manifesto. Many scholars have tried to sum up the essence of the Symbolists' theoretical and philosophical views, to state what Symbolism is in twenty-five words or less, but the generalizations offered thus far, however neat and harmonious they may seem, have not entirely grasped the complexity of the task.

Because there were not only different authors espousing individual views, but also because some of the authors' views changed in the course of the two and a half decades of what can be called Symbolism's existence, the arrangement of the essays and the introduction to them emphasize chronology. The original versions of the essays were chosen instead of possible later revisions; the purpose of this choice was to show the authors' initial feelings and thoughts because these fresher impressions were what the other authors saw, and responded to, at the time.

The Introduction tries to place the essays in the context of Russian Symbolism, to help fit the various pieces together; it cannot serve as a history of this movement, which is indeed the subject of another volume, *A History of Russian Symbolism, 1892-1917*. The personal relationships of the authors, which often had an effect on ideological statements, and the different classifications that were current at the beginning of this century, which often took on a somewhat exaggerated importance, are highlighted in the Introduction. The notes at the end of the volume seek to illuminate obscure or difficult passages in the texts, including quotations, statements in other foreign languages, and references to people who are not well known. There is also a bibliography of the more important works about Russian Symbolism and the individual authors.

I am responsible for the selection and translation of the texts. Three of the works have appeared earlier in *Russian Literature Triquarterly*:

Bryusov's review of Balmont's *Let's Be Like the Sun* (translated by Rodney Patterson), the Gippius essay "Peredonov's Little Tear" (translated by Sharon Leiter), and Ivanov's "Thoughts on Symbolism" (translated by Samuel Cioran). In the case of these works, I have revised the existing translations to make the English versions more consistent and to mop up a few unfortunate "elephant tears." It almost goes without saying that translating these writings has presented a formidable challenge. Following the example of Vladimir Nabokov, who aimed for total accuracy of meaning at the expense of other considerations in his English version of *Eugene Onegin,* I have attempted to convey the author's thoughts as directly as possible, and in the case of quoted poetry, I have given the sense only, not the meter or the rhyme. Other conventions I have observed are: noting omissions (usually poems or comments not relevant to Symbolism) by means of ellipsis marks enclosed in square brackets — [...]; using Symbolism with a capital letter to signify the literary movement and symbolism with a lower-case letter to stand for the literary practice of using symbols; and using J. Thomas Shaw's System I for transliterating Russian words and names.

A grant from the University of Oregon's Office of Scientific and Scholary Research helped me in collecting the necessary materials for this book. I would like to acknowledge this assistance and thank my wife, Nadya, for her helpful comments about the translations.

INTRODUCTION

The era of Symbolism in Russia can be broadly defined as a quarter of a century, from its beginnings in 1892 to the 1917 Revolution. Strictly speaking, it was a major force in Russian literature and cultural life for only about ten of these years, from the beginning of this century to 1910.

For our purposes, the more comprehensive delineation of its time span is the most useful, especially since the importance of the Symbolists' actions and writings was greater than it might seem from a simple accounting of the readership of their books and journals.

It is generally agreed that the beginning of Symbolism in Russia can be dated from the lectures delivered by Dmitry Merezhkovsky (1865-1941) about the decline of Russian literature, as he perceived it, in 1892. These lectures, which were expanded and published as a book the next year, are considered one of the many manifestos of modernism in Russian literature. Merezhkovsky attacked the trends current then, the dead positivism, and the power of the honorarium. He was nostalgic about Dostoevsky, Turgenev, Tolstoy, and Goncharov (and even reinterpreted their works to fit his ideas); he praised Ibsen, Poe, and in particular the French Symbolists, for their mysticism, symbolism, and impressionism.

In 1894 and 1895, Valery Bryusov (1873-1924), along with a few of his friends and acquaintances, published *Russian Symbolists,* three collections of poems written by them and translations of French and Belgian Symbolists. The books themselves were not widely read (only 200 copies of the first and third, and 400 copies of the second, were printed), but they created quite a sensation in the press and gave a name to the new movement. Bryusov tried to give the impression, through the use of several pseudonyms, that there were many Symbolist authors actively involved in this new movement.

His introductions to the first two collections were rather polite in tone, but by the time he issued the third one, he had grown tired of critical attacks. One critic who helped to make Russian Symbolism better known, through his bemused reviews of *Russian Symbolists,* was the philospher and poet Vladimir Solovyov (1853-1900). Solovyov was not strictly speaking a Symbolist and was in fact not very sympathetic to several of the early Symbolists. He was later claimed as a forerunner and even a father of Symbolism, and although his reviews of the initial efforts of this movement were not as harsh as those of others, against whom Bryusov railed, Solovyov's parodies of these attempts at Symbolist versifying had a penetrating and deadly accuracy.

Many previously unknown "decadents" were first published during the years 1892-95. Konstantin Balmont (1867-1942) published his first major books of poetry. Zinaida Gippius (1863-1945) began to have her poetry and stories published, and Fyodor Sologub (pseudonym for Teternikov, 1863-1927) had his first poetry and prose printed. Merezhkovsky also published poems and began seeing his novels in print. At this time, however, there was no central journal or other unifying point, and in fact it is not really possible to speak of a single Symbolist "school" at any time in Russian literature; the movement can be more easily characterized as a series of loose groupings, whose members usually (though not always) agreed on the main topics. Bryusov was eager to lead the new movement, and toward the end of the nineteenth century he was able to help found the Skorpion publishing house, where Russian Symbolists' works and translations of European authors highly regarded by the Symbolists were printed.

* * *

The authors who appeared during this early period are generally known as the "older" generation of Symbolists, as opposed to another group of authors who began to publish a few years later. The distinctions between these two groups are often portrayed in quite strong terms: the first is depicted as more decadent, more egocentric, and somehow more "French," the second wave is seen as more idealistic, more "ecumenical," and more "Germanic," though a closer look at what the authors themselves wrote reveals that these distinctions are not easily supported and can in fact give a false impression.

Briefly, the main representatives of the group that began publishing before the end of the century include Merezhkovsky, Hippius, Balmont, Bryusov, and Sologub. Innokenty Annensky (1855-1909), a poet, essayist, and dramatist, is usually included in this group, although he began to publish his major works only after the turn of the century; he is in fact not closely related to either "wave" of Symbolism and will be further discussed later.

Merezhkovsky was active as an author of poetry, novels, drama, and essays. He was instrumental in publishing philosophical writings, which included playing a major role in the journal *Novyi put* (*New Way,* 1903-1904). His novels and other writings display an interest in world history, religion, art, and literature; his household was always a center of intellectual discussion and polemics.

His wife, Z. Gippius, was an accomplished poet, essayist (under the pen name Anton Krayny), prose writer, and memoirist. She was one of Russian literature's greatest women authors and was in some ways a better writer and leader than her husband. She participated in the activities mentioned above with her husband and was considered a spokesman for

Russian Symbolism in France in the early years of this century.

Balmont was one of the most popular poets of the Symbolist era. He published many volumes of verse and wrote essays on various topics in world literature, in addition to a novel, a drama, and short stories. He translated poetry from a number of languages, chiefly English and French, but also less well-known languages such as Mongolian, Lithuanian, and Armenian. His poetry quickly received a broad readership and was much imitated from 1895 to 1904.

Bryusov was without question the "master" of Russian Symbolism; without him, the Symbolist movement would not have had the prominence it achieved. He published a good deal of poetry, as well as stories, novels, essays, and memoirs. One of his most significant contributions to Russian Symbolism, though, was his administrative and editorial ability, best displayed in his successful efforts with the publishing of *Vesy* (*Libra,* 1904-1909) and the Skorpion house. His audacity, demonstrated very early in the title of his first volume of verse *(Chefs d'oeuvre,* 1895), was also a critical factor in getting the movement started, and his later coolness to others' views of Symbolism as a religious or mystical world view aided in the movement's decline.

Sologub was not as actively involved as Bryusov and the Merezhkovskys in founding the Symbolist movement and was able to develop his own reputation without the need to refer to literary or aesthetic platforms. His poetry, novels, short stories, and dramas are filled with pessimism and often display some of the strongest decadent tendencies of any of these authors. His chief novel, *The Petty Demon* (1907), is one of the most important prose works of the early twentieth century; it gives a very bleak and disturbing picture of life in a provincial town, which is indicative of Sologub's general view of the world.

* * *

The period from 1900 to 1903 saw a flowering of many Symbolist talents. Balmont was at that time "king" of poetry. His most significant statement about Symbolism, excerpted here, was seen as another manifesto of the Symbolist movement, though he was certainly not a theoretician like Bryusov, Andrei Bely (pen name for Boris Bugaev, 1880-1934) or Vyacheslav Ivanov (1866-1949). Balmont's best known book of poetry, *Let's Be Like the Sun* (1903) was widely praised, by Bryusov and Annensky among others. Bryusov later revised his opinion of the book and its author, but Annensky's view did not change.

Also during this time, one of the major journals, though not really a Symbolist organ, was *Mir Iskusstva (World of Art,* 1899-1904), which was also the name of a group of artists. Some of the Symbolists had articles published in this journal, and it became clear that Symbolism was not limited to literature, but extended to art and philosophy as well.

In January, 1904, Symbolism in Russia truly began to blossom. That month the major unifying force in the movement, the journal *Vesy,* began publishing. The lead essay published in the first issue was Bryusov's "Keys to the Mysteries," another of the countless "manifestos" of Symbolism, though it was mostly devoted to a summation of past art and literature. The next year, 1905, saw the publication of another important essay by Bryusov, "A Holy Sacrifice," in which he states what it means to be a Symbolist.

The failed revolution of 1905 was a significant event in the consciousness of many Symbolists. Balmont, Sologub, Bely, and Aleksandr Blok (1880-1921), for instance, took to writing poetry with a stronger social and political content. This same year also saw Z. Gippius attacking decadents and calling for greater social concern to combat the disease of individualism. Bely deftly responded to this essay and others published in her *Literary Diary* (1908) by pointing out her own decadent pedigree.

The years from 1905 through 1908 were both the high point of Symbolism and a time of increasing fragmentation of the Symbolist movement, especially with the introduction of two journals, *Zolotoe runo* (*The Golden Fleece,* 1906-1909) and *Pereval* (*The Divide,* 1906-1907). The attack by Gippius on the leading "decadents," including Sologub, Balmont, Bryusov, Bely, and Blok, was only one indication.

One of the causes of this division within the already loose ranks was the somewhat different view of Symbolism that was, at times, shared by the so-called second wave of Symbolists. The three main figures of this "younger" generation were V. Ivanov, Blok and Bely. Lesser lights were Ellis (pseudonym for Lev Kobylinsky, 1879-1947) and Georgy Chulkov (1879-1939).

V. Ivanov was an important theoretician, poet and scholar. Though he was somewhat older than the other writers in the "second generation," his views were more similar to theirs, and his residence was another intellectual gathering place. Ivanov was well educated, and his erudition is apparent in all his works. Blok was the best poet of the Symbolist movement and has been called the best Russian poet of this century, not without reason. In addition to his poetry, he wrote dramas and essays. Bely was one of the most prolific and multi-faceted of the Symbolists. In the first half of his career, he published poetry, short stories, travel notes, outstanding novels (*The Silver Dove, Petersburg,* and *Kotik Letaev,* for example), numerous essays, and four works called Symphonies (attempts to write "lyrical" prose in a musical form). He took an active role in the Symbolist journals and never tired of explaining the true nature of Symbolism.

Ellis is not remembered so much now for his writings as for his attempts to realize the precepts of Symbolism in his own life. He helped to edit Symbolist publications, including *Vesy,* and in 1909 was one of the founders of the Musaget publishing house, another organ for publishing works by Symbolists. He became interested in occult organizations before the Revolution, left for Italy in 1913, and lost touch with Russia after that, though he wrote monographs about Russian literature. G. Chulkov is mainly known for his "anarchistic" essays, critical studies of Dostoevsky and Tyutchev, and later memoirs of the Symbolist era. He was an editor of *Zolotoe runo* and was often the object of attacks by other Symbolists.

Though the members of this "younger generation" were universal in their denunciations of the excesses of decadence, there arose a very divisive topic in 1906-08—mystical anarchism, the tenets of which are outlined by Chulkov in the essay included here and attacked by Bely in one of his major statements about Symbolism and Russian literature. It was a rather violent disagreement for a few years, with Bryusov, and especially Bely and Ellis at *Vesy,* attacking Blok, Ivanov, and Chulkov at *Zolotoe runo* for the latter authors' supposed heresy. This quarrel about the proper path of Symbolism was later resolved, however.

Sologub continued in his own way during this period, publishing important works and offering his major statement about theater. Sologub wrote several dramas which were performed, as did Blok and Annensky, among others. Annensky, after singling Balmont out for praise in 1906, summed up current trends in Russian lyric poetry in 1909. He covered many poets; the excerpts printed here deal primarily with the authors included in this volume. He died before ultimately finishing this important essay and in fact gained a good portion of his fame, and respect, only after his death.

In 1910, especially in the months immediately after the last issue of *Vesy* in December, 1909, the so-called crisis of Symbolism became quite apparent. By that time, the three main "younger" Symbolists had become more or less reunited, both on a personal and ideological basis. When Ivanov and Blok proclaimed their fairly similar views in lectures printed in the journal *Apollon* (*Apollo,* 1909-1917), this evoked the wrath of Bryusov, who had not been afraid to attack these authors before. This time, however, the split became more of a gulf, in part because Bryusov had moved away from theoretical considerations of Symbolism to a more aloof position, where he could examine and comment on art from a more purely aesthetic point of view. Bely later joined Blok and Ivanov in condemning Bryusov's view of Symbolism as only art. These three then espoused the view of Symbolism as a world view, as something spiritual and greater than simple art.

Ellis forecast a bright future in the final chapter of his book about three Russian Symbolists, Balmont, Bryusov, and Bely, and although the movement suffered an irreversible decline after the major polemic of 1910, individual authors continued to produce some of their best work during the seven years preceding the Revolution in 1917. In 1912, an attempt to restore Symbolism to its former prominence was begun in the form of the journal *Trudy i dni* (*Works and Days*, 1912-1916) by the "second wave" Musaget publishing house.

The last three essays are retrospective in the sense that they all look back on the evolution and achievements of Symbolism. Gippius comments on Sologub's most influential novel, *The Petty Demon* and its hero Peredonov. The two statements by Ivanov and Sologub about Symbolism after the "crisis" help to give some perspective, from two very different points of view, on the movement. By the time of Sologub's statement, however, offered at a public "dispute" about Symbolism in 1914, it was obvious to most people concerned that Symbolism was not in fact going to predominate as a world view or even regain its former prominence as an artistic method.

* * *

As with everything else, the Symbolists had their individual reactions to the Socialist Revolution; some stayed in Russia and greeted the Revolution, others emigrated to Western Europe. It is now evident, many decades later, that these decisions about the Revolution affected not only the later careers of these writers but also their critical evaluation and the republication of their works. Some of the authors have had their works reprinted in the USSR, in part because of political views (Bryusov, Blok), some have had a few of their works reissued there (Bely, Sologub), and others have had works reprinted and evaluated by scholars only in the West (Merezhkovsky, Gippius).

Gippius and Merezhkovsky left for Paris in 1919, after suffering through the early deprivation after the Revolution. Both became fervently anti-Communist and frequently attacked the Bolsheviks. He continued to write novels and give speeches and died in 1941. She wrote essays and memoirs, in addition to tracts against the Soviet government and died in 1945. Balmont also left Russia though he was initially positive about the Revolution. He lived the rest of his life in France, did not contribute anything essential to literature in his last ten years, and died in 1942. Annensky, partly because he died early, has had most of his major works reprinted in the Soviet Union, but Ellis, who died in Locarno, Switzerland, in 1947, is not mentioned very frequently there.

Ivanov went to Baku after the Revolution and taught Greek at the university there until 1924, when he went to Rome, where he continued to write until his death in 1949. Some of his poems have been reprinted in the Soviet Union, but in recent years the bulk of his work has appeared only in Belgium.

Bryusov not only stayed in Russia, but was the only former Symbolist of any standing to join the Communist Party. In the early years of the Soviet era, he wrote a good deal and taught young Soviet writers. He died in 1924 and is one of the more revered Symbolists in his homeland. The other revered Symbolist is Blok, who greeted the Revolution with enthusiasm and wrote his most famous poem, "The Twelve," about it. According to many accounts, however, he was rather disillusioned with the new order when he died in 1921.

Chulkov also remained in the Soviet Union, wrote his memoirs about the Symbolist era, and died in 1937. Sologub was not very active in literary or political life after the Revolution, though he continued to write, and died in Leningrad in 1927. Bely shared Blok's view of the Revolution and hoped for the best, but he too was soon disillusioned. He left the Soviet Union briefly, partly for personal reasons, but returned after spending about two years (1921-1923) in Berlin. After his return and until his death in 1934, he continued to write but led a more isolated life, vastly different from the way he and others had lived in the early years of this century.

* * *

In the current Soviet view of literary history regarding the end of the nineteenth century and the beginning of the twentieth, Symbolism is relegated to a secondary position behind more politically acceptable (and popular) realist authors of the time. In the West, Symbolism is presented in a much more favorable light and its significance in Russian literature is usually unquestioned. The Western position is not exaggerated though; the time of the movement's prominence in Russian literary and cultural life deserves the various titles given it: the Time of Symbolism, the Silver Age of Russian Culture, and even the Second Golden Age. It was indeed a time of great cultural advancement for Russian, an age of richness that has not been equalled since.

Ronald E. Peterson
Occidental College, Los Angeles
1985

ON THE REASONS FOR THE DECLINE, AND THE NEW CURRENTS, IN CONTEMPORARY RUSSIAN LITERATURE
D. Merezhkovsky

In the epoch of naive theology and dogmatic metaphysics the area of the *Unknowable* was constantly confused with the area of the *Unknown*. People did not know how to demarcate them and did not understand the full depth and hopelessness of their ignorance. A mystical feeling intruded on the boundaries of exact empirical investigations and destroyed them. On the other hand, the coarse materialism of dogmatic forms subjugated religious feeling.

The newest theory of cognition has erected the indestructible dam, which had for ages divided terra firma, accessible to people, from the limitless and dark ocean that lies beyond the limits of our own cognition. And the waves of this ocean can no longer penetrate into inhabited land, into the area of exact science. The fundament, the first granite blocks of a cyclopic building—the great theory of cognition of the XIX century, was laid by Kant. Since then work on it has gone on uninterrupted, the dam rises higher and higher.

Never before has the boundary between science and faith been so sharp and inexorable, never before have people's eyes experienced such an unbearable contrast of darkness and light. In the meantime, while the firm soil of science on this side of phenomena is flooded with bright light, the area that lies on the other side of the dam, "the depths of holy ignorance," in Carlyle's expression, the night where we all came from and to which we must inevitably return, is more impenetrable than at any time before. In the past, metaphysics threw its brilliant and misty cover on it. The primal legend lit this abyss a little with its dim but consoling light.

Now the last dogmatic cover has been torn away forever, the last mystical ray has gone out. And now contemporary people stand defenseless—face to face with the indescribable darkness, on the boundary between dark and light, and nothing protects their hearts any longer from the terrible cold that blows from the abyss.

No matter where we go, no matter how we try to hide behind the dam of scientific criticism, we feel with our whole essence the proximity of the secret, the proximity of the ocean. There are no boundaries! We are free and alone!...It is not possible to compare any subjugated mysticism of past ages with this horror. Never before have people felt with their hearts the necessity of believing and understood with their reason the impossibility of believing. The most characteristic feature of XIX century mystical aspiration is contained in this ailing, insoluble dissonance, this tragic contradiction, in the unheard-of intellectual freedom, in the audacity of negating.

Our time must be defined by two opposing features—it is a time of extreme *materialism* and, at the same time, of the most passionate *idealistic* outbursts of spirit. We are present at a great, significant stuggle of two views of life, two diametrically opposed world views. The last claims of religious feeling are colliding with the last conclusions of empirical knowledge.

The intellectual struggle that filled the XIX century could not help being reflected in contemporary literature.

The prevailing opinion of the crowd has been realistic until now. Artistic materialism corresponds to scientific and moral materialism. The vulgar side of negation, the absence of a higher idealistic culture, the civilized barbarism amid the grandiose discoveries of technology—all of this put its particular stamp on the relationship of the contemporary crowd to art.

Recently, E. Zola spoke the following very characteristic words about France's young poets, the so-called *Symbolists,* to Monsieur Huret—a newspaper interviewer, who wrote the book *L'enquête sur l'évolution littéraire en France.* I will quote these words in the original, lest I weaken them in a translation:

> Mais que vient-on offrir pour nous remplacer? Pour faire contrepoids à l'immense labeur positiviste de ces cinquante dernières années, on nous montre une vague étiquette "symboliste," recouvrant quelque vers de pacotille. Pour clore l'étonnante fin de ce siècle énorme, pour formuler cette angoisse universelle du doute, cet ébranlement des esprits assoiffés de certitude, voici le ramage obscur, voici les quatre sous de vers de mirliton de quelques assidus de brasserie . . . En s'attardant à des bêtises, à des niaiseries pareilles, à ce moment si grave de l'évolution des idées, ils me font l'effet tous ces *jeunes* gens, qui ont tous de trente à quarante ans, de coquilles de noisettes qui le chute du Niagara.

> [But what can they offer to replace us? As a counterbalance to the immense positivist labor of the past fifty years they show us a vague "Symbolist" label that stands for shoddy verse. As a conclusion to the marvelous end of this vast century, as a formulation of this universal anguish of doubt, this disturbance of minds that are eager to know something certain, there is instead obscure prattle, cheap doggerel, composed by beer hall regulars . . . At such an important moment in the evolution of ideas, all these *young* men who are in their thirties and forties, lingering over trifles and similar foolishness, remind me of nutshells dancing on Niagara Falls.]

The author of *Rougon-Macquart* has a right to exult. It seems that none of the past works of genius has enjoyed a material success, or had a halo of thunderous acclaim in the newspapers, like that of the positivistic novel. Journalists recount with reverence and envy how high a pyramid could be made of the yellow tomes of *Nana* and *Pot-Bouille.* Zola's last novel has been translated with astounding zeal five or six times into Russian, and even the greatest works of world literature have not been translated in a similar manner into our language. The same inquisitive

Huret searched out the chief poet-Symbolist, Paul Verlaine, in his favorite cheap cafe on the Boulevard Saint-Michel. Before the reporter stood a man no longer young, crumpled by life with a sensual "face of a fawn," with a dreamy and tender gaze, and a huge, bald skull. Paul Verlaine is poor. Not without the pride characteristic of "the insulted and humiliated," he names as his only mother "l'assistance publique"—welfare. Of course, this person is far from the Academic chairs next to P. Loti that Zola dreams of so ardently and jealously.

Nevertheless, the author of *Débâcle,* as a true Parisian, is too carried away with contemporary life, noise, and the vanity of the literary moment.

It is an unforgivable error to think that artistic idealism is some recent discovery of Paris fashion. It is a return to the ancient, eternal, never-dying.

That is why these young rebels should be frightening for Zola. It's no business of mine that one of the two is a beggar, who has spent half his life in prisons and hospitals, and that the other is a ruler of literature, if not today, then tomorrow, a member of the *Académie?* Is it my business that one has a pyramid of yellow volumes and the Symbolists have "quatre sous de vers de mirliton?" Well, four lyrical verses can be more beautiful and truthful than a whole series of grandiose novels. The strength of these dreamers is in their *revolt.*

In essence, the whole generation of the end of the XIX century bears some type of revolt in its soul against suffocating, deadly positivism, which lies like a stone on our hearts. It's quite possible that they will perish, that they will not succeed in doing anything. But others will come, nevertheless, and continue their work because their work is *vital.*

"Let people be called to account soon, and with great craving for the pure and noble, which has been completely banished at this time." That is what the author of *Faust* predicted sixty years ago, and now we notice that his words are beginning to come true. "And what is reality all by itself? Its true depiction, which can give us a more precise knowledge about certain things, can bring us pleasure; but actually the higher utility that is in us is contained in the ideal that emanates from the heart of the poet." Then Goethe formulated this thought even more strongly: "the most immeasurable and inaccessible (to the mind) the given poetic work is, the more beautiful it is." It wouldn't hurt Zola to recall that these words do not belong to capricious Symbolists, pitiful nutshells dancing on Niagara Falls, but to the greatest poet and naturalist of the XIX century.

The same Goethe said that a poetic work should be *symbolic.* What is a symbol?

In the Acropolis above the architrave of the Parthenon some traces of a still extant bas relief depict a most common and evidently insignificant scene: nude, well-built youths are leading young horses and taming them calmly and joyfully with muscular arms. All of this is executed with great realism, if you want, even with naturalism, with a knowledge of the human body and of nature. But there is, after all, hardly more naturalism in Egyptian frescoes. And they affect the viewer, however, completely differently. You look at them as you would a curious ethnographic document, as you would a page of a contemporary experimental novel. Something completely different draws you to the bas relief of the Parthenon. You sense in it a breath of *ideal* human culture, a *symbol* of the free Hellenic spirit. A human tames a beast. This is not simply a scene from everyday life, there is in addition a whole revelation of the divine side of our spirit. That is why there is such ineradicable greatness, such calm and wholeness of life in the deformed piece of marble, above which millenia have flown by. A similar symbolism penetrates all the creations of Greek art. Isn't Euripedes' Alcestis, dying to save her husband, a symbol of maternal compassion, that inspires the love of a man and a woman? Isn't Sophocles' Antigone a symbol of the religious-maidenly beauty of female characters that is reflected in medieval Madonnas?

Ibsen's *Doll's House* has a characteristic detail: during a very significant dialogue between two characters a servant comes in and brings a lamp. The tone of the conversation in the well-lit room suddenly changes. It is a trait worthy of a physiologist and naturalist. The shift from physical darkness to light influences our inner world. An artistic *symbol* is hidden under a realistic detail. It's hard to say why, but you will not quickly forget this significant correspondence between the altered conversation and the lamp that lights the misty twilight.

Symbols should naturally and unintentionally pour from the depths of reality. If the author contrives them artificially, in order to express some idea, he turns them into dead allegories that evoke nothing but revulsion, which everything that is dead does. The last minutes of Madame Bovary's agony, accompanied by a banal ditty about love that is sung by an organ grinder, the scene of insanity in the first rays of the rising sun after the tragic night in *Ghosts,* were written with more merciless, psychological *naturalism,* with greater penetration into reality, than the boldest human documents of the positivistic novel. But with Ibsen and Flaubert, besides a current of thoughts expressed with words, you involuntarily feel another, deeper current.

"Any thought that is uttered is a lie." In poetry, what is unsaid and twinkles through the beauty of a symbol acts more strongly on the heart than what is expressed by words. Symbolism makes the very style, the very artistic substance, more inspired and transparent, something that shines all the way through, like the thin walls of an alabaster amphora in which a flame is burning.

Characters can be symbols. Sancho Panza and Faust, Don Quixote and Hamlet, Don Juan and Falstaff are, according to Goethe's expression, *Schwankende Gestalten.*

Dreams that haunt mankind are sometimes repeated from century to century and accompany it from generation to generation. It is impossible to convey the idea of these *symbolic characters* with any words, for the words only define, delimit a thought, and symbols express the limitless side of thought.

We cannot, at the same time, content ourselves with the crude photographic exactness of experimental snapshots. We demand and foresee new, still undiscovered worlds of sensitivity according to the hints of Flaubert, Maupassant, Turgenev and Ibsen. This craving for the unexperienced, this pursuit of nuances, of the dark subconscious in our sensibility, is a characteristic feature of the approaching ideal poetry. Baudelaire and Edgar Allen Poe have already said that the beautiful should *astonish* us a little, should seem unexpected and rare. French critics, more or less successfully, called this feature—*impressionism.*

Those are the three main elements of the new art: *mystical contents, symbols,* and a broadening of artistic sensitivity. [...]

Dmitry Merezhkovsky
1892

RUSSIAN SYMBOLISTS
V. Bryusov

From the Publisher

Not wishing at all to give any special preference to Symbolism and not considering it the "poetry of the future," as its followers who get carried away do, I simply feel that even Symbolist poetry has its own *raison d'être*. It is remarkable that poets who do not consider themselves followers of Symbolism have involuntarily come close to it when they wanted to express refined, barely perceptible moods.

I feel, moreover, that it is necessary to remind the reader that the language of the decadents, their strange and unusual tropes and figures of speech, are not at all a necessary element of Symbolism. It is true that Symbolism and decadence often merge, but it is also possible for them not to. The aim of Symbolism is to sort of hypnotize the reader with a series of juxtaposed images, to evoke in him a certain mood.

Subsequent installments of this edition will appear as enough material is gathered. Authors who wish to include their works are asked to address themselves, with a delineation of terms, to   Vladimir Alexandrovich Maslov, Moscow Post Office, *Poste restante*.

Publisher
1893

A Reply

Charming stranger!
First of all I beg you not to be angry with this form of address. That you are charming—I permit myself to guess from your handwriting and envelope that you are a stranger to me—it is impossible to deny, because in your letter there is not only no signature, and not even the slightest reference by which I could recognize you. It consists mainly of reproaches and censure, with the exception of a few lines of praise at the beginning, the number of which in my opinion seemed quite insignificant.

However—I must be fair—you are more condescending than our critics. They simply offered to send me to an insane asylum. You assume that I became a Symbolist by mistake, "perhaps because of involuntary imitation." By this you explain that there are three types of Symbolists: mystificators, who cannot rely on talent, who like to captivate with originality; mentally ill people; and the unfortunates who have strayed, among whom you magnanimously placed me, and who can still return to the true way.

"Works by such people," you exclaim further, "could not form a new school! Really! What is there in common between these heterogeneous creations that are called Symbolist? Do not these separate poets unite in only one thing, the desire to write something stranger and more unintelligible? Simply let someone try to answer the question, 'What is the essence of Symbolism?'—and I am certain that he will fail."

I am going to "try," meanwhile, to answer precisely that question in my letter, at least so that you do not count me among that group of unfortunates who have strayed, since for me it would be even less insulting to be among the charlatans. Only I must warn you that the views I will espouse do not at all constitute the usual Symbolist credo. It is quite possible that many simply will not agree with me since in *theory* Symbolists are actually divided into many separate circles. It is even more remarkable, however, that they come up with the same results in their works.

The first peculiarity of my view of Symbolism is that I pay absolutely no attention to its extremes. A school that is just beginning always tends toward extremes, which are not, of course, its essence. Besides—I must say, many people agree with me on this—it is necessary to separate certain doubtlessly foreign elements from Symbolism, elements that are associated with it in France. Such as mysticism, such as the aspiration to reform versification and the introduction of antiquated words and meters in connection with it, such as the semi-spiritualistic theories propagated by Sar Peladan. All of these are accidental admixtures to Symbolism.

Having separated them, I will divide all Symbolist works into the following three types:

1. Works that give a complete picture, in which, however, something incompletely drawn, half-stated, is perceptible; as if several essential signs are not shown. Such as, for example, Mallarmé's sonnets.

2. Works which have been given the form of a complete story or even drama, but in which separate scenes have a significance not so much for the development of the action as for a certain impression on the reader or viewer.

3. Works which seem to you to be an unrelated grouping of images and with which you became acquainted, probably, in Maeterlinck's poem "Greenhouses in the Forest," which has been translated several times here.

You, of course, are hurrying to object that I have not covered all of Symbolism, that it has many other forms.

To that I will say to you, first of all, that my three categories have a multitude of varieties. The connection of images, for example, can be completely imperceptible or it can be very easily recalled.

In the second place, I am compelled to refuse to apply this name to a number of works that are usually called Symbolist or decadent. So, I do not consider symbolic those works which are distinguished only by the strangeness of their metaphors, similes, audacious tropes and figures in general. The desire to renew the poetic language is noticable, it is true, among nearly all the Symbolists, but it does not belong to them exclusively. They are just more daring in their innovations. T. Gautier, however, was far from being shy in this regard, and there is no reason for calling him a Symbolist.

Further, I do not consider those works symbolic which shine only because of the novelty of their plots. Symbolism really disposes a poet to address the feelings and moods of the contemporary person, but it does not follow from this that any similar work is symbolic. I have come across quite a few poems that were written in a strange language with crazy metaphors, in which some amazing mood of the "fin de siècle" was depicted and about which I could not say—"here is a Symbolist poem."

Finally, I consider the famous rapprochement of poetry with music one of the means that Symbolism uses, but not its essence. A Symbolist tries to evoke a definite mood in the reader with the melody of verse, which could help him to grasp the general sense, and to do only that. Such as, for example, Maeterlinck's poem "Peacocks," which you probably know from various journals. It is true that certain Symbolists have surrendered to the play of sounds, so that the chief, and sometimes the only meaning is obtained by the sound complexes of words in their poetry, but these are extremes, which I will not touch upon, as I said earlier.

In this way, each Symbolist work can come under one of my three categories. You, of course, have already noticed by my delineations, what I find in common among them. Obviously, in all three cases, the poet transmits a series of images, not yet formed, into a complete picture, sometimes forming them into a whole, arranging them in dialogues and scenes, or simply enumerating them one after another. The connection given to these images is always more or less accidental, so that one must look on them as markers on an invisible path, opened up to the reader's imagination. Thus Symbolism can be called, as you illogically do, the "poetry of hints."

And so, something general has been found in "those varied works that can be called Symbolist," that permits us to consider them as belonging to one school. Now it is possible to pass on to your strongest accusation, which will help us to explain finally the essence of Symbolism: "In any case, why speak in hints when it is possible to speak directly?" I would only put this question as follows: "Is the essence of a poetical work destroyed if, instead of a whole image, only hints are given?" Poetry, like art, clothes thoughts with images. But in every thought it is possible to observe a whole process of development from the first conception to the completed development. The essence of the difference in a school of literature consists of precisely the degree of development with which a poet realizes his thought. So, in the Neo-Romantic school every image, every thought appears in its extreme conclusion. Symbolism, on the contrary, takes the first gleam, or embryo, which still has no sharply defined features, and in this way does not essentially differ any more from any other literary school than they do among themselves. Try to observe yourself, when you daydream, and transfer the same thing into words; you will get the first image of a Symbolist work, and a work in the spirit of the prevailing school.

From this it follows that not only the poet-Symbolist but also his reader must have a sensitive soul and in general a finely developed organism. One has to read into a Symbolist work; imagination must recreate just the thought hinted at by the author. For this reason, your last accusation, that the "circle of readers of Symbolist poetry must be quite small," remains in force, but I do not think that this is a powerful argument against Symbolism. Even Heine's poems are not for everyone. Symbolism has its areas and its readers, let other schools recognize this, and let it be content with what belongs to it.

You see that I am not in that group you condemn for being "dreamers," who want to make all poetry Symbolist. According to some data, however, I foresee that in the near future Symbolism will take the leading position, although I personally do not want this. According to my view, all literary schools have their own significance—let them develop in a friendly manner, not let one gain strength at the expense of the others.

You, of course, do not believe in the approach of such a golden age, and you probably do not agree with much of what I say. If—as I allow myself to hope—our correspondence is not cut off at the beginning, I will try to reaffirm my conclusions with a series of examples, which will always explain matters well; I will try to demonstrate that such a form of poetry as Symbolism had to appear now. But this, I say, will be later. For now I am satisfied that my letter, in one way or another, has answered the question, "what is the essence of Symbolism," and thus I have at least swayed your view a little, even though I do not know you, but at the end of the letter, of course, I am yours respectfully,

Valery Bryusov
1894

TO THE CRITICS
(ZOILUSES AND ARISTARCHUSES)
V. Bryusov

Our editions have been subjected to such merciless criticism from major and minor journals that it seems necessary for us to explain our view of it.

First of all, we feel that the majority of our critics were completely unprepared for the task they have taken on. They were not able to evaluate something *new,* and thus they had to content themselves with common phrases and ready exclamations. All the indignant little articles and notes not only failed to strike a blow at the new school, but in large part did not even give the readers any idea about it. And the indignation related mostly to the name, and we are convinced that if the same poems were to appear without the name of the school, they would not be greeted with such horror. The matter has not proceeded without curiosities. Thus one review avowed that only our translations are tolerable, and another one—that the translations are the weakest of all. Someone seriously offered to consider as Symbolism everything about which one could exclaim, "The Devil knows what it is"; there were those who doubted the very existence of Bryusov and Miropolsky: it seemed so insolent to call themselves Russian Symbolists.

Analyzing the first two issues, the reviewers tried, at least, to prove their words, to make citations, to show what, in their opinion, were errors in language; however, even then several of them found it possible to talk about our little books without having read them. The appearance of *Romances without Words* put the reviewers in a more difficult position: they did not know the original, and so they had to fall back on unsubstantiated condemnations.

It is difficult to glean serious accusations in the chorus of reproaches and derision, but it seems that there are three main points to which our judges address themselves most often. 1) Symbolism is an illness in literature with which people struggle even in the West; consequently, it is completely useless to innoculate us with it. 2) In our Russian literature, Symbolism is no more than an imitation that has no firm soil beneath it. 3) Finally, there are no moods that cannot be expressed outside of Symbolism.

The first accusation is too ill-defined; it does not directly indicate the shortcomings of Symbolism because we cannot consider the reviewers' lamentations that they cannot understand our poems any sort of indication; before referring to the theorem that poetry should be understood by the public, one must first prove it. Besides, similar complaints are too frequent when a new school in literature appears, and history has sufficiently shaken their authority. To the second accusation we answer that for us only one pan-human poetry exists (this understandably does not contradict the previous statement) and that a poet familiar with Western literature can no longer be a follower of the Meys and the Apukhtins; Russian Symbolism, however, had its own predecessors—Fet, Fofanov. The third accusation was particularly directed against the theory of Mr. Bryusov, stated in the second issue, which he did not present as our general program; we will point out, however, that the example of Fet, to whom the reviewer refers, speaks more for us; many of Fet's poems could be bravely called Symbolist, such as, for example: "The night and I, we both breathe...," "The garden is all in bloom...," "I won't say anything to you...," "For long there has been little joy in love...," and "You are all on fire...."

We have come across one more very definite accusation: "Behind French decadents there were novelty and audacity in their ideas—to write nonsense and laugh at readers, when Mr. Bryusov writes 'golden fairies,' this is not new, only boring and not very witty." To consider all of Western Symbolism, with the number of journals devoted to it, with its followers in Germany, Denmark, Sweden, Czechoslovakia—the result of the mystification of a few jesters—is also a sufficiently audacious idea, but an opinion that is, at least, less frivolous.

The reviews of Vladimir Solovyov aroused some interest in their time. Serious remarks actually pop up in them (e.g., about the imitativeness of many of Mr. Bryusov's poems in the first issue), but Mr. Vl. Solovyov was carried away by the desire to amuse the public, which led him to a number of witticisms of doubtful value and to a deliberate distortion of the sense of the poems. We say "deliberate"; Mr. Vl. Solovyov, of course, should easily catch the poet's most delicate hints because he has himself written Symbolist poems, as for example, "Why words..." (*Vestnik Evropy,* 1892, No. 10).

On this note we conclude and will not discuss the other remarks because they (perhaps we do not know some of them) offer only reprints from other newspapers and magazines, or unfounded derision and censure; after all, we are not obligated to argue with everyone who stands in the highway and begins to curse.

(Unsigned)
[*Valery Bryusov*]
1895

REVIEWS OF *RUSSIAN SYMBOLISTS*
Vl. Solovyov

1st Issue. Valery Bryusov and A. L. Miropolsky
(Moscow, 1894, 44pp.)

This notebook has undoubted merits: it does not burden the reader
with its dimensions and partly entertains with its contents. The pleasure
begins with the epigraph, taken by Valery Bryusov from the French
decadent Stéphane Mallarmé:

Une dentelle s'abolit
Dans le doute du jeu suprême.

[Lace is abolished
In the doubt of the highest game.]

And here is Bryusov's Russian "prologue:"

Pink colors die down
In the pale sheen of the moon;
Tales about spring's suffering
Freeze in the ice floes.
From the end to the beginning
Dreams are wrapped in mourning,
And their garlands are twined
With the silence of its coloring.
The roses of harmonies don't bloom.
In the flowerbeds of emptiness
Under the rays of a young daydream.
But through the windows of incoherent dreams,
Scattered daydreams
Won't see diamond stars.

The words, "the roses of harmonies in the flowerbeds of emptiness,"
and "windows of incoherent dreams" can be seen as at least symbolic, but
they are also a rather true definition of this type of poetry. However,
actual Russian "Symbolism" is represented rather weakly in this little
collection. Except for the poems directly designated as translations, of the
remaining poems, a good half are clearly inspired by other poets, and not
even Symbolist poets at that. The one, for example, that begins with the
lines:

> She and I met accidentally
> And I shyly dreamed about her,

and ends:

> There's an old tale that was once
> Condemned to be young forever.

undoubtedly came from Heine, although they are transplanted in the "flowerbed of emptiness." The following:

> An indistinct dream climbs the steps,
> It slightly opens the door of the moment—

is an involuntary parody of Fet. His poems without verbs have inspired:

> Starry, passionless sky,—

but are we to take such a lack of successful imitating as originality?

> The stars gently whispered—

is a free translation from Heine.

> Boy your little head—

idem.

And here is a poem which I would have equal difficulty calling original or imitative:

> *Little eyes* sparkling with tears
> And *little lips,* pitifully pursed,
> And *little cheeks* burn with caresses
> And curls mussed and tangled—etc.

In any case, is it really Symbolism to enumerate, in diminuitive forms, the different parts of the human organism, and even ones that are familiar to everybody?

I have a different type of objection to Mr. Valery Bryusov's "conclusion:"

> Golden fairies
> In a satin garden!
> When will I find
> The icy avenues?
> Silvery splashes of
> Infatuated naiads,
> Where are the jealous boards
> That will block your way.
> Incomprehensible vases

Lit by fire,
The dusk has frozen
Over the flight of fancies.
Beyond the gloom of curtains
There are funeral urns,
And an azure vault of
Deceitful stars doesn't wait.

Despite the "icy avenues in a satin garden," the subject of these verses is as clear as it is reprehensible. Attracted by a "flight of fancies," the author peeked into wooden bathing cabins, where persons of the female gender whom he calls "fairies" and "naiads" were bathing. But is it possible to smooth over such vile acts with magnificent words? And this is what Symbolism leads to in *conclusion!* We will hope at least that the "jealous boards" were up to their task. In the opposite case, the "golden fairies" would have had to pour water on our shameless Symbolist with the "incomprehensible vases," which are called wash tubs by common folk who use them to wash their legs in bathing cabins.

It is impossible to pronounce a general judgment of Mr. Valery Bryusov without knowing his age. If he is no more than 14, then he could become a rather good versifier, or maybe not. If this person is a grownup, then of course all literary hopes are out of place. I have nothing to say about Mr. Miropolsky. Of the ten small pages that belong to him, eight are taken up by prose fragments. But reading decadent prose is a task greater than my powers. The "flowerbeds of emptiness" would be tolerable only when the "roses of harmonies" are growing in them.

2nd Issue. Pub. by V. A. Maslov
(Moscow, 1894)

The species of beings called Russian Symbolists has as its chief feature extremely quick reproduction. Just last summer there were only two, now there are a whole ten. Here are their names in alphabetical order: A. Bronin, Valery Bryusov, V. Darov, Erl. Martov, A. L. Miropolsky, N. Novich, K. Sozontov, Z. Fuchs, and two more, one of whom is concealed under the letter M, and the other under three asterisks. I would be prepared to think that this species reproduces by arbitrary conception *(generatio aequivoca),* but such a hypothesis will hardly be accepted by exact science. Russian Symbolism, however, is enriched for now by more melodious names than melodious works. In the second issue, a total of 18 original poems have been included; with ten authors that comes out to one and a fraction apiece (1.8 or 1 and 4/5). The reader will agree that my critical method for now is distinguished by its strongly scientific character, which leads to completely indisputable results. I would like to keep the same method for evaluating the qualitative merits of the Russian Symbolists, but this is much more difficult; you cannot get by with just arithmetic here. It is necessary to establish common principles or norms of artistic activity and check the given work by the postulates that come out of them.

Unfortunately, this solely scientific method has one inconvenience: it would demand many years of study for me and it would have to be presented by me in many volumes, but what is required of me is a little review of a little notebook with verse of problematic merit. I'll have to reject the scientific method, but on the other hand, I would not want to be subjected to a justified reproach for being subjectively arbitrary and tendentious. However, is there not really any middle path between strict science and personal impression? There is, no doubt. Without ascending to unconditional principles, it is possible to take the intention of a criticized author or artist, instead of a personal opinion, as the norm for judging. Thus, for example, when a painter personally writes: "Behold—a lion!" on his picture—while anyone can see that a poorly drawn dog is there, and the painter's intention to depict a lion has, in his realization, been limited to the yellow color of dog's fur, then every witness to this failure, without falling into subjectivism, can call the picture unsatisfactory. For, independent of personal opinions, it is clear from the essence of things that neither a yellow color nor a poor drawing are sufficient by themselves to make a dog a lion. This method of judging, based on the objective difference between the two mammals, I call a relatively scientific method. Its application to Russian Symbolists is made easier because they have seen to finding the most definite form for expressing their intentions. In the introduction, Mr. Bryusov explains that the poetry which he and his comrades serve is the *poetry* of hints. Following our relatively scientific method, we will see how representative of the poetry of hints the poems of the Russian Symbolists really are.

> The strings rust
> Under a damp hand,
> Dreams grow mute
> And are covered with gloom.

This is the beginning and concluding stanza of a little poem by Mr. Miropolsky, which opens this anthology. Here, reference is made, with exaggerated *clarity,* to that sad and hardly interesting fact that the guitarist depicted by the author suffers from a well-known pathological phenomenon. There are no hints and there is no poetry here. The first verse, "the strings rust," contains another reference, but again a clear *reference,* not a hint, to Mr. Miropolsky's low level of literacy.

The second poem, "I am waiting," consists almost entirely of repeating two verses: "A resounding heart beats within my breast," and "My dear friend, come, come!" What is unclear here, where are the hints? It's easier to notice an excessive desire for clarity here, for the poet explains that his heart beats in his *breast*—so that no one thinks that it beats in his head or his abdominal cavity.

Mr. Valery Bryusov, the same one who described his reprehensible peeking in women's bathing cabins in the first issue of *Russian Symbolists,* now depicts his own bathing. This is of course harmless, but the bad thing is that Mr. Bryusov says such words about his own bath that clearly, without any hints, demonstrate the author's not completely normal mood. We warned him that the indulgence of base passions, even under the guise of Symbolism, will not lead to a good end. Alas! Our premonitions have come true earlier than expected! Judge for yourself:

> The midnight moisture in the silvery dust
> Intoxicates tired daydreams with rest,
> And in the *supple silence of a river sarcophagus*
> A *great man* hears no slander.

To call a river a sarcophagus, and oneself a great man—this is a quite clear sign (and not just a hint) of a sick condition.

> The corpse of a woman, rotting and putrid,
> The great steppe, a cast iron sky...
> And a long moment, resurrected by mockery,
> Rises with reproaching laughter.
>
> A diamond dream... A burnt sketch above...
> And aroma, and tears, and dew...
> The rotting and putrid corpse is abandoned
> And a raven has pecked out its eyes.

In this poem, signed by Z. Fuchs (we will hope that the Z. stands for Zakhar not Zinaida), it's possible, I think, to find a hint, only not a poetic one, but a hint that three councillors in the Tambov assembly were, perhaps, not quite correct in their opinion, that they should direct it not to peasants who had not finished their grammar school, but to certain versifiers who call themselves Symbolists. However—

> *In jene Sphären wag' ich nicht zu streben...*

I think that Mr. Fuchs has sufficiently punished himself by appearing in print with such a work. Nevertheless the impression produced by the poem of this Symbolist is so strong that I do not have enough spiritual calm for a relatively scientific analysis of further Symbolist pearls. And our Symbolists announce three forthcoming new editions on the last page, one of which is called *Les cshefs d'oeuvre.* We will postpone final judgment until the appearance of these "cshefs d'oeuvre," but now for the sake of fairness we will note that in the notebook discussed there is one poem that reminds us of real poetry:

> Child, look! there at the end of the avenue
> The bushes of nighttime beauty are spread...
> The fairies of the spring night have taken their image...
>   You did not understand my melancholy!

> The ray of the sun from dawn to night
> Pours passionate spells on the sleepy flowers...
> In vain he tries to look them in the eye just once...
>   You don't understand my melancholy!

> In the evening, hiding behind the mountain
> With the burning melancholy of a deceived dream,
> Powerless, he sees them kissing the moon...
>   You'll understand my melancholy, for sure!

Russian Symbolists.—Summer, 1895.
(Moscow, 1895, 52pp.)

In the preface to this new issue, the young sportsmen who call themselves "Russian Symbolists" have "found it necessary to explain their attitude" toward the critics. In the opinion of Mr. Bryusov and Co., the majority of their critics were completely unprepared for this important task, and those who were prepared turned out to be malefactors. Such is the reviewer for *Vestnik Evropy*. "The reviews of Vladimir Solovyov," the Symbolists write, "aroused some interest in their time. Serious remarks actually pop up in them (e.g., about the imitativeness of many of Mr. Bryusov's poems in the first issue), but Mr. Vl. Solovyov was carried away by the desire to amuse the public, which led him to a number of witticisms of doubtful value and to a deliberate distortion of the sense of the poems. We say 'deliberate': Mr. Vl. Solovyov, of course, should easily catch the poet's most delicate hints because he has himself written Symbolist poems, as for example, 'Why words...' (*Vestnik Evropy*, 1892, No. 10)."

Why, however, are the Symbolists so sure that this poem—whether Symbolist or not—belongs to the author of the reviews. The poem is signed "Vladimir Solovyov," but the reviews are designated by the letters Vl. S., which could perhaps stand for Vladislav Syrokomlya or Vlasy Semyonov. I do not have to answer for Mr. Vladimir Solovyov and the accusation of his printing a Symbolist poem in *Vestnik Evropy*. But the accusation that I deliberately distorted the sense of the poems of Mr. Bryusov and Co., I, Vlasy Semyonov, have to explain that even if I were inspired by hell's own spite, even then it would be impossible for me to distort the sense of those poems—because of the complete lack of sense in them. With their new issue, the Symbolists have placed this matter beyond all doubt. Well, just let someone try to distort the sense of such a work:

> The shadow of uncreated creations
> Sways in a dream
> Like fans of latanias
> On an enamel wall.
> Violet hands
> On an enamel wall
> Outline sounds sleepily
> In ringing-sonorous silence.
> And transparent kiosks
> In ringing-sonorous depths
> Grow up like sparkles
> In the azure moonlight,
> *The naked moon rises*
> *In the azure moonlight;*
> Sounds flutter sleepily
> Sound caress me,
> Secrets of created creations
> Caress me with a caress
> And the shadow of latanias quivers
> On an enamel wall.

If I wrote that it is not only indecent for a naked *moon* to rise in the azure *moon*light, but also completely impossible, since the moon *(mesyats)* and the moon *(luna)* are two names for one and the same thing, then would that really be a "deliberate distortion of the sense?"

Well then, take this "chefs d'oeuvre":

> The heart's ray from the silver of agitation
> Rises over the space of hoar frost,
> And, shaking, sounds the crystal of lightning
> And it floats, splashed with foam.
> It floats... like a moaning pouring
> It beckons the ice of the stars from the abyss...
> A star sleeps, distant in the proud calm,
> A star twinkles and sleeps.

Or another:

> Colonnades of songs hung in the air,
> And the crystal of accord rings like a fountain,
> White masses in the azure
> And a matte granite in the rays of mist died down.
> The glow of languors beats like foam in thoughts,
> Dear features flash like lightning,
> Resonant bridges bent over like an arch,
> Bright garlands entwined the facades,
> The aromatic gleam of Carrara's marble...

And serenades resound victoriously and disappear,
And an inspired splash spreads an echo.

Some Symbolists lessen the difficulty of writing senseless poems with a rather successful device: having written one line, they then turn it inside out—and a new one appears:

Over the dark ravine,
The ravine dark,
Like an immodest picture,
A picture immodest,
Hung mists,
Mists hung,
Like deceits,
Deceits without thought,
Without thought or connection
In a passionless story.
In a story passionless,
In a story obscure,
Where the pale colors
Of a sad ending
Are sad like the tales
Of a homeland distant.

And here is a poem in which there is neither sense nor rhyme—as if it were written to illustrate the phrase—*ni rime, ni raison* [neither rhyme nor reason]:

Cadavers, lit by gas!
A vermillion ribbon on a sinful bride!
Oh! we're going to the window to kiss!
Do you see how pale the dead people's faces are?
This is a hospital, where children are in mourning...
This is oleanders on ice...
This is the cover of *Romances without words*
The moon isn't visible through the windows, dear.
Our souls are a flower in your boutonniere.

The Symbolists rebuke people for being carried away by the desire to amuse the public, but they can see that this enthusiasm only leads me to simply reproducing their own pearls.

I should note that one poem in this collection has a clear, indisputable sense. It's very short—just one line:

Oh, cover your pale legs.

For complete clarity, I would say, "For otherwise you'll catch cold," should be added, but even without this, the advice of Mr. Bryusov, evidently directed to a person suffering from anemia, is the most intelligent work of all Symbolist literature, not only Russian, but foreign as well. Of the examples of poems translated for the present issue, the following masterpiece by the famous Maeterlinck deserves attention:

My soul has been ill all day,
My soul is sick of farewells.
My soul is struggling with silence.
My eyes meet a shadow
And under the knout of reminiscences
I see the specters of desire.
A half-forgotten track leads
Dogs of secret desire.
In the depths of forgetful forests
Packs of lilac dreams rush by,
And yellow arrows—reproaches—
Punish the deer of false dreams.
Alas, Alas! desires are everywhere
Returned dreams are everywhere,
And breath is too blue ...
The image of the moon on the heart grows dim.

Perhaps "a dog of secret desire has barked in the heart" of another stern reader long ago—exactly that desire that authors and translators of such poems would, in the future, write not only "under the knout of reminiscences" but also "under the recollection of the knout ... " But my own critical pack is more distinguished by "friskiness" than by "spite," and the "blue breath" evoked in me the orange desire to the lilac composition of yellow verse, and the multicolored peacock of vainglory prompts me to share with the public three examples of my gris-de-perl, vert-de-mer and feuille-morte inspiration. Now at least Mr. Bryusov and Co. have the real right to accuse me of printing Symbolist poems.

I.

Vertical horizons
In chocolate skies,
Like half-mirror dreams
In laurel-cherry forests.
The specter of a fire-breathing ice floe
Has died out in the bright twilight,
And a hyacinth Pegasus stands,
Not hearing me.
Immanent mandragoras
Rustled in the rushes,
And rough-decadent
Doggerel in wilting ears.

II.

Above the green hill,
Above the hill green,
Above the couple in love,
Above the in love couple,
A star shines at noon,
At noon it shines,
Although no one ever
Notices this star.
But a wavy mist,
But a mist wavy,
From a radiant land it,
From a land radiant,
It slips through between the clouds,
Above a dry wave,
A motionless flyer
And even with a dual moon.

III.

In the skies church chandliers burn
    And below—darkness.
Did you go to him, or didn't you go?
    Say yourself!
But don't tease the hyena of suspicion,
    The mice of melancholy!
Don't look at how the leopards of vengeance
    Sharpen their teeth!
And don't call the owl of wisdom
    In this night!
Donkeys of patience and elephants of meditation
    Ran away.
You alone have given birth to a crocodile
    With your fate here.
Let the chandeliers burn in the sky
    In the grave there is—darkness.

Vladimir Solovyov
1894-1895

AN ELEMENTARY STATEMENT ABOUT SYMBOLIST POETRY
K. Balmont

If you have renounced the everyday cares that bore you to tears, if you are sitting alone by a big window, and outside, like the flowing and ebbing tides, a crowd of people passing by is constantly moving, in a few moments you will be drawn into the pleasure of contemplation and will mentally merge with this moving diversity. You will unintentionally come to know, with the swiftness that comes easily only by stimulation, those familiar strangers, who appear for a moment in order to disappear immediately. In the fleeting smiles, in the casual movements, in the profiles that appear for a moment, you will divine hidden dramas and romances, and the more you look, the more clearly the invisible life beyond the visible exterior will be sketched for you, and all the specters which seem to be alive will appear before you merely as moving tissue, as creations of your own daydreams. They will all finally merge into one common stream, directed by your thoughts, and having perceived the beauty and complexity of your soul, they will form with you one unbroken unity, like radii from a center. The world will become a phantasmagoria, created by you because, sitting alone by a big window, you have looked too long and too fixedly at the inexhaustible stream of people.

Meanwhile, if you found yourself in this crowd, taking equal part in its spontaneous movements, bearing the yoke of everyday life, you would, I think, not see anything in this crowd besides the usual gathering of people at a certain time and on a certain street.

Such are the two different manners of artistic contemplation, two different systems of artistic perception—realism and Symbolism.

The realists are always simple observers, Symbolists—always thinkers.

Realists are gripped by concrete life, like the breakers on the seashore, and they see nothing beyond this life. Symbolists, aloof from real actuality, see only their dreams in it, they look at life through a window. This is because every Symbolist, even the most minor one, is more mature than every realist, even the greatest one. The one is still enslaved by matter, the other has passed into the sphere of the ideal.

The two different manners of artistic perception that I am talking about always depend on the individual characteristics of each writer, and the external circumstances of the historical situation only sometimes correspond to one manner or another that becomes predominant. In the sixteenth and seventeenth centuries, almost simultaneously, two different geniuses appeared as the living incarnation of both literary manners: Shakespeare created a whole series of brilliant examples of real poetry;

Calderon was the precursor of our times, the creator of dramas that are noteworthy for the beauty of Symbolist poetry. Of course the essential national qualities of these writers to a great degree determined their manner of creativity. England is a country of positive acts, Spain—a country of improbable undertakings and religious madness. But the historical atmosphere, in the sense of influencing a personality, was filled with similar elements, both in England and in Spain: national power, individual brilliance, and dreams about worldwide supremacy. In addition, if we take one entirely analogous situation, we can say that in the same Spain there were simultaneously the realist Lope de Vega and the Symbolist Calderon, in the same England there lived simultaneously the realist Shakespeare and the decadent John Ford.

In exactly the same vein, we see in the course of the nineteenth century the simultaneous existence of two opposing literary schools. Next to Dickens we see Edgar Allan Poe, next to Balzac and Flaubert—Baudelaire, next to Lev Tolstoy—Henrik Ibsen. It's impossible, however, not to recognize that the closer we are to the new century, the Symbolists' voices resound more persistently, the need for more refined modes of expressing feelings and thoughts (which make up the distinguishing feature of Symbolist poetry) becomes more tangible.

How can I define Symbolist poetry more precisely? It is a poetry in which two contents merge organically, not forcibly: concealed abstraction and apparent beauty—they merge as easily and naturally as a river's waters merge harmoniously with sunlight on a summer morning. Despite the hidden sense of one Symbolist work or another, however, its directly concrete contents are almost always complete in themselves, they have an independent existence, rich with nuances, in Symbolist poetry.

Here is the point where Symbolist poetry is sharply delimited from allegorical poetry, with which it is sometimes confused. In allegory, on the contrary, the concrete sense is a completely subordinate element. It plays an auxiliary role and is usually combined with didactic problems that are completely foreign to Symbolist poetry. In one case we see a kindred merging of two senses arising spontaneously, in the other, their forced coupling is evoked by some external considerations. Allegory speaks with the same monotonous voice of a minister or the witty didactic tone of a street singer (I'm using this term in its medieval sense). Symbolism, filled with hints and reservations, speaks with the tender voice of a siren or the hollow voice of a Sybil, evoking presentiment.

Symbolist poetry is inseparably connected with different varieties of contemporary literary creation, known by the names decadence and impressionism.

I feel completely powerless to strictly differentiate between these shadings, and I think that in reality this is impossible and that, strictly speaking, Symbolism, impressionism, and decadence are nothing more than *psychological lyrics,* which change their composite parts but always remain unified in their essence. In fact, these three currents sometimes go in parallel, at other times they diverge and merge in one stream, but in any case they rush in one direction (and there is not the difference between them that there is between river and ocean water). If it's absolutely necessary to offer a definition, however, I would say that an impressionist is an artist who speaks with hints that are subjectively experienced and with partial references, who creates in others the impression of what he sees as a whole. I would also say that a decadent in the true sense of the word is a refined artist who perishes because of his refinement. As the word itself demonstrates, decadents are the representatives of an epoch in decline. These are people who think and feel at the edge of two periods, one finished and the other not yet born. They see that the dusk has darkened but the dawn is still sleeping somewhere beyond the edge of the horizon. Because of this, the decadents' songs are songs of twilight and night. They debunk everything old because it has lost its soul and has become a lifeless diagram. But, having a premonition of something new, the people who have grown up with the old are not able to see the new for themselves—because there is so much of the most painful yearning, together with the most ecstatic outbursts, in their moods. A type of this person is the hero of a drama by Ibsen, the Master Builder, Solness; he falls from the tower he has built himself. The philosopher of decadence is Friedrich Nietzsche, an Icarus who perished, who was able to make wings for himself, but who couldn't give his wings the strength to withstand the burning fire of the all-seeing sun.

Those who think that decadence is a reactionary phenomenon are deeply mistaken. It is sufficient to read one little poem by Baudelaire, "Prière," in order to see that we are dealing with a liberating force:

> Praise the great, holy Satan!
> You ruled in heaven. Now you're in the depths
> Of the rejected abyss of desecrated hell.
> Now your pleasure is in silent intentions.
> Eternally thinking spirit, be merciful with me.
> Take me under your protection; take me under the tree of knowledge
> At that hour, when like a temple, like a sacrificial building,
> It spreads the rays of its branches
> And again your brow is shaded by radiance.
> Sovereign of revolt, freedom, and consciousness!

The ones who think that Symbolist poetry was created largely by Frenchmen also stray very far.

This straying was conditioned by the unjust hegemony of the French language, because of which everything written in French is immediately read by a large public, while talented and even brilliant creations, written in English, Russian, or one of the Scandinavian languages, until recently had to wait decades before entering the broad channel, and to take a definite place among that number of works read by thousands.

I stress this fact: everything brilliant created in the field of nineteenth century Symbolist poetry, with a few exceptions, belongs to English, American, Scandinavian, and German, not French, Symbolists [...]

While realist poets regard the world naively, as simple observers, subservient to its material basis, Symbolist poets, re-creating materiality with their complex sensitivity, rule the world and penetrate its mysteries. The realist poets' consciousness goes no further than the limits of earthly life, defined with exactness and with the deadly boredom of mileposts. Symbolist poets never lose Ariadne's mysterious thread that connects them with the worldwide labyrinth of Chaos. They are always fanned by whiffs that come from a place beyond the limits, so that, as if against their will, the dull roar of still other voices, not theirs, seems to be heard beyond the words they pronounce. One senses the speech of the elements, fragments from choirs, resounding in the Holy of Holies, of the Universe we imagine. Realist poets frequently give us valuable treasures, but these treasures are such that, having gotten them, we are satisfied, and something has been reduced. Symbolist poets give us a magic ring in their creations, which makes us happy, as a jewel does, and at the same time it calls us to something else. We feel the proximity of something new and unknown for us, and looking at the talisman, we go, we depart for someplace further along, further and further.

And so, these are the basic outlines of Symbolist poetry: it speaks its own special language, and this language is rich with intonations; like music and painting it arouses a complex mood in the soul—more than any other kind of poetry, it affects our aural and visual impressions, forces the reader to pass along the *reverse path of creativity:* a poet, creating his Symbolist work, goes from the abstract to the concrete, from idea to image. Whoever becomes acquainted with his works ascends from a picture to its soul, from spontaneous images, beautiful in their independent existence, to the hidden spiritual perfection that ascribes a double power to them.

They say that Symbolists are incomprehensible. In every school there are degrees, and features can be taken to absurdity, in everything that boils there is scum. But it is impossible to determine the depth of a river by looking at its foam. If we will judge Symbolism by worthless writers who create weak parodies, we will decide that this manner of creation is a distortion of common sense. If we will take true talents, we will see that Symbolism is a powerful force, that aspires to divine new combinations of thoughts, colors, and sounds, and frequently they divine them with irresistable persuasiveness.

If you love a spontaneous impression, enjoy in Symbolism the characteristic novelty and all the splendors of its pictures. If you love a complex impression, read between the lines—secret lines will step forth and speak to you eloquently.

Konstantin Balmont
1900

A REVIEW OF K. D. BALMONT'S *LET'S BE LIKE THE SUN*
V. Bryusov

Our days are exceptional—some of the most remarkable in history. One should know how to evaluate them. Unexpected and marvelous possibilities are being revealed to mankind. That which has for centuries seemed inert, dead, fundamental matter is beginning to tremble with life in the depths of our souls. It is as though some kind of windows had slammed shut in our existence and some sort of obscure shutters had parted. Like stems of plants we involuntarily, unconsciously turn our faces toward the source of light. Soothsayers of the new are everywhere—in art, in science, in ethics. Mysteries that we have not known before are revealed in everyday life. Events which we had passed by, paying no heed, now attract our full attention. Through their coarse thickness the radiance of another existence manifestly shines.

But there is no need to exaggerate the power of the movement attracting us. We are the crest of a risen wave, but it will break. It is still far to the sea, although from our height its salty scent is already evident. The caravan of humanity, traveling its course, has ascended to the top of a hill and the goal of its travels is visible. The youths, walking on ahead, are already shouting "Jerusalem! Jerusalem!" They kiss the earth and weep with joy. But the elders sternly stop them. They know how the desert mirage brings distant vistas closer. They know that they will have to descend the other side of the hill, that they will have to pass through another plain, ford rivers, conquer new hills, again lose their way and fall into despair.

Yes, the route is still long. That in which we now find promise will not soon come to pass. The flowers of mystical contemplation that were on the verge of reviving in us will yet again wither and die. More than once humanity will return in its intellectual designs to what is closest to it, the earthly, and more than once glorify it as unique.

There have already been epochs like ours in the past. Quite recently, during the years of Romanticism, these same distances were visible which are now being revealed to us—true, from a lesser height and more obscurely. The seventeenth century was such an epoch of insight. Our books, the creations of our art, are fated to experience years of oblivion in the graveyards of immeasurably expanded museums and libraries. It may be that they will have to wait whole centuries for their triumphant resurrection. Occasional madmen, chance dreamers for whom life at that time will be stuffy and confining, will begin searching through these dusty covers, these semi-abandoned canvases and bronzes, and, drinking in our words and songs, meeting echoes of their own dreams in the distant past, will say with amazement, "They already knew all this! They already dreamed of this!"

But while recognizing this inevitable, albeit temporary, loss of all our hopes, we must scrutinize the present all the more vividly. In it throb the first convulsions of what will unfold completely and perfectly centuries later. In today's man there are signs of those cravings and slakings that will fill the souls of our future brothers like a wild whirlwind. We will catch those signs. In the man of tomorrow they may not exist. We can perceive and surmise that life which we cannot participate in.

Tyutchev speaks precisely of this:

> Fortunate is the person who has visited this world
> During its fateful moments.
> He has been summoned by the most high
> As an interlocutor at their feast.
> He is a spectator of their great spectacles;
> He has been admitted into their councils.
> While still alive, yet like a heavenly dweller,
> He has drunk immortality from their chalice.

* * *

In few people does this tremor of the future manifest itself so clearly and powerfully as in K. D. Balmont. Others recognize perhaps more clearly the entire mysterious meaning of contemporaneity, but rarely does anyone carry this contemporaneity within himself, in his personality, or experience it more fully than Balmont. Balmont is first of all a "new man"; there is a new soul in him, new passions, ideals, expectations—different from those of earlier generations. To a certain extent he is already living that "tenfold" life, about which another contemporary poet has dreamed. And it is this *new* life that makes Balmont a poet of the *new* art. He did not arrive at it through a conscious choice. He did not reject the "old" art after rational criticism. He does not set himself the goal of realizing an ideal rationally discovered at an earlier time. In forging his verse, Balmont is only concerned about whether it is beautiful in his own mind, interesting in his own estimation, and if his poetry belongs all the same to the "new" art, it happened without his wanting it. He simply relates what is in his own soul, but his soul is among those that have only recently begun to flower in our land. It was the same with Verlaine in his day. In this lies all the power of Balmont's poetry, all the vitality of its trepidation, although in the very same quality lie its weakness and limitation.

> I want to do everything in everything
> In order to tremble ever and anon.

In these two lines A. Dobrolyubov expressed what is most inalienable in the new understanding of life. To live means to be in moments, to surrender to them. Let them take the soul imperiously and draw it into their impetuous rush as a whirlpool seizes a small pebble. That which has resulted now is true. What existed before this is already nonexistent. Perhaps there will be no future at all. People who harmonize their actions with stable convictions, with plans for their lives, with different convictions, somehow stand outside of life, on the shore. To freely submit to the replacement of all desires is the precept. To place the entire fullness of existence in every moment is the goal. To gain an extra glimpse of a star is worth falling into the abyss. One could sacrifice the love of an entire life to kiss just once the eyes of her who, among the passers-by, has pleased you. Everything—even pain, even horror—is desirable so long as it has filled the soul with trembling.

"I am consumed to ashes by each moment, I live in each betrayal," Balmont confesses. "Everyone knows how momentary I am," he says in another place. And in individual images he lets you see through, as though with your own eyes, those moments which absorb the whole world.

> You and I were drunk on fragrant cherry blossoms.
> Suddenly we forgot the morning.
> Suddenly we entered into dreams.
> And the morning turned into a shoreless sea—
> Seas of floating clouds, branches, shrubs, greenery.
> Flowers, trees, and grass, grass and flowers.
> Seas of colors, flowers, love and you and I.
> Face to face we bent together; hand in hand
> We were suddenly filled with the joy of lightly trembling grass.
> With immeasurable light the sun shone in the heights
> And there was ecstasy, surprise and you and I.
> The brief hour lived in us,
> Eternity reigned in us,
> Morning waxed for us, for us, for us.
> Dual radiations, we were two phantoms of spring—
> Dreams prompted by the fragrant bird-cherry trees.

But in order to yield to each moment one must love them all. Behind the exterior, the appearance of things, one must surmise their eternally beautiful essence. If one sees around oneself only what is accessible to ordinary human vision, one cannot pray to everything. But from the most insignificant thing there is a passage to the most magnificent. Every event is a boundary between two infinities. Every object is created by myriad wills and is an indispensible link to the future fate of the universe. Every soul is a deity and every meeting with a person reveals a new world to us. Nothing is petty: all phenomena are like a light fabric covering fathomless abysses. Only one who does not see them, who is blind, boldly walks near them, among them. One able to look into their depths knows the sacred horror before the abysses surrounding life.

Sleep, half-dead, withered flowers,
Like the beauties that knew no blossoming;
Nurtured by the Creator beside well-traveled routes,
Crushed by a sightless, heavy wheel.

When everyone is celebrating the birth of spring,
When unrealizable dreams are coming into being,
When everyone can be delirious, and only you cannot—
Beside you spreads the cursed path.

And, half-broken, you lie in the dust—
You, who could have brightly looked into the distant sky,
You, who could have met happiness like everyone—
Lie in feminine, inviolate, virginal beauty.

Sleep now that you've looked upon the fearsome, dusty road;
Your equals may reign, but you must sleep forever—
Arranged by God for a festival of dream—
Innocent of the blossoming of beauty, sleep.

The symbolism of this poem attains an all-embracing compass. It forcefully compels us to feel that, close beside us all, that "fearsome" path lies, where every person may perish under a fateful, heavy, "sightless" wheel.

Nowhere does the mystical side of the world reveal itself so manifestly as in love. In the moment of passionate confession, in the moment of passionate embrace, one soul peers directly into another. The mysterious roots of love, its sexual origin, go deep into the very core of the world, sink into the fundamental principle of the universe, where the difference between I and not-I, between you and he disappears. Love is the absolute limit of our existence, and the beginning of a new existence, a bridge of golden stars, over which a person crosses to that which is "not man," or even "not yet man"—to God or beast. Love allows one, even only for a moment, to break away from the conditions of one's existence, to inhale air from another sky, a fusion of all feelings, all thought, all life, the whole world, into one outburst.

"Wandering through countless cities, I am always charmed by love alone"; these are Balmont's words. "Like the Sevillian Don Juan," he passes in love from one soul to another in order to see new worlds and their mysteries. His poetry glorifies and celebrates love, all the rites of love, its entire rainbow. He says that, going along the path of love, he can attain "too much—everything!" And here love and voluptuousness are incorporated into the image of a destructive flower—the arum:

Tropical flower, splendid crimson arum.
Your blossoms burn with ecstatically joyful fire.
Your leaves are threatening, they cannot be forgotten—
Like lances, made deadly instruments by fate.

Flower-monster, evil-eyed and haughty,
With unkind fire, dual-hued and languishing,
Outwardly gleaming with the radiance of dawn,
Brightly violet and black inside.
Baneful flower, invincible arum,
I am devoted to your powerful charms.
I know what they lavishly promise me:
To breathe their burning poison with amorous festivity.

Neither in love nor in other ways, however, is the thirst for the fullness of the moment ever completely slaked, for by its very nature it is insatiable. It requires each moment to disintegrate into an infinite number of sensations, but in man everything is finite, everything has an end. For all the brightness of life, for all its madness, the feeling of hopeless and fateful dissatisfaction must grip each soul. Only in ecstasies does the soul truly and entirely surrender itself, but it lacks the power to undergo such ecstasies with any kind of frequency. Some portion of consciousness usually remains on guard, follows the whole turmoil of life in a detached way, and destroys the integrity of the moment, splits it in half with its barely perceptible but relentless gaze. From this tormenting awareness, envy invincibly arises for everything that lives without the form of human life: clouds, wind, water, fire. In the elements there is none of our consciousness: they can completely surrender themselves to every moment, without remembering what has flashed by, without knowing what will follow. They do not have to exclaim bitterly, as we do, about every changing moment: "They're the wrong ones, the wrong ones!"

Songs to the elements are one of the favorite themes in Balmont's lyrics. "I am unfamiliar with what is human," he notes. He writes hymns to Fire, the Sun, the planets. An entire section of his book is devoted to the "four voices of the elements." He calls the wind his "eternal brother," and the ocean the ancient "progenitor" of all human generations.

Ocean, my ancient forebear,
Keeper of a millenial dream,
Bright dusk, giver of life, avenger,
Watery sky going far into the depths!

Mirror of primordial inceptions,
Seer of the first dawn,
Knower of more than we may know—
I am speaking with you, immortal one!

You are a wholeness forged by no one.
The world of land is empty and dead for the heart—
But you breathe eternally in boundlessness
With thousands of youthfully ravenous mouths!

Gracefully solemn, quiet, stormy, tender,
You are like life: truth and deception.
Let me be a damp grain of your sand,
A drop in the eternal... Eternity! Ocean!

Four fundamental currents in Balmont's art are the thirst for the completeness of every moment, sensing the abysses that surround us, the feeling of mystery in passion, and merging with elemental life. They draw all of his impressions into their channels. Indeed, they determine his literary sympathies as well ("We like the poets who are like us"). In quest of the full life, of integral, impetuous characters, he turned to Calderon, to the Spanish drama of the seventeenth century. "The sense of mysteries" makes him akin to the poet of horror, mad Edgar; his attitude toward love, passion, and women draws him close to Baudelaire and today's "decadents"; and finally his penetration into the life of the elements allies him with Shelley and Indian pantheism. Adjunctive to the basic currents are secondary ones; these are rather tributaries with semi-independent lives of their own, yet essentially nourished by the same currents. Hence, in consequence of his belief in the possibility of a "full" life, and thus its opposite, he hates life that is lusterless and temperate. This leads him to stinging, barely lyrical satires (e.g., "In Houses"). Hymns to the elements, on the other hand, often resolve into quiet children's songs—gentle, meek, and beautiful songs about fields, springs, dawns, and snowflakes. But the four voices remain fundamental in Balmont's entire being and in all his poetry. And they all somehow blend into the full-voiced exclamation of his *rusalka,* who has managed to swim up "from the deep sea floor" and look at the sun, although it burned her eyes:

I have seen the sun, she said:
Does it matter what the future holds?

* * *

What "we now consider an idle dream"—all manner of presentiments, suggestions, foretelling, and sympathy, all that is now in us feebly and fortuitously—will someday constitute, of course, the real essence of man's spiritual life. The present turtle's pace of thought, our causal cognition, will be replaced by an ardent intuition. The limits of consciousness will expand and be submerged by that immensity which we now call the unconscious. But in that barely conceivable future these mysterious powers will attain their full flowering and make man in all aspects of life more discerning, more sensitive, more commanding. But now, having barely awakened from a sleep lasting centuries, they cannot replace the coarser but more conventional (for us) means of cognizing the world. It is easier for us to move ahead in thought at a crawl from situation to situation, like a worm surveying the land, than to try to fly like birds on unsteady wings. Thus a blind person who has just regained his sight still relies on his sense of touch (and rightly so!).

In Balmont the unconscious life predominates over the conscious. But, proud of his bright eye, this blind man who is recovering his sight depends too much on the power of his vision. He dares to venture where there can be no path, sometimes slipping pitifully and falling where many walk freely with a stick. Wherever there is power in consciousness and clarity of thought, Balmont is weaker than the weak. All of his efforts to achieve breadth of thought, to imbue his verses with broad generalizations, to encompass centuries in a concise image, end in failure. His epic effort, the long poem "Artist Devil," except for several beautifully formulated thoughts, and a few truly lyrical fragments, is completely composed of rhetorical commonplaces rising from that scream with which singers strive to conceal vocal insufficiencies. And in his lyrics Balmont can never survey his creations with the impartial view of a critic. He is either in them or hopelessly distant from them. Hence Balmont can never correct his verses. His corrections are distortions. If he fails with a certain verse he rushes on to the next, satisfied—in the interests of association—with any kind of approximate expression. This obscures the meaning of some of his verses and the obscurity is of the most undesirable kind: it is occasioned not by the ambiguity of the content but in the imprecision of the selected expressions. In such cases Balmont is satisfied even with empty, hackneyed phrases that say nothing. For all the subtlety of the general construction of his poems he reaches the limits of banality in individual verses.

* * *

In one of his poems Balmont speaks of himself:

> I am the refinement of the leisurely Russian tongue;
> Other poets before me are precursors.

If Balmont said this with his individual line in view, its musicality, he is right. Balmont's equals in the art of verse have not existed in Russian literature and do not exist. It might have seemed that in the melodies of Fet Russian verse reached maximum ethereality and airiness, but where others saw limits, Balmont discovered the boundless. Such an unattainable model of euphony as Lermontov's "On an airy ocean" pales completely in comparison with Balmont's best songs. Yes! He was the first to discover "inclinations" [*uklony*, "inflections," "deviations," "divagations"] in our poetry, to discover possibilities that no one had suspected, unprecedented "reprises" [*perepevy,* "echoes"] of vowels blending into one another like drops of moisture, like crystal ringing.

And yet Balmont's verse has retained the whole construction, the entire framework of conventional Russian verse. One might have expected Balmont, in his impetuous craving for changing impressions, to surrender his verses to the will of the four winds, to shatter them, to cut them up into small, glittering pieces, into a pearly dust.

But this simply has not happened. Balmont's verse is the verse of Pushkin and Fet—perfected, refined, but essentially the same. The movement that created *vers libre* in France and Germany, which sought new artistic devises, new forms in poetry, a new instrument for the expression of new feelings and ideas, left Balmont almost completely unaffected. To make things worse, when Balmont attempts to adopt the features of the new verse from others, his success is poor. His "broken verse" [*preryvistye stroki*], as he calls his meterless verse, loses all the charm of Balmontian musicality without acquiring the freedom of the poetry of Verhaeren, Dehmel, and D'Annunzio. Balmont is Balmont only when he writes in strict meters, correctly alternating strophes and rhymes, observing all the conventions developed during two centuries of our versification.

And new content far from always fits into the Procrustean bed of these correct meters. Madness, forced into an excessively rational stanza, loses its elementality. Lucid forms impart a vulgarizing clarity to all the vague chaotic elements which Balmont attempt to pour into them. It is as though he accept Pushkin's "Until Apollo calls the poet . . ." in reverse. The Pushkinian poet's soul awakened like an eagle responding to divine summons. In Balmont it loses some of its power and freedom. Balmont is free and unlimited in life; in art he is fettered and entangled in thousands of rules and prejudices. He is a "genius of the elements" and a "bright god" (his own words) in life, but in poetry first of all a man of letters. His transports and passionate experiences pale in passing through his art. For the most part only fading embers remain of the fire and light; they are still fiery and bright for us, but they are already wholly different from the sun that they were.

Such are the limits of Balmont's poetry.

* * *

Let's Be Like the Sun is Balmont's sixth collection of verse (if the one published in 1890 is not counted). His last collection, *Burning Buildings,* was a momentary flare, a glittering display of fireworks. It was almost entirely composed in a few weeks. It had the poignancy and tension of rapture. *Let's Be Like the Sun* is the art of several years. Here Balmont's poetry has spread out to its full expanse and apparently reached its eternal banks. Here and there it has attempted to splash over these banks in a kind of turbid, weak wave, but without success; it is fated to remain under this horizon. But in his own world Balmont will of course reach even newer depths, for which he now merely yearns.

Let's Be Like the Sun places Balmont immediately after Tyutchev and Fet in the ranks of our lyric poets. He is their nearest and only successor. Among contemporary poets Balmont is indisputably the most significant, both in the power of his elemental gift and his influence on literature. All of his contemporaries will have to be careful first of all not to fall into the orbit of his gravity, to guard their independence. To vie with Balmont in the realm of the pure lyric is a dangerous feat. There is little hope of surviving even as a cripple, like Jacob.

Valery Bryusov
1903

KEYS TO THE MYSTERIES
V. Bryusov

I

When unsophisticated people are confronted with the question "What is art?" they do not try to comprehend where it came from, what place it holds in the universe, but accept it as a fact, and only want to find some application for it to their lives. Thus arise the theories of useful art, the most primitive stage in the relationship between man's thought and art. It seems natural to people that art, if it exists, should be suitable for their dearest small needs and necessities. They forget there are many things in the world that are completely useless in terms of human life, like beauty, for example, and that they themselves constantly commit acts that are totally useless— they love and they dream.

It seems ridiculous to us now, of course, when Tasso assures us that poetic inventions are similar to the "sweets" that are used to coat the edge of a dish with bitter medicine; we read, with a smile, Derzhavin's poems to Catherine the Great, in which he compares poetry to sweet lemonade. But did not Pushkin, partially under the influence of echoes of Schelling's philosophy and partially arriving at the same opinions independently, reproach the dark masses for seeking "usefulness" and say that they were worth less than a "cooking pot," and didn't his tongue slip in "Monument" when he wrote these verses:

> And I will long be the favoite of the people,
> Because I aroused good feelings with my lyre.

And didn't Zhukovsky, adapting Pushkin's poems for print, furnish the following line in a more direct way: "That I was useful because of the vital charm of my verses...," which gave Pisarev cause for rejoicing.

In the greater public, the public that knows art in terms of serialized novels, operatic productions, symphonic concerts, and exhibits of paintings, the conviction that art's function is to provide noble diversion prevails, indivisibly, to this day. Dancing at balls, skating, playing cards— these are also diversions, but less noble ones; and people who belong to the intelligentsia, meanwhile, read Korolenko, or even Maeterlinck, listen to Chaliapin, go to the Peredvizhnaya, and to decadents' exhibits. A novel helps to pass the time in a train or in bed, before falling asleep, you meet acquaintances at the opera, and find diversion at art exhibits. And these people attain their goals, they really relax, laugh, are entertained and fall asleep.

None other than Ruskin, an "apostle of beauty," speaks out in his books as a defender of "utilitarian art." He advised his pupils to draw olive leaves and rose petals, in order to discover for themselves and to give others more information than we have had up to now about Grecian olives and England's wild roses. He advised them to reproduce cliffs, mountains, and individual rocks, in order to obtain a more complete understanding of the characteristics of mountainous structure. He advised them rather to depict ancient, disappearing ruins, so that their images could be preserved, at least on canvas, for the curiosity of future ages. "Art," says Ruskin, "gives Form to knowledge, and Grace to utility; that is to say, it makes permanently visible to us things which otherwise could neither be described by our science, nor retained by our memory." And more: "the entire vitality of art depends upon its being either full of truth or full of use. Great masters could permit themselves in awkwardness, but they will never permit themselves in uselessness or in unveracity."

A very widespread, if not prevailing, school of literary historians treats poetry in the same way that Ruskin does the plastic arts. They see in poetry only the exact reproduction of life, from which it is possible to learn the customs and mores of that time and country where the poetic work was created. They carefully study descriptions of the poet, the psychology of the characters he has created, his own psychology, passing on then to the psychologies of his contemporaries and the characteristics of his times. They are totally convinced that the whole sense of literature is to help in the study of life in this or that century, and that readers and poets themselves fail to realize this, as uneducated people, and simply remain in error.

Thus the theory of "useful art" has rather eminent supporters, even in our time. It is more than obvious, however, that it is impossible to stretch this theory to cover all the manifestations of art, that it is ridiculously small for it, as a dwarf's caftan would be for the Spirit of the Earth. It is impossible to limit all art to Suderman and Bourget, just to please the good bourgeois, who want "noble diversions" from art. Much in art does not come under the concept of "pleasure," if one considers this word only in its natural sense, and does not put the term "aesthetic pleasure" under it, because it does not say anything and itself demands an explanation. Art terrifies, it shakes us, it makes us cry. In art there is an Aeschylus, an Edgar Allen Poe, a Dostoevsky. Just recently L. Tolstoy, with his customary accuracy of expression, compared those who seek only pleasures in art to people who would try to convince us that the only goal of eating is the pleasure of taste.

It is also just as impossible to please science and knowledge by seeing only reflections of life in art. Although the most divine Leonardo wrote essays about *come lo specchio è maestro de' pittori,* and although until recently in literature and the plastic arts, "realism" seemed to be the final word (that is what is written in today's textbooks)—art has never reproduced but has always changed reality: even in da Vinci's pictures, even among the most ardent realist authors, like Balzac, our Gogol, and Zola. There is no art that can repeat reality. In the external world, nothing exists that corresponds to architecture and music. Neither the Cologne cathedral nor Beethoven's symphonies can reproduce what surrounds us. In sculpture there is only a form without any paint, in a painting there are only colors without form, but in life, however, the one and the other are inseparable. Sculpture and painting give immobile moments, but in life everything flows in time. Sculpture and painting repeat only the exterior of objects: neither marble nor bronze is able to render the texture of skin; a statue has no heart, lungs, or internal organs; there are no hidden minerals in a drawing of a mountain ridge. Poetry is deprived of any embodiment in space; it snatches up only separate moments and scenes from countless feelings, from the uninterrupted flow of events. Drama unites the means of painting and sculpture with the means of poetry, but beyond the decoration of the room there are no other parts of the apartment, no streets, no city; the actor who goes off into the wings stops being Prince Hamlet; what in actuality lasted twenty years can be seen on the stage in two hours.

Art never deceives people, with the exception of anecdotal cases, like the foolish birds pecking at fruits painted by Zeuxis. No one believes a picture is a view through an open window, no one greets the bust of his acquaintance, and not one author has been sentenced to prison for an imaginary crime in a story. Besides, we refuse to call artistic precisely those works which reproduce reality with a singular resemblance. We recognize neither panoramas nor wax statues as art. And what has been accomplished if art succeeds in mimicking nature? Of what use can the doubling of reality be? "The advantage of a painted tree over a real one," says August Schlegel, "is only that there won't be any caterpillars on it." Botanists will never study a plant according to drawings. The most expertly depicted marina will never replace a view of the ocean for the traveler, if only because a salty breeze will not blow in his face and the sounds of waves crashing against the beach rocks will not be heard. We will leave the reproduction of reality to photography and the phonograph—technicians' inventions. "Art belongs to reality as wine does to grapes," Grillparzer said.

The defenders of "utilitarian art" have, it's true, one refuge. Art does not serve the goals of science. But it can serve society, the social order. The use of art could be that it unites separate personalities, transfusing one person's feelings into another, so that it welds the classes of society into one whole and helps their historic struggle among themselves. Art from this point of view is only one means of communication for people among a number of different means, which are, first of all, the word, then writing, the press, the telegraph, the telephone. The common word and prose speech render thoughts, art renders feelings... Guyau defended such a sphere of thought with force and wit. Here in Russia, L. Tolstoy has recently preached the same ideas, in a slightly altered form.

But does this theory really explain why artists create and why audiences, readers, and viewers seek artistic impressions? When sculptors knead clay, when painters cover canvases with paints, when poets seek the right word in order to express what they have to—not one of them sets his mind on transmitting his feelings to others. We know of artists who have scorned humanity, who have created only for themselves, without a goal, without the intention of making their works public. Is there really no self-satisfaction in creation? Did not Pushkin say to the artist: "Your work is your reward?" And why don't the readers cut this telegraph line between themselves and the soul of the artist? What is there for them in the feelings of someone they don't know, who may have lived many years ago, in another country? The task of scholarship about art is to solve the riddle of what consolidates the artist's dark cravings and the corresponding cravings of his listeners and viewers. And there is no solution in the scholastic answer: "art is useful because it facilitates the intercourse of feelings; and we want intercourse by feelings because we have a special instinct for communication."

The stubbornness of the advocates of "utilitarian art," despite all attacks on them by European thinkers of the last century, has not weakened yet and will probably not run dry as long as arguments about art continue to exist. There is always the possibility of pointing to its usefulness in one way or another. But how easy it is to use this object, that force! Archeologists learn about ancient life from the remains of buildings, but we don't build houses so that their ruins can help archeologists in the twenty-fifth century. Graphologists affirm that it is possible to learn about the character of a person from his handwriting. But the Phoenicians (according to the myth) invented writing for an entirely different purpose. The peasant in Krylov's fable condemned the ax to cut chips. The ax noted with justification that it was not guilty of being dull. In Mark Twain's book about the prince and pauper, poor Tom, once he is in the palace, uses the state seal to crack nuts. Perhaps Tom cracked nuts very successfully, but the state seal was meant to be used for other things.

II

People who think differently, who put aside the question of what art is needed for, what use it is, have asked themselves another metaphysical question: What is art? Separating art from life, they examine its creations as something self-important, self-contained. Thus arose the theories of "pure art"—the second stage in the relationship between man's thought and art. Carried away by the struggle with the defenders of applied, utilitarian art, these people have gone to the other extreme and have affirmed that art need never have any kind of utility, that art is diametrically opposed to all profit, all purpose: art is purposeless. Our Turgenev has expressed these thoughts with merciless frankness: "Art has no purpose other than art itself."And in a letter to Fet he is even more explicit "It's not that useless art is rubbish; uselessness is precisely the diamond in its crown." When the supporters of these views asked: what unites into one class the creations that people recognize as artistic, the pictures of Raphael, and Byron's verses, and Mozart's melodies—why is all of this art?—what do they have in common? They answered—Beauty!

This word, first uttered in the same sense in antiquity, then seized upon and repeated thousands of times by German aestheticians, has become an incantation *sui generis*. They have satiated themselves, made themselves drunk with it, not even wanting to fathom its sense.

> A genius should admire
> Only youth and beauty...

Pushkin said. Maykov repeated his precept almost word for word when he said that art:

> Is like revelations
> From the heights above the stars,
> From the kingdom of eternal youth
> And eternal beauty.

Baudelaire, who it would seem would be foreign to them, created a stunning image of Beauty, destructive and attractive:

> Je suis belle, ô mortels! comme un rêve de pierre,
> Et mon sein, où chacun s'est meurtri tour à tour,
> Est fait pour inspirer au poète un amour
> Eternel et muet ainsi que la matière
> ....
> Et jamais je ne pleure et jamais je ne ris.

When the theory of pure art had just been created, it was possible to understand that beauty meant exactly what it means in the language. It was possible to apply the word "beautiful" to almost every work of ancient art and to art of the time of pseudoclassicism. The nude bodies of statues, the images of gods and heroes were beautiful; tragedies' myths were sublimely beautiful. There were, however, hanged slaves, incest, and a Thersites in Greek sculpture and poetry—which did not fit too well with the concept of beauty. Aristotle and his later imitator Boileau had to advise artists to depict ugliness in such a way that it seemed, nevertheless, attractive. But the Romantics and their successors, the realists, rejected this embellishment of reality. All the world's ugliness invaded artistic works. Deformed faces, rags, the pitiful conditions of reality stepped out into pictures; novels and poems changed their place of action from regal castles to dank cellars and smoky attics. Poetry took on the hustle and bustle of everyday life, with the vices, horrors, and vanity of the petty, commonplace, little people of today. When the talk turned to Plyushkin, there was not any possibility of referring even to spiritual beauty. Beauty, like the virgin Astrae of mythology, the *ultima coelestum,* evidently abandoned art once and for all, and after Gogol, after Dickens, after Balzac, one was able to praise revelations only with an eye completely blind to the surroundings:

> From the heights above the stars,
> From the kingdom of eternal youth
> And eternal beauty.

In addition, even the very concept of beauty is not immutable. There is no special, universal measure of beauty. Beauty is no more than an abstraction, a common notion, similar to the notions of truth, good, and many other widespread generalizations of human thought. Beauty varies with the centuries. Beauty is different for different centuries. What was beautiful to the Assyrians seems ugly to us; fashionable clothes, which captivated Pushkin by their beauty, arouse laughter in us; what the Chinese now consider beautiful is foreign to us. But in the meantime, works of art from all ages and all nations conquer us equally. History was recently a witness to how Japanese art subjugated all of Europe, even though beauty in these two worlds ls completely different. There is inalterability and immortality in art, which beauty doesn't have. And the marble statues of the Pergamon altar are eternal not because they are beautiful, but because art has inspired its own life in them, independent of beauty.

In order to reconcile the theory of "pure art" with the facts somewhat, its defenders have had to violate the notion of beauty in every possible way. Since ancient times, when speaking about art, they began to give the concept of "beauty" different, often rather unexpected meanings. Beauty was identified with perfection, with unity in diversity, it was sought in undulating lines, in softness, in moderateness of dimensions. "The unfortunate notion of beauty," says a German critic, "has been stretched in all directions, as if it were made of rubber . . . they say that, in relation to art, the word 'beauty' should be understood in a broader sense, but it would be better to say too broad a sense. To affirm that Ugolino is beautiful in a broader sense is the same as avowing that evil is good in a broader sense and that a slave is a master in a broader sense."

The substitution of the word "typicality" for "beauty" has enjoyed particular success. People have assured us that works of art are beautiful because they represent types. But if you lay these two concepts one on top the other, they are far from congruent. Beauty is not always typical, and not everything typical is beautiful. *Le beau c'est rare,* says one whole school of art. Emerald green eyes seem beautiful to too many people, although they are rarely encountered. Winged human figures in Eastern pictures are striking because of their beauty, but they are the fruit of fantasy and themselves create their own types. On the other hand, are there not animals that are ugly by their very distinguishing marks, which are impossible to depict typically in any other way than ugly? Such as cuttle-fish, skates, spiders, and caterpillars? And the types of all inner ugliness, all vices, all that is base in a man, or stupid, or trite—how could they become beauty? And isn't the new art, more and more boldly entering into the world of individual, personal feelings, sensations of the moment and of just this moment, breaking absolutely and forever with the specter of typicality?

In one place Pushkin speaks about the "Science of love," about "love for love," and notes:

> this important amusement,
> Praised in our forefathers' time,
> Is worthy of old apes.

These same words can be repeated about "art for art's sake." It separates art from life, i.e., from the only soil on which something can grow into humanity. Art for the sake of aimless Beauty (with a capital letter) is dead art. No matter how irreproachable the sonnet's form, no matter how beautiful the marble face of a bust, if there is nothing beyond these sounds, beyond the marble, what will attract me to it? Man's spirit cannot be reconciled with peace. *"Je hais le mouvement qui dèplace les lignes"*—I hate any movement that displaces lines," says Baudelaire's Beauty. But art is always seeking, always an outburst, and Baudelaire himself poured not deathly immobility, but whirlpools of grief, despair, and damnation into his chiseled sonnets. The same state seal that Tom used to crack nuts in the palace probably sparkled very prettily in the sun. But even its beautiful shine was not its purpose. It was created for something greater.

III

People of science have approached art in completely different ways. Science has no pretensions about penetrating the essence of things. Science knows only the relations of the phenomena, knows only how to compare and contrast them. Science cannot examine anything without knowing its relation to another thing. Science's conclusions are observations about correlations between objects and phenomena.

Science, approaching works of art with its special methods, first of all has refused to consider them by themselves. It understands that works of art without any relation to man—to the artist/creator and the person who is perceiving someone else's creation—give no more than a painted canvas, chiseled stone, words and sounds connected into periods. It is impossible to find anything in common between Egyptian pyramids and Keats' poems if you forget about the designs of the builder and the poet, and about the impressions of the viewers and readers. It is possible to identify one with the other only in the human spirit. Art exists in man and nowhere else. The honor of recognizing this truth belongs to the philosophers of the English school. "Beauty," wrote Brown, "is not anything that exists in objects independently of the mind which perceives them, and permanent therefore, as the objects in which it is falsely supposed to exist. It is an emotion of the mind, varying, therefore, like all our other emotions, with the varying tendencies of the mind, in different circumstances."

Relying on this truth, science has naturally discovered two ways of studying art: studying the emotional excitement that seizes the viewer, reader, or listener when he surrenders to artistic impressions, and studying the emotional excitement that prompts an artist to create. Science started out on these two paths, but almost from the first step it lost its way.

We must recognize as hopelessly unsuccessful the attempt to connect the study of aesthetic excitement, those impressions that works of art give us, with physiology. The connection between psychological and physiological facts poses a riddle for science even in the most elementary phenomena. It still cannot explain the transition between the prick of a pin to the sensation of pain. The desire to reduce immeasurably complex artistic emotions to something like the pleasant or unpleasant movement of the eyeball cannot provide us with anything but a subject for ridicule. Every physiological explanation of aesthetic phenomena goes no further than dubious analyses. We could achieve the same measure of success looking for answers to the questions of higher mathematics in physiology (at its present stage of development).

Psychology could do no more here. But even this science, which Maeterlinck said had "usurped the beautiful name of Psyche," is also still far from maturity. Up to now it has investigated only the simplest phenomena of our spiritual life, although with a flippancy characteristic of children, it hastens to affirm that it already knows everything, that there is nothing else in the human spirit, and if there is, it is carried out according to the same models. Finding itself confronted by one of the most mysterious phenomena of human spiritual existence, the sphinx-like riddle of art, psychology began to solve this complex mathematical problem, which demands the most refined methods of advanced analysis, using only the four principles of arithmetic. The problem remained unresolved, of course, the answer obtained was most arbitrary. But psychology announced that the work had been done. And if the facts themselves did not fit the pattern, so much the worse for the facts!

Psychological aesthetics gathered a number of phenomena, which it recognized as "direct producers of aesthetic sensation," such as, for example, in the area of vision: combinations of chiaroscuros, harmonies of colors and their unification with luster, the beauty of complex movements and forms, the proportions of parts, the firm and soft support of weight,— or in the area of sound: special combinations of tones called melody and harmony, tempo, emphasis, cadence. It added various pleasant sensations, procured by means of association, to these "producers." And psychological aesthetics now intends to solve the question of art with addition and subtraction, without even using "multiplication and division." They seriously think that every artistic creation can be divided, in its crudest sense, into these basic elements: brilliance, curvature, and melody, and that after this division there is no remainder.

Without even saying that the simplicity of many of these quasi-elements is extremely dubious, the whole matter comes down to the fact that only in art do these impressions evoke "aesthetic excitement." We all know the brilliance of the sun, it is often pretty, pleasant, one can find pleasure in it; but there is none of that unique thrill in it that works of art pour into everyone who truly knows how to cling to it. But in a poem, where the same sun is depicted, although it is made of verses and "does not enlighten" (Lotze's expression)—it shines for us with an entirely special brilliance, the brilliance of a work of art. And it is like this everywhere. If we break down Klinger's bust of Beethoven into its pieces, to the varicolored marble, the dull and lustrous metals, and even add the "associative" feelings about the creator of the Ninth Symphony, the rapture that grips us when we confront the creation of a new Phidias will not be there! And the non-artificial beauty of nature, the nicest, most elegant and triumphant landscapes that enchant and captivate us, will never give us just that which is called "aesthetic excitement." Only special divine emissaries are destined to evoke this sensation—the ones who have been given the significant name of creator—*poietes*.

Another path has led science to study the emotional excitement that causes man to sculpt statues, to paint pictures, to compose poems. Science has begun to try to find out what kind of desires attract the artist, compel him to work—sometimes to exhaustion—and find self-satisfaction in his work. And that spirit that wafted over science in the century just past, which in its time removed things and phenomena from their places, even though they seemed immobile to the philosophical eighteenth century, turned them into an uncontrollable stream of the eternally changing, eternally evolving world, the spirit of evolutionism—this spirit fixed the researchers' attention on the origin of art. As in many other cases, science substituted the word to "become" for the word to "be" and began to investigate not "What is art" but "Where did art come from," thinking that it was answering one and the same question. And so detailed research appeared about the origin of art among aboriginal people and savages, about the crude powerless rudiments of ornament, sculpture, music, poetry... Science thought it would solve the mystery of art by analyzing its genealogical tree. In its own way, the theory of heredity was applied here, with the assurance that a child's soul depends entirely on the combination of his ancestors' spiritual characteristics.

The investigation of art's ancestors led to the theory that was first expressed by Schiller with complete definiteness. Spencer picked up and developed this theory in passing, but with overwhelming scientific detail. The forefather of art was recognized as the game. Lower animals do not play games at all. Those who, thanks to better nutrition, have a surplus of nervous energy, feel the need to expend it—and they spend it on games. Mankind spends it on art. A rat that gnaws on things that are not good for it, a cat that plays with a ball of yarn, and especially children playing are already indulging in artistic activity. It seemed to Schiller that he was not debasing the significance of art at all with this theory. "Man," he says, "plays only when he is a person in the full sense of the word, and he is only a person when he plays." This theory adjoins, of course, to the theories of useless art, which Spencer realizes: "To seek an end, which would serve life, i.e., good and utility," he writes, "inevitably means to lose sight of its aesthetic character."

Similar to the other scientific solution to the enigma of art, this theory is also too broad to accurately define art, as the theories of "utilitarian" and "pure" art were too narrow. In its search for the simplest elements that make up aesthetic excitement, science has offered elements that are often not art and which completely fail to explain the idiosyncratic, unique influence of art. In its search for what causes us to be attracted to a creation, it has also named things that often do not lead to art at all. If all art is a game, then why is not every game art? How can we draw a boundary between them? Are not children playing with a ball more like adults playing cards than Michelangelo creating David? And why was this Michelangelo an artist when he sculpted his statues and was not an artist when he played knuckle bones? And why do we recognize aesthetic excitement when we listen to the flight of the Valkyries but are only amused when we watch kittens playing? How, finally, do we explain that admiration which artists of all ages arouse in mankind: we see them as prophets, as life's leaders, as teachers. Are Ibsen and L. Tolstoy only organizers of the great, universal games of our days?

Present-day science has until now turned out to be powerless in grappling with the enigma of art. The theories it has posited cannot stand because they conceal contradictions in themselves. But if we could even allow that the science of the future will luckily avoid all the submerged rocks and carefully, checking every step, feeling every inch of soil with the staff of its methods, come to all the conclusions that it can attain—will it give us the answer to what is art? But such a question cannot even exist for science, since it nonetheless asks about the essence of something. Science only answers about the position that aesthetic excitement occupies in the series of other emotional excitements that man has, and exactly what causes brought man, in the past millenia of his existence, to artistic creation. Will this satisify our intentions? Will we be calmed by these sober answers of exact science?

Of course not. Returning to the example that has already served us twice, we can say that science will only break down in a crucible the state seal that poor Tom took possession of. Science will tell him only how much gold and how much ligature are in it, will only explain how its brilliance influences human eyes and how heavy it is to carry. But as before, poor Tom will know nothing about the purpose of this thing. Who will solve the mystery of what art is, this state seal in the great state of the universe?

IV

The most striking thing is that all these theories posited have irrefutable facts behind them. Art gives us pleasure—who's going to argue! Art teaches—we know this from thousands of examples. But together with this there are often no easily attainable goals, no use, in art—only fanatics can deny this. Finally, art unites people, opens the heart, makes everyone communicants of the artist's creation. What is art? How can it be both useful and useless? serve Beauty and often be ugly? be a means of communication and seclude the artist?

The only method that can hope to answer these questions is intuition, inspired guessing—the method that philosophers and thinkers, who have sought the solution to the mystery of existence, have used in all ages. And I will point to one solution to the enigma of art that belongs precisely to a philosopher, which—it seems to me—gives an explanation to all those contradictions. This is the answer of Schopenhauer. The philosopher's own aesthetics are too closely tied to his metaphysics. But, tearing his guessing loose from the restricting chains of his thought, freeing his teachings about art from his accidentally entangled teachings about "ideas," the intermediaries between the worlds of noumena and phenomena—we arrive at a simple and clear truth: art is the comprehension of the world by other, non-rational ways. Art is what in other areas we call revelation. Works of art are doors half-opened to Eternity.

The world's phenomena, as they open up to us in the universe—extended in space and flowing in time, subject to the law of causality—must be studied by the methods of science, by rationality. But this study, based on the indications of our higher senses, gives us only approximate knowledge. Our eyes deceive us, attributing characteristics of a sunny ray to a flower that we are looking at. Our ears deceive us, reckoning vibrations of air as characteristics of a ringing bell. All our consciousness deceives us, transferring its characteristics, the conditions of its activity, to external objects. We live in the midst of an eternal, primordial lie. A thought, and consequently science, are powerless to expose this lie. The most that they could do is to point it out, to explain its inevitability. Science only brings order to the chaos of false concepts and arranges them according to rank, making it possible, making it easier to learn about them, but not to have cognition of them.

But we are not hopelessly locked in this "blue prison," using Fet's image. Signs are those moments of ecstasy, of supersensible intuition, that offer different comprehensions of worldly phenomena, that penerate more deeply under their external covering, into their core. The primordial task of art consists of fixing forever these moments of insight, of inspiration. Art begins at the instant when the artist tries to make his dark, mysterious sensations clear to himself. Where there is none of this clarification, there is no artistic creation. Where there is no mystery in a feeling, there is no art. A person for whom everything in the world is simple, clear, attainable, cannot become an artist. Art is only where there is audacity beyond the edge, breaking through the boundaries of the cognizable with the craving to scoop up at least a drop of

> An alien element, from the beyond.

"The gates of Beauty lead to cognition," said the same Schiller. In all the centuries of their existence, unconsciously, but unchangingly, artists have carried out their mission: to explain the mysteries revealed to them, and at the same time they have sought other, more perfect means of attaining cognizance of the universe. When the savage drew zigzags on his shield and affirmed that it was a "Serpent," he had already performed an act of cognition. In the same way the ancient marble statues, the images of Goethe's *Faust,* Tyutchev's poems—all of these are precisely renderings, in a visible, tangible form, of those insights that the artist had. True cognitions of things in them was revealed to the degree of completeness that imperfect materials of art (marble, paints, sounds, words...) allowed.

But in the course of long centuries, art has not given a clear and definite account of its purpose. Various aesthetic theories knocked artists off the path. And they raised idols, instead of praying to the true god. The history of the new art is primarily a history of its liberation. Romanticism, Realism, and Symbolism are three stages in the struggle of artists for freedom. They have finally thrown off the chains of enslavement to different random goals. Now art is finally free.

Now it is consciously devoted to its highest and singular purpose: to be the world's cognition beyond rational forms, beyond thinking about causality. Don't hinder this new art in its task, which at another time might seem useless and alien to present-day needs. You measure its use and modernity with standards that are too short. Our personal benefit is tied to the benefit of mankind. All of us live in eternity. Those questions of existence that art can answer will never stop being topical. Art is perhaps the greatest power that mankind possesses. At the same time when all the crowbars of science, all the axes of public life, are not able to break down the walls and doors that enclose us—art conceals within itself awesome dynamite, which can shatter those walls, and moreover it is the *sesame* that makes doors open by themselves. Let contemporary artists consciously forge their works in the shape of keys to the mysteries, in the shape of mystical keys that will unlock for mankind the doors of its "blue prison" to eternal freedom.

Valery Bryusov
1904

A HOLY SACRIFICE
V. Bryusov

Until Apollo calls for a
Holy sacrifice from a poet,
He is faintheartedly absorbed
By the bustle of a vain world.
His sacred lyre is silent,
His soul partakes of cold sleep,
And among the world's
Insignificant children, perhaps,
He is the least significant.

Pushkin

When Pushkin read Derzhavin's poem, "Let me be gnawed for my words, for my deeds the satirist will honor me," he said: "Derzhavin is not quite right. The words of a poet are his deeds." This is retold by Gogol, who added: "Pushkin is right." In Derzhavin's time, a poet's words, his works, seemed to be the *celebration* of deeds, something that accompanied life, that decorated it. "You are the glory, I will live by your echo," Derzhavin says to Felitsa. Pushkin placed the words of a poet not only on the same level as deeds, but even higher: a poet should reverentially bring his "holy sacrifice," but at other times he can be the "least significant," without demeaning his high calling. From this avowal it is just a short step to the recognition of art as something more important and more real than life, to the theory formulated with crude directness by Théophile Gautier:

Tout passe.— L'Art robuste
Seul à l'éternité

[Everything passes. Only powerful art is eternal.]

In Pushkin's poems the cry of one of Count Aleksei Tolstoy's letters before his death is already heard: "there is more worth living for than art!"

Pushkin has few works which are so foreign, so strange to us, as these verses about a poet, even with his keen hearing and ability to foresee the future quivering in our souls today!

Glorifying the poet's "words," as Derzhavin belittled them, Pushkin agrees with him in the certainty that these two areas are separate. Art is not life but something else. A poet is a dual being, an amphibian. That "among the world's insignificant children," he "rules vanity's affairs"—plays faro like an "eternally idle rake" (Pushkin), whether he serves as a minister, as a confidant of tsars (Derzhavin)—suddenly, by divine command, he is transformed, his soul takes wing, "like an eagle awakening," and he stands like a priest before the altar. In Pushkin's life this separateness was carried to the external differentiation of ways of living. Having "understood the rhymes," he "fled into the country" (Pushkin's own expression in a letter), literally on the "banks of wasteland's waves, in the broad, noisy oak groves. And all of Pushkin's school looked, with the same eyes, at poetic creation as something different from life. The duality was even carried to convictions, to a world view. It seemed completely natural that a poet would have one set of views of the world in his poems, and a different set in his life. It was possible to state with certainty that Lermontov, who wrote a poem about a demon, didn't believe in the actual existence of demons: a demon was for him a fairy tale, a symbol, an image. Only a very few poets of the time were able to retain the unity of their personalities in life and art. Such a person was Tyutchev: the world view which others professed only for creativity was in fact his belief. Such a person was Baratynsky: he was able to transfer his everyday understanding of the world into his poetry.

The road along which the artist who separated creativity from life travels leads straight to the barren heights of "Parnasse." "Parnassians" are those who bravely proclaimed the extreme conclusions of the Pushkinian poet, who agreed to to be "least significant" until Apollo's command "called him," a conclusion which of course would have horrified Pushkin. The same Théophile Gautier, who came up with the formula about the immortality of art, the last Romantic in France and the first Parnassian, left his own definition of a poet. "A poet," he writes, "is first of all a worker. The effort to put him on an ideal pedestal is utterly senseless. He must have precisely the same amount of intelligence as any worker, and is obliged to know his work. Otherwise, he's a poor day-laborer." The poet's work is polishing words and placing them in settings of verses, as a jeweler does— the processing of precious stones. And true to this precept, the Parnassians worked on their verses like mathematicians on their problems, perhaps, not without inspiration ("inspiration is needed as much in geometry as it is in poetry"—Pushkin's words), but most of all with attention, and in any case, without excitement. The young Verlaine, who had certainly been previously under the influence of Parnassianism, with his characteristic lack of restraint, noted straightforwardly: "we, who chisel words like bowls and very coldly write passionate verses. Poor people! Art is not for squandering one's soul. Is the Venus de Milo made of marble or not?"

> ...nous, qui ciselons les mots comme des coupes
> Et qui faisons des vers émus très froidement...

Pauvres gens! L'Art n'est pas d'éparpiller son âme:
Est-elle en marbre, ou non, la Venus de Milo?

But contemporary art, which is called "Symbolism" and "Decadence," did not pass along that deserted road. Two blossoms opened on the stem of Romanticism: Realism together with Parnassianism. The latter, although it perhaps "burns with eternal gold in chants," now has indisputably "dried up and collapsed," and the former gave seed to fresh sprouts. And everything that is new, that arose in Europe in the last quarter of the nineteenth century, grew out of those seeds. Baudelaire and Rops, who are still foreign to us in form, but familiar in their outbursts and experiences, the true predecessors of the "new art," appeared precisely in the epoch when Realism was the leading school: they would have been impossible without Balzac and Gavarni. They began within the ranks of the Parnassians, but they took only their understanding of form and its significance. Having left the Parnassians to collect their own *Trophées,* the "decadents" left them, in all the violence, all the grandeur and baseness of life, departed from dreams about the luxurious India of the rajahs and the eternally beautiful Hellas of Pericles, for the fires and hammers of factories, for the rumble of trains (Verhaeren, Arno Holz), for the customary arrangements of contemporary rooms (Rodenbach, Rimbaud), for all the torturous contradictions of the contemporary soul (Hoffmannsthal, Maeterlinck), for that contemporaneity that Realists hoped to realize. It's not accidental that the City of our time, which first entered art in the Realists' novels, found its best singers precisely among the decadents.

Romanticism tore away the ropes which Pseudoclassicism had used to bind the poet's soul, but it did not completely free it. The Romantic artist was still convinced that art should depict only the noble and the beautiful, that there are many things which do not belong to art, about which it must remain silent ("A genius should be an admirer of only youth and beauty," Pushkin wrote). Only Realism returned the whole world to art, in all its manifestations, great and small, beautiful and ugly. The liberation of art from its closed, prescribed limits was accomplished in Realism. After this it was sufficient for the thought that *the whole world is in me* to penetrate deeply into consciousness—and then our contemporary understanding of art arose. Like the realists, we accept life as the only subject for realization in art, but while they sought it outside themselves, we turn our gaze inwards. Each person can say of himself, with the same right by which all methodological conventions are affirmed: "Only I exist." To express one's experiences, which is the only reality accessible to our consciousness—this has become the artist's task. And this task has consequently defined the peculiarities of form—so characteristic of the "new art." When artists believed that their aim was to reproduce the external, they tried to imitate external, visible images, to repeat them. Realizing that an object of art is in the depths of feeling, in the spirit, called for a change in the method of creation. This is the path that led to the symbol. New, symbolic creativity was the natural consequence of the Realistic school, a new, further, inevitable step in the development of art.

Zola collected "human documents." He turned the writing of a novel into a complex system of study, simplified the work of an investigative attorney. Much earlier, our Gogol zealously filled his notebooks with materials for his future works, he wrote down conversations, bons mots, and sketched types he had seen. But the artist can only offer as a fateful image that which is in him. A poet can only reproduce his own soul; it's all the same whether it's in the form of a lyrical, frank confession, or if it fills the universe, like Shakespeare, with masses of eternally vital visions that he has created. The artist must fill up his own soul, not notebooks. Instead of making piles of notes and clippings, he must throw himself into life, into all its whirlwinds. The abyss between the artist's "words" and "deeds" disappeared for us when it turned out that creation is merely a reflection of life and nothing more. Paul Verlaine, standing on the threshold of the new art, already personified the type of person who did not know where life ends and art begins. This repentant drunkard, who had fashioned hymns to the flesh in taverns, and to the Virgin Mary in hospitals, did not renounce himself, bringing his "holy sacrifice," and did not scorn himself, his past, when he heard the "divine word." Whoever accepts Verlaine's verses must accept his life; whoever rejects him as a person, let him reject his poetry: it is inseparable from his person.

Pushkin, of course, was only taking refuge in the formula "until a poet is called" to a significant degree . . . It was necessary for him, as an answer for his enemies, who spitefully whispered in each other's ears about his "debauchery," about his passion for cards. Despite Pushkin's own confession that he was "least significant," his image seems much more lofty to us in life than does Yazykov's, who posited the totally opposite ideal for a poet ("Be majestic and holy in the world"). But it cannot be argued that as a Romantic (in the broad sense of the term), Pushkin gave us access to only certain sides of his soul in his works. At certain moments in his life *he* did not consider himself worthy to stand before the altar of his divinity for a "holy sacrifice." Like Baratynsky, Pushkin divided his experiences into "revelations of Purgatory" and "heavenly dreams." Only in those creations, so accidental for Pushkin, like "Hymn in Honor of the Plague," "Egyptian Nights," and "I remember school at the beginning of my life," are hints about the dark side of his soul preserved for us. The storms of passion that he experienced in Odessa or during the days that led to his tragic duel— Pushkin hid them from people, not only because of his personal pride, because he didn't want to exhibit his suffering for "the simple-minded to gape at," but also with the modesty of an artist, who separated life from art. What revelations perished in this enforced silence! It seemed to Pushkin that these confessions would debase his work, although they did not debase his life. By force, he tore himself, as a poet, away from himself, as a person, compelled himself to write "Angelo" and all the while dreamed about fleeing "to a pure refuge of works and peaceful delights," thinking that there he would find a second Boldino. There was no "refuge of delights and works," but days of painful separation from his bride, nightmares of his "criminal youth" that arose in solitude, and the threat of death drawing near!

We, for whom Edgar Allen Poe revealed the whole temptation of his "imp of the perverse," we, for whom Nietzsche reappraised old values, cannot follow Pushkin on this path of silence. We know only one precept for an artist: sincerity, extreme and ultimate. There are no special moments when a poet becomes a poet: he is either always a poet or never one. And the soul does not have to wait for the divine word in order to take wing like an "awakened eagle." This eagle must look at the world with eternally sleepless eyes. If the time has not come for bliss in this insight—we are ready to compel him to be watchful at any rate, at the price of suffering. We demand from a poet that he tirelessly bring his "holy sacrifices," not only with his verses, but with every hour of his life, with every feeling—his love, his hate, accomplishments and failures. Let the poet create, not his books, but his own life. Let him keep the altar fire burning, like Vesta's fire, let him kindle a great bonfire, unafraid of burning himself and his life in it. We throw ourselves on the altar of our divinity. Only a priest's knife, cutting our breasts, gives us the right to be called a poet.

Valery Bryusov
1905

DECADENCE AND SOCIETY
Z. Gippius

There's so much nonsense everywhere; everything has turned around and gotten so muddled that no one understands anything. Words have completely lost their original sense. Just pronounce something and someone has to ask: "But what do you mean by that?" "I—thus and so." Let's agree at the beginning.

I was somehow able to be present at an argument by three people about asceticism. One rejected it, another permitted it, and the third fervently affirmed it. They argued "for a long time, until they shed tears of strain," as Nadson writes, but in the end it turned out that all the tears were shed in vain: each of the arguers understood the word "asceticism" quite differently from his neighbor. If there were thirty people arguing, instead of three, it's quite possible that each would shout only about *his own* "asceticism."

Of course, to begin to get to the root of things and rework the meaning of every word is impossible; you risk never finishing. But, nevertheless, it doesn't hurt to agree on just which concept will be called by this or that word.

What is "society?"

Not wanting to go into complexities and particularities, nuances and transitions, I will first of all define "society" as the unification of human interests, i.e., their transformation into something whole—united human efforts directed towards that whole thing.

A bunch of people are pulling a loaded cart in the middle of the road out of the mud. The ones on the right side, I'm sure, can argue with the ones on the left; they'll shout that it must be pulled like this—not from there, from here; some will bother others, I dare say; but the cart is the same for them, they all have to tug at it, and if they are friendly or if they quarrel—they are nonetheless together, and all of them are somehow concerned with this one common cart. Not only "public argument" but also "social struggle" enters into "society."

But one must speak truthfully: society is such that, in this one notion, it is still not *public life;* that is, life as it is, as a whole, and it cannot be included in such a society of common interests. There is as much in common among people as there is not in common. Our jealous, narrow "society" has nothing to do with human differences. And "society" just starts out—and so begins the inclination to turn people into a flock of sheep, into a crowd that lives only by this common cart, by common (in relation to the cart) agreements and discords.

> ...Personalities have been erased, generic typicality has smoothed everything sharply individual, *restless,* eccentric. People, like goods, have become something handled wholesale, by the dozen, cheaper, worse separately, but stronger and more numerous *en masse.* Individualities have been lost, like the spray of a waterfall, in the common stream, not having even the faint comfort of "glistening and being distinguished, passing through the colors of the rainbow." Hence the natural, though it seems repugnant to us, indifference to the life of one's neighbor and to the fate of people: we deal with types, kinds, matters, not with people. Today a hundred people were buried in a coal mine, tomorrow only fifty will be; today ten people were killed on one railroad line, tomorrow only five will be.... and everyone looks on it as a minor evil. Society offers insurance ... What more can it do?.. There can be no shortcoming of goods being transported because someone's father or son is killed; neither can there be in the live rounds used in digging coal. You need a horse and a worker; it doesn't matter at all if the horse is a roan or if the worker is named Anempodist. The whole secret of the replacement of individuals by the masses, of the absorption of personal peculiarities by class, is in this *"doesn't matter at all!"*
>
> (Herzen)

And "society" ends in this replacement of individuals by the masses, where people, uniting, feel chiefly and even only like a crowd, a compact mass, where you can't distinguish anything and can't recognize anyone. Unwillingly and unconsciously, people themselves prune and erase their own peculiarities, their differences, don't want to know about them, and renounce them in the name of community. But, meanwhile, just this renunciation finally leads the community to destruction.

Not all the truth of life is in "community," only half the truth. The other half, the reverse—but only a half—is held by those people we now call "individualists."

II

There are more and more of them lately. The consciousness of individuality is being refined, in spite of everything, is growing and, as if dividing people, it is pulling them away from common work, from the very consciousness of their community. But this division only seems to exist. It is only temporary.

An individualist (I am speaking about actual individualists, not "decadents," about whom more later) has understood or perhaps felt that humanity is not a compact, homogeneous mass—but a mosaic picture, where each piece should not resemble another, but should be differentiated by color, form, size, and still each piece is nevertheless needed for the whole, fits tightly and wholly in *its own place.*

But one needs to know one's place, to see one's form and color; only then is it possible to compose one picture and not fall into a common heap. Individualists break away from "humanity," and suffering, scramble out of the heap. An individualist cannot *not* be separated, even for a moment; he has to feel his separateness, to have it totally in himself, only in order to find his separate place, that corresponds to him alone, in the true community.

A real consciousness of "individuality" does not destroy the consciousness of "humanity." The more deeply the difference is perceived, the more clearly the unity, the community, is felt.

This moment of retreat from the common into the personal, into one's self, into individual life, into one's own distinctiveness—this is the half-truth, the other half of the truth of the contemporary "social people." Just this moment of splitting life's truth in two is now very clear; this is our "present."

And a great, painful confusion, tragic nonsense, is the result. Individualists have not seen each other yet, because they are isolated and hate the herd-like society from which they have torn loose; they thirst for something else, but they don't find it. Social people hate individualists fiercely, totally misunderstand them, confuse them with decadents, who themselves are not mixed in with anyone else and cannot even mix. And so absurdity is piled on top of absurdity. Abuse on abuse. Pain on pain. Blood on blood. The cry of loneliness is covered by the roar of the herd. You can't make out anything, or anyone. People, who are essentially more distant from each other than I am at this minute from any black in South America, unite and agree in an external way. Those who should and could be together cannot see each other.

A matter that is, at its root, personal—centripetal—tries, abnormally, to put on societal clothes, leaps pitifully out into the open. On the contrary, matters that are by their very nature common, societal—centrifugal— appear as some kind of grimace directed at community, like a pile of felled logs that naively thinks it is a forest.

If Herzen were alive, how he would shout, with trebled force, that everything is "all to the bad." Herd-like society is to the bad. Individualists with their lost contact, decadents with their innocent indolence, identical obtuseness of senseless sleep or senseless blood, hunger and satiation, well-being and suffering, everything is to the bad. Belief in good despite everything is a pitiful illusion; you have to "know and see," and Herzen would see and know that this stifling and improbable confusion is to the final detriment of society and this final detriment is already beginning.

It is not an accident, however, that he does not see this. It is not an accident that he lived in his own time, and not ours. If he were living now— would the contemporary Herzen not see farther than the old one? And would he not say, as the same person but not quite the same, because he is a new model: "Yes, it's bad, but this bad is not to the bad, but to the good. This illness is not fatal. It's painful but it will grow wings. *Now I see.*"

III

Let us look, however, a little closer at the common nonsense. Let us examine just one little chunk of it, let us take one of its innumerable parts, and from this part, narrowing it more and more, only one concrete example.

Let us take a look at the decadents: what place do they occupy in the inflamed struggle between "humanity" and the "person," between these two inimical (for the time being) halves of one truth—and do the decadents actually occupy any place?

I will speak about literature, and even very narrowly, about literary decadents, but this does not mean at all that a decadent is chiefly a literary phenomenon, or generally involved necessarily with the field of art. A decadent, like a "social person" or "individualist," can be where he wants and who he wants to be: a doorman, a civil servant with special credits, a monk, a country doctor, a minister, a factory worker, a king, a store-keeper, a poet. People involved in one form of art or another are more accessible for observation, the particularly characteristic decadent disposition is expressed by these artistic types.

Decadents are in their own way—eunuchs—"which were so born from their mother's womb." A born eunuch is innocent: a decadent is innocent because he is born without the most basic traits of a human soul: the sense, as incontestable as the knowledge, that *I am not unique in the world, but I am surrounded by people like me.* This is as primitive and natural as having a nose, two eyes, two hands, seeing, hearing, the five normal senses. A decadent born without this sense is like a person born without the sense of hearing. No matter how much sounds are explained to him, he will never understand anything about them, and will not even believe, as he should, that they exist, because to have faith in something it is necessary to have an inner essence that somehow corresponds to it—that *there is something* to answer with, even in the darkest depths of the essence. An individualist, no matter how painfully he was torn from the compact mass of humanity, no matter how he cursed the "herd-like" society—he understands it and sees it, and curses it in the name of another, a new society, in the name of (let us say) unconscious unification of the two halves of one truth. That is, in the name of a "common life," without which it is impossible for him to breathe. As with a "herd-like" social person, sometimes the feeling of individuality heaped up in the soul, but always ready for insurrection, begins to stir. The individualist refines his consciousness of individuality on the basis, never changing for him, of a sense of community, of connection with other individuals. The decadent does not have this foundation, there is no feeling of community, of connection—not the slightest. He simply *doesn't suspect* that there are others besides him. Not having the necessary foundation, the background, he has no *consciousness* of personality in the proper sense of the word. There is nothing for him to refine. He has only a *sense* of personality, immobile, rounded, self-satisfying, and blind. He does not need the sense of sight; after all this individual remains equal and identical to himself, after all he cannot correspond to any other individual because there is no other.

If this really is an "individual," and what the value of such an individual is, whether this existence of an individual is real or not—this is another question and it seems that it is not even a question; it's too easy to answer. But we are not concerned with that. We are just exploring.

A real, complete decadent, "from his mother's womb," is truly a "child of nature." If he somehow incarnates in some form his spiritual experiences, reveals them—he does it as a person who is walking all alone in a meadow and singing a song. He walks and sings. If people pass by accidentally beyond the forest, they hear the song. But the singer never learns of it. He sings alone.

> I seek my joy
> In myself, loving myself,
> And I shape this
> Serenade for myself.

Or, close to these lines, by the same author, after many years:

> I alone will find joy,
>   Here everything is mine, only I am here.
> I'll light a quiet lamp...
>   I love it. It's mine.

Whoever looks in the window sees the lamp because it's lit. But who will look? There is no one.

"I am the free wind, wind, wind...," Balmont pours into his best, most complete poems. Tender Blok, from the newer ranks, only sings to himself about a "Queen," a "Maiden," that he alone sees, who comes only to him.... He sees himself and her, fashions hymns for himself and her. Alone, you will always understand what you sing, understand what you want to say when you speak; the Queen will understand because after all she is Blok; there are enough hints tossed out, half-expressed images, half-incarnate movements of the soul, signs, almost no words; and thus decadent poetry is poetry, but for all its deep, sometimes holy, sincerity, it is half-poetry, half-art. It is something half-developed, it is a child half-born, still-born—in the huge majority of cases.

There are good decadent poets and bad ones; there are strong voices and weak ones. A strong voice flies more quickly to the person accidentally passing by the forest. Perhaps the passer-by will say: "What a fine voice. What a nice song." But this is an accident, something that could also not have taken place. The singer sang for himself, and the passer-by did not see him, as if he weren't there.

"The city, forests, sunsets, factory smokestacks, the railroad, clouds, people—all of this is one thing. I am something else. I observe people, clouds, and smokestacks, and these things are distributed around me equally, but I sense only myself. In this way I alone really exist."

It's clear that with this innate defect of the soul there can be no struggle, no falls, no uprisings, no movement, except in a circle. And no achievements. What kind of struggle can there be, when there is no opponent? What kind of society, if there is no one and you need no one? And why try particularly to express your soul more fully? It exists and everything in it is expressed. Go and sing—the meadow is green, you're alone—go on and sing, if you want to.

"If you feel like singing." That's why there are so many decadents in poetry and in all the arts. Many are genuine, many are fake, imitators of form, half-expressed thoughts and hints. But there are many imitators and falsificators everywhere. All sincerity can be obtained from outside, like a fashion.

I am speaking about the correctness of real, innate decadents, but, of course, I am sorry and afraid that they are now supported and surrounded by multitudes of imitators and falsificators; they now have such a complete command of poetry and literature that all of it has sort of fallen out of society. Almost all poetry and literature, insofar as it is decadent, is outside the flow of history, humanity, outside the struggle between "we" and "I"; this literature has no relation to the flow of life and thought, neither has life any relation to it. I am speaking about literature, art, about its inclination.

How did this happen? With the general nonsense, confusion, unification of the ununitable, division of the united, with the general distortion of concepts—one need not be surprised about anything. Say what you want—all words are still turned upside down and roll along—what you catch is yours.

The personal fights like the common, the common like the personal; everyone doesn't say what he means, and finally doesn't know what he wants.

Only the decadent has everything he wants—he "sings in the meadow." No one hears him, but it turns out that he seems to be singing neither alone nor in a meadow, that decadence seems to be literature . . . and after all, literature is common to all . . .

. . . In conclusion, looking back once more on the whole tragic and bloody absurdity of recent times, on the truth split in two, on the struggle of the (herd-like) "social types" with individualists, on the fruitlessness of their struggle, in particular, with all the external conditions of life, subject to destruction, looking back on all this "bad" that Herzen croaked about—I want to say, why does it not seem so "bad" to us?

The "herd" principle of society that hates individuality (either openly or secretly) leads to "bourgeois crystallization," as Herzen expresses it. Individualism that stops can lead to an artificial decadence that is more terrible than the innate variety. But we trust that the individualist will not stop with himself; expanding, he struggles with the old union of people in the name of a new one, such a one where, while he is not cut off from them, he can still feel his own lack of confluence with them. And all the while, he wants to find his own soul, so that he will have something to give in return.

Herzen thought only goals close at hand unite people. Yes they unite, but what of their achievements tomorrow, the day after tomorrow? Either a new de-unification or bourgeois, crystallized well-being. Individualist-rebels, it seems, understood or at least felt not that "distant goals are a trap" (as Herzen thought), but precisely that nearby ones are, that people can be united, not by a distant goal, but by the *ultimate* goal, that it is the primary, chief and necessary condition—that it is the *ultimate* goal. And not only are the "nearby goals," and unity in them, not thrown overboard, do not disappear in the presence of the ultimate goal, but on the contrary, they themselves, as passing goals, will always be achieved, replacing each other simply and naturally. They will form themselves, as the stubborn icicles in Andersen's tale formed the word "eternity" when Kay understood something distant and higher. But when he tried (in vain) to arrange them earlier with his frozen hands, when he didn't understand yet, nothing happened, everything collapsed.

If there actually are people who are already beginning to perceive this simple truth, which Herzen failed to see, the truth of unity by means of distant, ultimate goals, if there is already a consciousness of this truth in the soul of people now living on the earth, does this not mean that the truth is on the earth? And can *descend* to the earth and can *be* on it?

Herzen saw a gloomy, black corridor. We see a white spot from deep inside it. What is it? The exit? How far away it is! Is it not all the same? Just to know that it exists. We will not get out, only the others will.

Herzen said, "Seek nearby goals." And he sadly thought at the end of his life: "nevertheless, nothing will come of it." We recall different words: "Seek ye the Kingdom of God, and all these things shall be added unto you."

We will seek and will think, even at the end of our lives, that "something will come of it."

Anton Krayny
[*Zinaida Gippius*]
1905

A REVIEW OF GIPPIUS' *LITERARY DIARY*
A. Bely

Anton Krayny is armed with a light critical rapier that whistles elegantly. The rapier draws beautiful monograms, it whistles playfully near his opponent's nose, provoking an attack, but then it whines spitefully and gets even with a lissom brilliance. It teases with a light, silken whistle, and it seems it would be easy to overwhelm him—just try: take the offensive; not all Russian critics have learned the art of fencing. The majority of them have fought with their fists from the beginning of time; well, and the others, a cut above, they set out for a battle like heavily armed soldiers; when will they be ready? They will certainly drag a thirty-six pound harquebus after them, and they will take a prop for the harquebus; nobly, honorably, traditionally—but My God!—while they are loading the harquebus (ten printed pages!), and setting up the prop (ten more pages!), and aiming their hand-held cannons at the enemy (ten pages!), and striking a spark (ten pages!) and firing (ten pages: fifty in all)—two or three of Anton Krayny's lines (the silken whistle of a sparkling blade!) are able to inflict serious wounds on one or another of these armed venerabilities. And Anton Krayny's rapier literally mows down rows of Russian criticism's fistfighters. It's no wonder they used to arrange for landslides to fall on an elegant publicist in bygone days.

Now several of his articles have been collected in one book; and the collection reveals a vulnerable spot in the publicist: it's a forced carelessness he uses to deal with a number of questions. What would happen if an opponent who knew how to fence would step forth? They would sprinkle summer lightning and brilliance, running down from their blades, and then the opponent would propose that they switch to *backswords*. Heavy is the backsword of methodological investigation for the elegant hand of our talented poetess, who hides under the pseudonym of Anton Krayny! What would happen if the opponent threatened with the backsword, transferring the question of freedom, or of predeterminateness of creativity, into the field of the analysis of the basic concepts of "freedom," "inevitability," "creativity," or "art?" Poor Anton Krayny, who has gotten used to a careless regard for his opponents because of his former skirmishes with the fistfighters and the poor shots with their harquebuses: the heavy backsword (too heavy for an elegant hand that holds a whistling rapier) would soon fall from her hand!

And the opponent would attack as follows:

You mount your attack on a number of poorly thought out judgments; you do not put forth any question in all its seriousness; meanwhile you conclude that individual art is obsolete, that it is just a transitional form from a lower type of tendentiousness to a higher one. Your attacks are just, perhaps, if you are dealing with Emelyanov-Kokhansky or Machtet, but Bryusov is standing before you. And I will not even mention Goethe: where are you going to order him to go? What are you going to do with him? Anton Krayny, defend yourself; where is the whistling brilliance of your rapier? The backsword dangles awkwardly in your hands.

The opponent would advance and Anton Krayny would retreat:

You affirm that aesthetic individualism has played its role, you operate arbitrarily with a concept that demands methodological treatment; the problem of individuality is complex: there are psychological, empirical, metaphysical, social, and religious individualities. What does the concept "individuality" contain, in your opinion? What is the process of individual development, and what are the norms of this process? Or do not the problems of individuality, raised by the scientific-philosophical disciplines, exist for you? Or do you simply cross off the works of Helmholtz, Fechner, Volkelt, Lipps, and Ostwald that concern art? Individualism in art—this is a debatable and obscure question that demands a complex elaboration. And it will not be solved by the whistle of your beautiful but—alas—weak rapier, but by a war or a union of methodological fortresses, armed with long range weapons; I would like to see what steps you would take when just one serious shell bursts over you. And we will not answer you: we will spare a lady. You thought you were fighting with us, with individualists—oh no—you did not fight with us, but with little boys from a preparatory school who were threatening you with paper airplanes. Crash—the backsword fell from your hands; defend yourself, we won't take advantage of your awkwardness.

You reveal an ignorance of terminology: when you are speaking about individualism you mean solopsism. What are you demanding from contemporary art, you who count yourself a representative of it? Do you really want the collective creativity of Christian values? And so you attack the complexity of methodological questions with Christ and the Antichrist? In this way you are emasculating culture, and it is not up to the "eunuch" (your definition of decadents) to teach you that culture is multi-faceted.

Enough of this fighting with backswords; we will not forget that we are dealing with a lady; we will not attack her with gnoseology; let us take up the rapiers again; let us fence on an equal basis. And so, where do you put Pushkin, Byron, Goethe, Nietzsche? Are they representatives of ecclesiastical art? Or did they write the canons? Crack—the end of my rapier broke against you: another rapier please!

Well, forget it: let's talk about decadent-idealists, whom you called at one point Grinkas (after the name of your dog), at another "eunuchs," and other extremely polite names. Poor individualist-decadents: while you were ignoring culture, science, and art, you were laboring over the construction of an unprecedented ecumenical art, which should evoke such a pleasant recollection in us (do you recall your recent articles?), and you abused us with the name of your dog Grinka because you were bored, individualists created works that will always remain in Russian literature, sat over treatises on the history of art, culture and the theory of cognition, at the same time admiring the zigzags of a harmless rapier, and ignoring the word "eunuch" that the rapier had written above them. Oh your poor rapier, so subjective in its attacks on individualists, so individualistic in its "super-individual" prophesying! It broke again, another rapier, please!

Z. N. Gippius is a "decadent" poetess; Mr. Anton Krayny—who is she, in your opinion, is she not "Grinka the dog," a "eunuch?" No, Mr. Krayny, let us, natural or tactical individualists, take up her defense amicably. Oh, Mr. Krayny, the mask has flown from your face: the respected poetess stands before us. What can a gallant cavalier do other than lower his rapier, or offer his breast to the blows of an elegant hand!

That's what a real opponent would say, then he would begin to analyze Anton Krayny's positions, without playing around. But he will not do that. The litigation once begun by the provocative A. Krayny against the decadents has been—alas!—decided, and not in his favor. Together with the "stupefied" Moscow decadent, Bryusov, "who penetrates through all the doors" ("you know how to penetrate them all immediately"), and the not yet sour A. Bely, the talented publicist has rewarded, with the blows of her rapier, Petersburgian "super-individualism"—flesh of the flesh of Krayny's aspirations. But "dulled" decadence has more "pointedly" understood the motives of the sharp critic in his morbidly-"dulled" relation to his comrades of the pen. These comrades—"eunuchs, which were so born from their mother's womb"—turned out to be suddenly not deprived of the "sense of the incontestible knowledge that I am not unique in the world, but I am surrounded by people like me." But now A. Krayny, who has reproached us for a lack of feeling of solidarity, has committed that sin, by reprinting old, scandalous utterances that have been disproved by evidence.

And the "not yet sour" individualist, Bely, does not need to point this out to the "overly sour" Christian consciousness of Anton Krayny.

And if Anton Krayny has any honor of thought, should not his rapier, so elegant, so light, fall from his hand when he turns it against us? In the hands of capricious subjectivism the rapier of a super-individualistic publicist is only useful for a barely literate crowd of fistfighters, or for a poor shot with a harquebus.

Andrei Bely
1908

BALMONT AS A LYRIC POET
I. Annensky

I.

Among the varied peculiarities, or perhaps under developments, and sometimes distortions, of our spiritual nature, for which we are obliged to Russian history, one has always occupied me—the narrowness of our view of the word. The originality and even more the audacity of the Russian word still embarrasses us a little even now, even in those cases when we sense its indisputable beauty. We are too used to looking at the word from top to bottom, as we would at some colorless, service-oriented thing, as if it were some stenography or Esperanto, and not an aesthetically valuable phenomenon from the area of the most ancient and refined of arts, where world types live in all the splendor of it; emotional and picturesque expression. [...]

The extreme carelessness and fundamental colorlessness of language in the journals makes the attempts of the Russian poets of most recent time especially interesting for an investigation into our literary language. In one way or another, these attempts have forced the Russian reader to think about language as he would about art—consequently, they raise our feeling for language. Personally, I have more or less succeeded in looking into the work of one of the new poets—K. D. Balmont. Balmont has translated and written a lot of poems, but the most definitive ones for his poetry are, in my opinion, the collections: *Burning Buildings, Let's Be Like the Sun,* and *Only Love;* what follows will be mainly about them.

II.

Of the two varieties of our artistic word, prose developed under conditions incomparably more favorable than those which have fallen to the lot of poetry. Our journals' critics would rather forgive the belletrist Andreev all his Mists, Walls, and Abysses, than the poets Balmont and Bryusov the games they celebrate. Something solemnly sugary and mincing seems to have stuck to Russian verse. And we do not even want to look at poetry seriously, i.e., as art. I think that poetry will be, in words: serving and accomplishment, a fire and an altar, and any other kind of as yet undisturbed emblem, but in deeds, we still value the sweet lemonade in it, not deprived, however, of a usefulness that is highly valued even by the stern and distressed Russian reader. Is it really possible to think about verse? What's left for algebra then? And here a troubled mind, seeing that the ready formulas do not apply to the new poetry, the formulas so dear to him in all their vulgarity, hurries to caricature, if not alienate, everything that cannot be subjected to translation into the service-oriented language. Let even the rainbowy mist of poetry enchant him—in the best case there will be a shrug of the shoulders and a "yes! beautiful form." Oh, enough of this "poetical form," and which pedant thought up this expression anyway?

But the affairs of poetry are in even worse shape if the poem seems immoral to the reader, as if *moral* is one and the same as *virtue,* and as if the preservation of this in words, at least in the most heroic meters, has something in common with feats and even a kind smile. The poetic art, as with all the others, is defined first of all by the fact that a gifted person aspires to experience the rare and high pleasure of creation. Creation by itself is amoral, and to enjoy it or something else in no way means to sacrifice and limit oneself for the sake of one's neighbors, no matter how much good they would later obtain from our pleasure.

I will stop at one example, characteristic, in my opinion, of our stubborn lack of desire to understand the new poetic word.

In K. D. Balmont's collection of poems, *Let's Be Like the Sun,* in the section called "The Snake's Eye," the following piece is printed:

> I am the refinement of the leisurely Russian tongue
> Other poets before me are precursors,
> I first discovered inclinations in this speech,
> With reprises, angry and tender ringing.
> > I am a sudden break,
> > I am thunder playing,
> > I am a transparent brook,
> > I am for all and for no one.
> A splash very foamy, torn-together,
> Semi-precious stones of the original earth,
> Forest roll call of a green May,
> All this I'll grasp, I'll take, bereaving others.
> > Eternally young as a dream,
> > Strong because I'm in love
> > With myself and with others,
> > I am refined verse.

It seems that I have not heard or read that anyone liked this piece. I am not speaking, of course, about the representatives of the new school. Mockery, hints about delusions of grandeur, triumphant smiles because of the *inclinations* and the *reprisiveness* and thund*er* rhyming with some break*er*—all of this is *en premier lieu.*

Meanwhile, the poem is clear to transparency and can seem like delusions of grandeur only to those people who do not want to see this form of mental illness beyond the banality of Romantic formulas. [. . .]

But we have had enough of this. A reader who has learned "Exegi monumentum" by heart in school is ready to forgive the poet this proud desire for praise: we are all just folks and who has not caught himself in a passing daydream ... But by what right? But permit me to say: perhaps this *I* is not K. D. Balmont under the guise of verse. What do I mean, not him? Are the inclinations and reprises not all written in prose in the preface to *Burning Buildings?* Well, okay, if you like, that is a piece of evidence. But what if, perhaps, we do not mean Balmont as a single person here, but something like Pythagoras and his school. No matter what, the reader is upset. And then this "all the other poets are precursors" here. What nerve, just imagine!... Pushkin, Lermontov?... But worst of all, for our humility, is this unbearable, overt self-infatuation.

> Strong because I'm in love
> With myself and with others.

Why with himself?

For people who don't see poetry as the passive self-enjoyment of swinging on swings, but as a distinctive form of beauty, which has to be taken by attention, aroused and attuned to it. The *I* of Mr. Balmont is not personal or collective, but most of all our *I*, merely realized and expressed by Balmont.

It is all the same to me whether Balmont was the first to discover inclinations and reprises; for me the intuition and revelation of my soul at the creative moment are important in the piece; for this we are all obligated to the insight and tender musicality of Balmont's lyrical *I*. It is most of all important that the poet has merged his being with verse here, and that this is not Quintillian's decoration at all—but the very essence of the new poetry. *Verse is not the creation of the poet,* if you wish, it does not even belong to the poet. Verse is inseparable from the lyrical *I*, this is its connection with the world, its place in nature, perhaps its justification. The poet's *I* manifests itself in this only when it made verse *refined and beautiful.* The leisureliness of refined speech does not entirely belong to it, since this is the rhythm of our rivers and May sunsets in the steppe. However, the refinement of the poet's *I* is also limited by the national element and perhaps to an even greater extent than the poet would like: it transports us to the gilded tops of Vladimir's palace in the *byliny,* to those traveling heroes whose every movement leads, in writing and studying, to the pedantic Churilo, to the factual games of the buffoons and the whiteness of Zabava's face, which the wind does not dare to fan. But is this not really the same call for refinement in Pushkin's slogan "the beautiful must be majestic," or Lermontov's fountains and his slow steps along the siliceous road sparkling in the moonlight? Is this all not the same *refinement,* only not just called such? Why was Balmont the one to name it?... Well, okay, let it be refinement, but why so bizarre? "Splash very foamy, torn-together." Would not *mountain-fountain, moon-June* be simpler? Like rolling off a log. Yes, the poet does not name the *sea,* he does not impose the sea, in all the unwieldiness of a pontian impression, on us. But for that one mysterious connection between the playing of the waves and our *I* sounds symbolically in these four words. *Very-foamy-ness* is the *touch of life* on the secret of the soul, a *re-splash* is the *restless music of creativity;* and *torn-apart-together* is our impossibility of separating our *I* from nature and together with this its unceasing aspiration for originality.

Further, the poet's verse can be *unclear* for you, since the poet is not obligated to cope with the level of your aesthetic development. But verse must be *transparent,* it is as *fluid as a brook.*

It belongs to no one because it serves no one and nothing, because from time immemorial, by the very airiness of its nature, verse is free, and because verse is a thought that belongs to no one and is created by everyone, but it does not hide from anyone—it is for all who want to read, sing, learn, scold, or ridicule, it is all the same. Verse is the bright, new word that falls into the sea of eternally creating things.

New verse is strong because of its infatuation with itself and others, while self-infatuation is here sort of exchanged for the poet's classical *pride* in its merits.

What could be more sincere than a confession of self-infatuation and more legitimate than feeling itself, without which lyrical poetry could not even come into existence, and I am not talking about its Romantic stage, on which we were all raised. But why, you see, does Balmont not calling it the sea, like all good folks, on the contrary, call it something we prefer to be silent about? Although, of course, Victor Hugo...

But verse is also in love with others, i.e., it wants to merge with everything that is *similar in nature* to it, that is fluid, bright and ringing. It grasps everything and is even ready to take from others. Eternally young as a dream, in all pouring, splashing, and singing, it keeps only its own independence and refinement.

This last means that verse not only doesn't impose anything on us, but it also doesn't give us anything, because its beauty, like a treasure, must be sought out and discovered. Before, for those who were *precursors of our verse and our I,* nature was an object, a favorite being, perhaps sometimes even an idol. They celebrated it, they sought sympathy from it, and a reflection of their *I* in it.

> The Ukrainian night is calm...

> I go out alone along the road...

Our verse, although it perhaps does not inaugurate a new poetic era, goes away from the irrevocably *conscious* aspiration and *symbolically becomes nature itself,* by representing the fluid inclinations of swan-like snowy whiteness, and all these splashes of nature's lives and desires, and the distinctiveness of stones, and everything that is eternally renewed, not ceasing to be a dream; finally, everything that is strong by virtue of its capacity for infatuation: not love, with its sacrifices, melancholy, reproaches, and despair, but precisely a merry and unscrupulous infatuation with itself and everything; and at the same time the poet doesn't impose his *I* on nature, he doesn't think that the beauties of nature should be grouped around his *I,* but on the contrary, he hides and sort of dissolves this *I* into all the impressions of existence.

Balmont's piece magically merged all the captivating verse of mobility and brilliance, and the poet was able to do this without a *single disuniting simile.*

Finally, about the meter. The refined, slow anapest, though not erasing, nevertheless weakens the sharpness of the word *I*; the poet delicately puts it into the thesis of the meter. Balmont's anapests are, moreover, in this piece totally devoid of the severe character of tragic parodes, which the Greeks softened with dance, and amid the multi-colored and raucous kingdom of splashes, peals of thunder, calls, and semi-precious stones, the poem like the soul of the poet, retaining its rhythm, moves peacefully and slowly among the edges, which he himself delicately outlines, along the tree-lined avenues of his rectangular garden, two long, and two short. [...]

IV.

Balmont's lyrical *I,* as far as I have been able to determine it, seems very interesting to me. I will begin an analysis of it with that feature which struck me earlier than others. Balmont wants to be both insolent and brave, to hate and admire crime, to combine in himself both hangman and victim and the siren with the spectral black monk. He makes even his own childhood reminiscences bloody, and meanwhile, tenderness and femininity are, so to say, the basic characteristics of his poetry, his *I,* and precisely in them, and in nothing else, one must seek explanations of both the lightness of his poetic touch on things, and of the freedom and singing of his lyrical speech, and, I dare say, of the capricious chageability of his mood. Among all the black revelations of Baudelairism, among the cold "snakinesses" and stupefying aromas, the attentive gaze easily discovers in Balmont's poetry the purely feminine modesty of the soul which does not understand all the dreariness of the cynicism that looks at it, although it seems to an inquisitive imagination and hothead that they were long ago and irretrievably defiled by the cold slipperiness of vice. [...]

I must confess that I can in no way find the notorious eroticism of Balmont's poetry. In my opinion we would rather take for eroticism the poet's desire to find taste in wine which he essentially does not like.

In any case Balmont as a lyric poet is not passionate, since he does not know the torment of jealousy and definitely alien to the exclusivity of yearning. I think it is organically impossible for him to create something like Pushkin's "Incantation." He is too much of an aesthete for that.

> I want to be insolent, I want to be brave.

But do these innocent rockets really still mystify anyone?

Yes, I want exactly to be insolent and brave, because I am neither the one nor the other.

Balmont's love is much more aesthetic, delicate, major, mysterious, than all these

> Go away, gods, go away, people. [...]

V.

[...] To conclude what I have said about Balmont's poetry and to give a belated motto to my essay—here are some words recently spoken by Henri Albert.

He said them about Nietzsche, I will say them about Balmont, the best representative of the new poetry.

"His influence on our young literature has already been considerable. It will grow more and more every day. Salutary? Inauspicious? It doesn't matter! It brings us new material to think about, new motifs for life..."

Innokenty Annensky
1906

THE VEIL OF ISIS
G. Chulkov

The tenth anniversary of Stéphane Mallarmé's death is this autumn. Many events have taken place in that time; the Slavic world, which anticipated in the person of Dostoevsky the secret aspects of Symbolism, now finds an exit from the decadent labyrinth, and we can no longer be satisfied with formulas and definitions that the great founder and theoretician of new art proposed: Mallarmé's brilliant aphorisms are truly only "disorder" for us, only wandering and dreaming, and in them there is no integral aesthetic, for which the contemporary soul thirsts, tired of philosophical skepticism and artistic dilettantism.

I don't know if we will find that integral aesthetic soon, but in any case we formed the firm conviction that it is impossible to build an integral aesthetic on idealism and only idealism, the type that Mallarmé believed in. But we would be unfair to the memory of the poet if we forgot about his thoughts on Wagner, his infatuation with music, his dream about "national" art. Evidently, these possibilities which are now being discovered by contemporaneity were already hiding in Mallarmé's soul. And the principle of aesthetic "suggestion" that Mallarmé talks about did not lose its significance, despite the fact that the nature of art received new enlightenment.

It's true that in our view this "suggestion" does not dominate in the process of creativity, but as a secondary feature it seems as necessary as it did before.

The definition of Symbolism, as given later by other theoreticians of the French school, added a little to what Mallarmé said. Thus, Remy de Gourmont sees Symbolism as one chapter in an idealistic world view, and underscoring the aspect of freedom, almost identifies Symbolism with art in general.

The Symbolism that seemed like a "new" poetic school during the years of Mallarmé's struggle with the Parnasse now tries to find objective criteria for general aesthetic evaluations, independent of the shifts in transient literary groupings.

Now we are occupied with Symbolism as the basic theme of general aesthetics. The word "symbol" did not have that meaning we now ascribe to it. Kant called a symbol the "contemplations" that a priori give an "indirect sensual representation of concepts." Hegel understood a symbol as a particular case of allegory and called the first stage in the development of art the symbolic stage; Schopenhauer stressed the symbol's conditionality and refused to accept any concealed significance for symbols of

Christianity, such as the fish. Despite the metaphysician's ignorance of this term, however, now we must accept it partially in the sense that the ancients gave to it. The worshippers of Demeter understood *symbalon* as a holy sign that stood for the secret of divinity. Let's decide to have a symbol signify that incarnation of aesthetic experience which opens up a number of mystical potentials that lead to the absolute.

In the aesthetic scheme proposed by Kant in his *Critique of Judgment,* Symbolism will correspond to that middle row which is defined by the feature of purposiveness. Thus from the formal side, Symbolism is like a bridge between the conformity to law of the given world and the final purpose, i.e., freedom.

Kant's aesthetic, his teaching about the beautiful *(das Schöne)* and the sublime *(das Erhabene),* cannot satisfy us by the strength of its formal character. The "antimony of the judgment of taste," discovered by him, permits a too abstract affirmation of a "supersensual substratum of phenomena." And the aesthetic idea, in the light of criticism, remains only an inexplicable representation of imagination—no more; the truly sublime, in Kant's opinion, must be sought only in the soul of a person who expresses a judgment, and not in an object of nature; in Kant's aesthetic, those absolute values that the contemporary soul craves are absent. And his last formula, "the beautiful is a symbol of the morally good," finally draws the dividing line between criticism and the contemporary understanding of Symbolism.

The successor and interpreter of critical aesthetics, Schiller, introduced substantial corrections in Kant's teaching about the beautiful and the sublime. He suspended the direct identification of the beautiful with the morally good, and as a poet defended self-sufficing beauty. Schiller expanded the critical basis of aesthetics with an "anthropological" basis. In Schiller's opinion, nature and freedom, and the sense and intellect in a person, form an aesthetically real unity and are not "conditionally" united, as Kant thought.

Hegel's aesthetic, his teaching about the incarnation of the idea in matter, his view of the world as a theater, on the stage of which a spirit acts, hardly brings us nearer to Symbolism.

The Hegelian identification of idea with form in art interests us even less than the thoughts of Schopenhauer, who anticipated what would most excite contemporaneity in his teaching about music, written with such genius. Music, as the *universalia ante rem,* as the objectification of what is innermost—this is the central theme of Symbolism, if we broaden the principle of music to include all the other arts and most of all poetry.

Symbolism accepts not what separates Kant, Schiller, and Schopenhauer, but what unites them—the aspiration to discover in art the objectivization of Plato's ideas. But Plato's opinion notwithstanding, human art is not a weak imitation of nature but something that overcomes it, the restoration of original images, a magic mirror that reflects the world of divine potentials in itself.

Schelling spoke out the most positively in this sense: he taught that beauty is "something infinite, expressed in a finite form," an opinion that almost coincides with Fichte's. Fichte thought that art introduces an actually transcendental point of view into life itself. The contemporary aesthetic theory of Vyacheslav Ivanov reveals two principles in Symbolism—idealism and realism. Thus, impressionism is the method of idealistic Symbolism, and the method of realistic Symbolism is pure symbolism (symbolics): its pathos *a realibus ad realiora.*

The evolution of idealistic Symbolism from Baudelaire to Maeterlinck was defined, in my view, by the pathos of illusionism: the poets made it their task to expose the illusiveness of empirical visibility.

The Symbolist-idealist knows no objective values, no innermost *res:* for him beauty is only a cold reflection of a dream, a petrified dream-vision: and it's no accident that Baudelaire puts exactly these words in the mouth of beauty:

Je suis belle, ô mortels! comme un rêve de pierre...

Or in the words of a Russian poet:

I am stone and dream, and I am beautiful, people!

These words are not only a formula of Parnassian poetry, but they also exhaust the contents of idealistic Symbolism. In order to free ourselves from the enchantment of snowy beauty, we have to listen again and again to Verlaine's precept: "de la musique avant tout chose..." His poetry is filled with premonitions of the new realistic Symbolism by force of the incarnations of this principle. The essence of the new aesthetic theory, in my view, is in this exit from idealistic captivity into the world of real symbolics.

Three years ago I wrote on the pages of *Voprosy zhizni (Questions of Life):* "We are experiencing a cultural crisis: we have to forge new values, to find a new mystical experience, if we don't the horror of abstraction threatens us." Even now I don't have to renounce my views from that time: if our dreams are not realized, if Symbolism does not go along the path of the new non-"decadent" experience, an epoch of cultural stagnation will ensue.

But fortunately the epigones of decadence are too sluggish to move towards these quests; and those among them who could, because of their souls' make-up, enter the circle of new experience, are hiding for the time being behind the backs of their recent masters.

If the predecessors of our contemporary idealistic Symbolists are

French—Mallarmé, Jules Laforgue, Maeterlinck, Vielé-Griffin, and several others, then the direct forerunners of our realistic Symbolists must be considered Vl. Solovyov and F. Tyutchev.

The French tied their poetic quests to idealistic tendencies in the spirit of Kant, Hegel, and Fichte; the pioneers of Russian Symbolism sought justification for their poetry in a mystical world view.

Vl. Solovyov's poems are inseparably linked with his philosophy, so close to Schelling in the last period of his religious searching. Tyutchev's poems are filled with premonitions and insights into that primal reality which only mystics can know.

Mallarmé and Maeterlinck almost always stand at the edge of idealism and mysticism, but they lack the courage to step across the threshold, beyond which true reality shines.

In essence, the themes of Maeterlinck's lyrics are entirely exhausted by a quiet lament:

> Les clefs des portes sont perdues,
> Il faut attendre, il faut attendre...
>
> [The keys to the doors are lost,
> We have to wait, we have to wait...]

The experience of such Symbolists as Mallarmé and Maeterlinck is the experience of solitary souls enclosed in a circle of idealistic contemplation. Vl. Solovyov's experience was different. He had the right to say:

> O ruler of earth, heaven and sea,
> I hear you through this gloomy moan...

The same voice and the same vision haunted Tyutchev.

> Who are you? Where are you from?
> How can I decide if you're heavenly or earthly?
> A heavenly resident, perhaps,
> But with a passionate female soul.

There are two paths before us: 1) from Mallarmé's "Divigations" to René Ghil's "Instrumentation" and the "contemporaneities" and "everyday-ness" of experimental poets (positivism is a natural degeneration from idealism), or another path: 2) from Vl. Solovyov and Tyutchev to quests for a new non-"decadent" experience. After the experience of such great decadent poets as Paul Verlaine and Fyodor Sologub, contemporary decadent experiments frequently seem like poor, childish amusements worthy of the hero of Huysmans' novel *A rebours*—and no more.

In opposition to unprincipled decadence, we see the search for ideas on the paths followed by Vl. Solovyov and earlier by Schelling. The great philosopher, who perfected a religio-philosophical synthesis of the systems of criticism and idealism, says in his teachings about the evolution of the ancient gods: "it is impossible to consider them like beings created only by poetry; only the end, not the beginning, of this process can have such a purely poetic significance. These images are transformed in poetry, but they do not arise thanks to poetry: poetry itself arises first in them and from them."

The theory of mytho-creation proposed by V. Ivanov is a direct continuation and development of Schelling's views of art and religion. It's natural that the principle of mytho-creation by itself occasioned a crisis in Symbolism. If we begin to search for any ideological content in idealistic Symbolism then the so-called decadence, i.e., "extreme individualism," will have to be accepted as this content. But genuine lyrics come out from a circle of solitary, individual experience. The decadents' unprincipled experimentalism becomes the property of topical satirists for the newspapers. Genuine decadents, who drank the bitter cup of Nietzscheanism and Baudelairism to the dregs, are lonely. Those who imagine themselves to be the representatives of contemporary decadence and lead a campaign against the principle of universalism are the epigones of an ideological movement which was at one time rich with deep content and creative wisdom.

But what does the exit from solitary decadent experience mean? The affirmation that some lyric poets have escaped the circle of solitary individual experience means that the experience of these lyric poets is linked by mysterious bonds to the universe. In this experience the principle that "a person is not the measure of things, but a moment is " is no longer triumphant. Another principle, the principle of affirmation of one's personality in the universe, is triumphant.

The crisis of individualism is not in that contemporary society has forgotten the precepts of Nietzsche, Baudelaire, and Edgar Allen Poe, but in that it has uncovered a new path, more direct than before, to the affirmation of these precepts. The great individualists of the nineteenth century did not realize that the genuine realization of their wills to the affirmation of personality is possible only by the affirmation of the principle of universalism. This is why the path of the new lyrics from the aspect of their internal contents is prepared by philosophy, or more precisely, by the prophetic insights of Vl. Solovyov and Schelling. In the light of these prophecies, the deep abyss that divides our contemporary poets becomes visible. And if some of our new lyric poets who are privy to these revelations still clutch at the rotting staffs of decadent banners, then this is evidence only of how terrifying it is for a poet consciously to cross over the boundaries of individualism, even if the fabric of his soul has changed.

False decadent individualism supposes the essence of the affirmation of personality is in the affirmation of separate moments, casual and torn apart. And this is the poet's confession:

I would have loved, but I'm not strong enough,
You don't seek, don't wait,
And all dreams, like ghosts, and all desires are a lie.

And further—

It's all the same, all the same to me,
I'm observing a shadow game.

But true individualism cannot be satisfied by false desires and a transient shadow game; the essence of the affirmation of personality is in uncovering its connections with the universe. An idividuum who is isolated from the universe is not an individual. An individuum becomes an individual only when he overcomes himself, recalling Nietzsche's words: a person is a bridge, not a goal.

Tomorrow's task is the justification of those contradictions that arise in the soul together with the crisis of individualism. Antimonic constructions in the circle of contemporary experience are more valuable for us than logical constructions, deprived of the poison of contradictions.

The antimonies of our reason are only a reflection of those mystical contradictions which make up the peculiarity of new religious experiences. The scepticism of old decadence went no further than the critique of given experience and the reevaluation of moral values. And in the area of religion, decadence went no further than agnosticism. But since the time when the circle of experience widened, from the time when the individual sensed his internal connection with "everything," and together with this was able to not get lost in pantheism, from that time, the triumph of more sublime, although perhaps more dangerous, experiences ensued. A person became not only a creator of myths, but also an investigator of all sides of his spirit. In decadence, the reappraisal of values was only partly accomplished, but beyond good and evil there was only amazement. There was no criticism, no action.

The new experience beyond good and evil saved people from idol worship. The myth incarnate is just as bright as a symbol, thanks to its reality, and it demands a vital justification.

The theme of mytho-creation posited by V. Ivanov as a religious and aesthetic theme has, in my view, another meaning: in this theme the essence of a religious social process is revealed. Considering history from the religious point of view, we see how myths are born, sometimes forming a part of culture, sometimes being the center of a common process. The Egyptian worship of Isis and Osiris, the Samothracian mysteries of Axierus, Axiocersus and Axiocersa, the Greek cults of Demeter, Persephone, Dionysus; the Roman cults of Ceres, Proserpina, Bacchus, and the religious teachings of recent time about the World Soul, Sophia, and the crucified Jesus, all these moments of high religious life, repeating within themselves common, analogous features, constitute one and the same way to a certain religious unity. The sense and goal of these and other mysteries and cults parallel to them is to find that common soil on which it is possible to break the circle of solitary experience and together with this to find the path that leads to a religious society.

The so-called "crisis of individualism" is not a sign of our time alone. In different epochs, from the most ancient to the end of the nineteenth century, we see the struggle between two principles taking place; the principle of individualism, disunification—and the principle of universalism, the principle of religious society. Every truly religious act already overcomes individualism. Thus the hysterical cries that it is impossible to overcome individualism only testify about the low spirits that are characteristic of certain corners of contemporary culture.

Is it possible to reconcile oneself with the fact that religious-social experience, already found more than once by history, is now irretrievably lost? What is this evidence of? The irreligiosity of our culture? But is that so? Perhaps those elements of culture which by their nature are religious slip away from our attention?

Religious-social acts are taking place before our eyes, and it is only possible to interpret their significance and appraise their high value by understanding them as mytho-creative acts.

Contemporary social acts are usually evaluated formally, victories and defeats are added up, chances are weighed, class and group interests are measured—and all this formal and external work, very necessary and honorable, makes up the facts from which certain sociological conclusions can be made. But this difficult and necessary work does not touch on the essence of these experiences, which are characteristic for the soul of a person who actively participates in social actions. The essence of a religious society is in an individual finding a personality for himself, i.e., beyond the transient psychological experiences, finding his *I* for himself, as a principle that unites him with the internal side of humanity and the world. A religious society leads one person to another person, unites them, not mechanically, but internally, with an unfathomable bond of love.

But despite the mysteriousness of religious action, it is possible and even obligatory to talk about it. It is possible because our reason, frequently powerless in the world of purposes, is strong enough when we are speaking about paths of attainment. And, on the other hand, it is necessary to speak about religious society because the triumph of a mechanical principle, gray and deathly, threatens our contemporary society; it is necessary to struggle with it, pointing to the path of sacrament.

And it is possible to say, not only by playing craftily with words, that the great French Revolution was the bearer of a myth about the incarnation of freedom on earth. And if we now realize that the goal of the revolution was not attained and the dream about freedom turned out to be a "myth" in the current and vulgar conception of this word, even then, despite this, we must confess that the great revolution was a necessary moment in history. The actors of that epoch did not understand what they were acquiring for humanity, but their gains, nevertheless, are not insignificant. After all, Columbus discovered America, not really knowing what he was discovering. And on the other hand there was a moment of true mytho-creation in the great French Revolution: people believed in future freedom, in the pathos of that belief, there was true mytho-creation. And in this pathos, religious by its nature, there was the internal justification of that epoch and that revolution, which we now consciously stigmatize with the name "bourgeois revolution."

In our time, people live by faith in the approaching social revolution. And our scepticism cannot diminish that faith. We know that if in the future mankind will ridicule our errors, it will never ridicule our faith in that social truth, which is not just a symbol for us, but a living reality: beyond that reality, the earth-mankind appears to us as an absolute in its formation. And aren't we repeating here the eternal myth about the earth in which participants in Samothracian mysteries, the priests of Demeter, the servants of Ceres and the Christians (who believe in the earth as Christ's bride) believed?

Scientific socialism, which affirms economic interest as the stimulus for struggle and progress, guesses only one facet of religious evolution. Raising the curtain of formal science a little, we see life in its unbrokenness, we see the magic poured into the universe, about which the philosophers speak. The revolutionary struggle takes on a theurgic significance; this is the earth itself striving for freedom.

The theme of revolution, however, is a cunning theme. It is not possible to include every revolutionary act in the chain of those historical phenomena that make up the living bridge from plurality to unity, from the transient to the absolute. The revolutionary struggle takes on theurgic significance only if it is Dionysian. We must listen to the rhythm of a given epoch in order to define its character in respect to the principle of Dionysianism. And Nietzsche says precisely: "in the music of a given nation its orgaistic experiences are perpetuated." The greatest musical works of modern times—almost all of Beethoven and Wagner's "Ring of the Niebelungs"—reflect in themselves religious moments of revolutionary enthusiasm.

And in lyrics, in addition to their ideological content, and even in spite of a clear tendency, it is sometimes possible to discover signs of oscillations of the popular element: the melodiousness and manner of the verse changes, depending on whether revolution raises its leonine head or not. Thus the spirit of rebellion and uprising soars in the strophes of Baudelaire and Verlaine, although neither one wrote verses about revolutionary subjects.

Not only objective investigation, but also a definite sermon are possible on this theme. It is true that contemporaneity does not possess such advocates but perhaps tomorrow they will come to us. They will call on us to struggle, but this call will not sound quite like the calls of contemporary agitators. The inspiration which sometimes illuminates events on the paths of history will become, perhaps, a constant satellite and guide for a nation.

Social movements, freed from hysterical and convulsive outbursts, will develop regularly, retaining the harmony of newly formed songs. And the more harmonious these songs will sound, the more dangerous they will be for the enemies of freedom.

If I am mistaken, if the spirit of revolution has nothing in common with those "orgiastic agitations," which are united with the spirit of the crucified God, with the spirit of Dionysus and Christ, if the analogies and symbols I have pointed out are only an accident, then in that case a deep schism between religion and progress is inevitable. But I believe that a religious spirit lives in revolution. And if this is so, then the victories and sacrifices of revolution draw us inescapably to the final liberation.

Thus we arrive at the problem of anarchism. In our time we meet attempts to base mechanical ideas on a mystical world view. The premonitions of these ideas are already scattered throughout the literatures of the eighteenth century, the period of "Sturm und Drang," and later in the poetry of the nineteenth century, in the poetry of Byron and Shelley.

From this same nineteenth century, two geniuses arrive at the threshold of contemporaneity and light our way with their torches. I am speaking about Ibsen and Dostoevsky. Nietzsche's individualism finds its resolution in the words of these wise men and prophets.

The "non-acceptance of the world," propogated by the German Romantics at the beginning of the nineteenth century, seems like childish dreaming compared to the themes advanced by Ibsen, Dostoevsky and Nietzsche. And if it is possible to speak about the rebirth of Romanticism in our time, then it is only in the sense of the recogntion of certain aesthetic principles of the Romantic school, and not in the sense of the affirmation of the Romantic world view. The Romantics' "rejection of the world" led them to reaction and blind servitude, and this idea takes on the opposite meaning and entails new consequences in the new enlightenment of eschatological ideas. The Romantics were not logical in their judgments, but the experience of the end of the nineteenth century could not pass without a trace on the contemporary world view. One of the critics has called contemporary anarchism, which arose on the basis of a mystical world view, the most logical of the Romantics' teachings. I think that the rapprochement of contemporary anarchism with Romanticism hardly enlightens the essence of this theme. Contemporary anarchical ideas are separated from Romanticism by such an impenetrable wall of philosophical criticism, refined by scepticism, and such a rich world of new psychological experiences, that this rapprochement seems forced. After all, even the very expression "rejection of the world," which has become a contemporary slogan, belongs to Dostoevsky and is not found among the Romantics.

And this is not accidental. Romantics went out of this world—contemporaneity carries on a struggle with it. Romanticism lived on dreams of the past—for contemporaneity the eschatological problems are the most fatal problems.

And only one thing brings contemporary mysticism closer to Romanticism: this is the aspiration to uncover the magic principle in man's nature. This connects the pioneers of decadence with Romanticism: in Baudelaire's quests for astral intoxication, and in Verlaine's prayers of love, there truly was magic. But there is none in the contemporary decadents' works. Only the lonely F. Sologub knows how to draw a magic circle around himself and is privy to secret knowledge: the magic of other decadents is an unmasked magic; it is impossible to remain on the edge of idealism for an indefinite period. One must either search for new heights or fall. And the fall of decadence has taken place. The epigones of decadence are in the plane of positivism. Even in the West we see a number of writers who share the fate of other epigones.

In Italy, Gabriele D'Annunzio, with the manners of a tired patrician and the tastes of a European bourgeois, vainly dreams with his lascivious writings of setting fire to his wasted soul; in Germany, the sweet and false Hofmannsthal equally offends lyrics and drama with his lyrico-dramatic experiments; and next to him Wedekind pretends to know sex and captivates the hearts of plump and obtuse petty bourgeois with his vulgar charlatanism.

. . . .

According to Kant beauty is like Isis. As the ancient mother of nature, she says about herself: "I am everything that is, that was, and that will be, and no mortal has removed my veil." But there are people nowadays who dare to affirm that the sense of art is in exposing real existence and that the path of art is *a realibus ad realiora*.

These two opinions, so different, come together however at one point. In essence, Isis' declaration does not contradict the basic principle of realistic Symbolism; yes, of course, none of the *mortals* will remove the veil of the mother goddess, but wasn't the divine principle put into us? And don't we, as immortals, have the right to see things face to face? It is true that we are not gods, we are enslaved by the norms of the given empirical world—and for this reason art is for us only a magic mirror, where an absolute world is reflected, as in fortune telling, as a promise, and not as the fulfillment of our hopes, but we already become acquainted with the secret in this mirrored magic, as reality, and not as a projection of our dream.

In idealistic Symbolism, we have a world of ideal things, desired and possible, but abstracted from true existence; in idealistic Symbolism we have the symbolics of actual existence. Here we touch on the theme of general odegetics, i.e., mystical anarchism. The analysis of the nature of Symbolism leads us to the problem of freedom in mysticism; we already understand that we, as slaves of the world, live exclusively by our belief in possible freedom. Without negating the immutability of the given world's laws, we however never reconcile ourselves to those laws, as to something that should be. All of us—who either accept or reject the principle of free will—unconsciously live by the single hope of this possibility. If someone were to take away this hope, if we believed that there were no free will, that our every act is predetermined in advance by the law of causality, we would perish in despair. And, of course, in that case our faith in free will is more real and unconditional than our consciousness of the laws of necessity. Here not only a philosophical but also a religious antinomy is revealed. And if the philosophical antinomy does not find its resolution in the methods of gnoseology, then the religious antinomy is resolved directly in a circle of our experiences. Bergson's newest theory, which tries to resolve this antinomy, seems probable to us only because this thinker has introduced the principle of free creativity into his system. In his book. *L'Evolution créatrice* [*Creative Evolution*] Bergson is guided by certain premises of a psychological rather than a gnoseological nature. The world is dynamic, a series of events unfold in time, and the adherence to past acts of newer and newer creative accomplishments testifies about the freedom put into the world.

An eternal struggle between normativeness and freedom is taking place in the world, and only because of this does it live and move.

We are on the border of life and art. Baudelaire was right when he affirmed that the world is a symbol. Realistic Symbolism discloses the symbolics of the world, but in art not only the moment of cognition but also the moment of creation is present. And this creation in realistic Symbolism is addressed not to the ideal world of the possible, although imagined, values, but to the subject itself.

In order to become acquainted with the world of real, not imagined, values, we must recreate ourselves. The essence of mystical anarchism is in this, as I propose to understand this philosophizing about the paths of freedom. Changing and freeing ourselves, we acquire secret knowledge. A person creates only himself, and every idealistic creation is an imaginary creation, like a dream vision, like a "shadow game." The evolution of Symbolism from decadence to realistic Symbolism—this is a path straight to the creation of the ultimate value—man.

Georgy Chulkov
1908

SYMBOLISM AND CONTEMPORARY RUSSIAN ART
A. Bely

What is Symbolism? What does contemporary Russian literature represent?

Symbolism is confused with modernism. Modernism implies a multitude of literary schools that have nothing in common. *Sanin's* bestialism, and neo-realism, and the revolutionary-erotic exercises of Sergeev-Tsensky, and preaching the freedom of art, and L. Andreev, and the elegant trifles of O. Dymov, and Merezhkovsky's preaching, and the Pushkinianism of Bryusov's school, etc.—we call this whole discordant chorus of voices in literature either modernism or Symbolism, forgetting that, if Bryusov is connected with anyone, then it is Baratynsky and Pushkin, in no way with Merezhkovsky; Merezhkovsky is related to Dostoevsky and Nietzsche and not to Blok; Blok is closer to the early Romantics and not to G. Chulkov. But people say: "Merezhkovsky, Bryusov, Blok—these are modernists," and oppose them to other people and other things. Thus, if we define modernism, we are not defining a school. What are we defining? A professed literary credo?

Or is Russian modernism perhaps a school, in which the irreconcilable literary currents of yesterday and the reconcilable currents of today mingle harmoniously in the same channel? In this case, modernism's uniformity is not found at all in the external features of literary works, but in the *means of evaluating them.* But then, for modernism, Bryusov is as new as Pushkin or Derzhavin, as is all of Russian literature. Then why is modernism— *modernism?*

Beginning with *Mir Iskusstva* [*The World of Art*] and ending with *Vesy* [*Libra*], the journals of Russian modernism have been conducting a battle on two fronts: on the one hand they support young talents, on the other—they resurrect the forgotten past. They arouse interest in the exceptional examples of Russian painting in the XVIII century, they renew the cult of the German Romantics, Goethe, Dante and the Latin poets, they bring Pushkin and Baratynsky to us in a new light, they write outstanding essays about Gogol, Tolstoy, Dostoevsky; they foster new interest in Sophocles, they are engaged in new productions of Euripides on the stage, and they renew ancient theater.

And so: modernism is not a school. Do we have here, perhaps, an external unity of various literary devices? The mingling of literary schools gives rise to a multitude of modernistic insipidities: impressionism is coarsened in Muyzhel's stories, populism is also coarsened: it's neither fish nor fowl, it's a little bit of everything.

But perhaps modernism is characterized by a deepening of the methods of any school, no matter which one: the method, taking on more depth, turns out to be something different than it first seemed. This transformation of a method is found, for example, in Chekhov. Chekhov departs from naive realism, but by deepening realism, he begins to come in contact with Maeterlinck and Hamsun. And he completely departs from the literary devices not only of Pisemsky and Sleptsov, for example, but also Tolstoy. But do we call Chekhov a modernist? Bryusov, in contrast to this trend, passes from the Romantic side of Symbolism to even more real images: finally in *The Fiery Angel* he paints life in ancient Cologne. But the public and the critics stubbornly rank Bryusov among the modernists. No—the true essence of modernism is neither in the mingling of literary devices nor even in deepening the method of working.

Is it, perhaps, refining the tools of the trade, or sharpening artistic vision in the bounds of this or that literary school, broadening the sphere of perceptions? The Symbolist and the Realist and the Romantic and the Classicistic author can deal with the phenomena of colored sound, the refinement of memory, the splitting of one's personality and so forth. The Symbolist and the Realist and the Romantic and the Classicistic author will each concern himself with these phenomena in his own way. But artistic images of the past—don't they display a remarkable refinement at times? And the Romantic Novalis is indeed more refined than Muyzhel, and Goethe's lyrics are indeed finer than those of Sergei Gorodetsky.

And so, does the character of the convictions we express remain the criterion for modernism? But L. Andreev preaches about life's chaos, Bryusov—the philosophy of the moment, Artsybashev—the satisfaction of sexual need, Merezhkovsky—a new religious consciousness, V. Ivanov—mystical anarchism.

Again modernism is broken down into a multitude of ideological currents.

The whole order and system of notions about reality has changed under the influence of the evolution that is taking place in science and the theory of knowledge. The order and system of thinking in regard to moral values has changed, thanks to the sociological treatises of the second half of the XIX century; the antimony between the individual and society has deepened; the dogmatic solutions to basic contradictions in life have again become problems and only problems. Together with the change in understanding yesterday's dogmas, the question about the creative attitude toward life has been put forth with special vigor; before an individual's creative growth was connected with this or that religious attitude toward life. But the very form for expressing this growth—religion—has lost its ability to get in touch with life; it has retreated into the area of scholasticism; science and philosophy negate scholasticism.

And the essence of a religious perception of life has passed into the area of artistic creation; when the question of a free, creative individual has been put forth, the significance of the application of art has grown. A re-evaluation of the basic ideas about the existing forms of art was needed; we recognized more clearly the connection between the product of creativity (a work of art) and the very process of creativity that transforms an individual. We began to derive the classification of literary works more and more often from the processes of creativity; this type of classification collided with the old classifications of views of art that were established on the basis of studying the works of art, and not on the basis of studying the very processes. Studying the processes of cognition shows us that the very cognitive act bears the character of the creative affirmation, that creation precedes cognition; the former predetermines the latter. Consequently, the definition of creation by a system of views, not tested by the criticism of cognitive abilities, cannot be at the base of judgments about elegance, and all that metaphysical, positivistic, and sociological aesthetics unconsciously gives us is a narrowly preconceived elucidation of these questions. Dogmas with these views are dependent on the tools of analysis, but these tools are often not tested by critical methods. We now consider the judgments of literary schools about literature as possible methods of relating to it, but not as commonly obligatory dogmas of literary creeds. True judgments should flow from studies of the processes of creation, free from the dogmatics of any school. We should find, at the base of future aesthetics, the laws of creative processes, combined with the laws for embodying these processes in a form, i.e., with the laws of literary technique. The study of the laws of the techniques, styles, rhythms, forms of depiction lies within the area of experiment. The future aesthetics is simultaneous and free (i.e., it recognizes the regularity of cognitive processes as goals in themselves, not as the application of these processes for the utilitarian goals of dogmatics). But it is exact in so much as it puts experiment at the base of literary technique. Thus it offers its own method, not a method drawn from disciplines that have no direct relation to creation.

People will object: symbolism of a certain type is peculiar to any literary school; what have contemporary Symbolists contributed that is special? Of course they have contributed nothing more valuable than Gogol, Pushkin, Goethe and others did in terms of images. But they realized that art is entirely symbolic, "to the limit," not just "to a certain degree," and that aesthetics relies on symbolism alone and takes all its conclusions from it. Everything else is not essential. This "everything else," meanwhile, has been considered the true criteria for evaluating literary works.

The principles of classification of literary works can be either a division made by schools or a division according to the strength of talent. It is important to know what kind of credo a writer has and how much talent he possesses. If a limited credo weakens a powerful talent, we struggle with his credo for him. This is the essence of the discord between us and the talented representatives of realism and mystical anarchism. We fight with Gorky and Blok because we value them; we accept *The Confession* and pass by Chulkov.

If I name Gorky, Andreev, Kuprin, Zaytsev, Muyzhel, Artsybashev, Kamensky, Dymov, Chirikov, Merezhkovsky, Sologub, Remizov, Gippius, Ausländer, Kuzmin, the poets, Bryusov, Blok, Balmont, Bunin, V. Ivanov, and others who approach them, and among the philosophers I name L. Shestov, Minsky, Volynsky, Rozanov, and the publicists, Filosofov, Berdyaev, Anichkov, Lunacharsky, and other critics, then everyone will agree with me that I touch on contemporary Russian literature (I make no reference to those modern belletrists, among whom there are a few talented authors, but even so there are talented readers like Kozhevnikov).

These names fall into several groups. The first group of writers is from *Znanie* [Knowledge]. Their center is Gorky. Their ideologues are a group of critics who at one time came out with the *Essays of a Realistic World View*. Artsybashev and Kamensky stand apart from this group because they have taken on certain features of cheap Nietzscheanism.

The former and the latter groups adhere to realism.

Then follows the group united around *Shipovnik* [Sweetbrier]. This group has two flanks; on the one hand there are writers here who form the transitional link from realism to Symbolism, i.e., impressionism; the left flank consists of writers who form the transition from Symbolism to impressionism; there are attempts to create schools of symbolic realism and mystical anarchism from this transition. The group of neo-realists has no ideologues of its own; they partially merge with realism (Zaytsev is one example), partially with Symbolism (like Blok). Mystical anarchists, on the other hand, have their own ideologues: first of all, A. Meyer, the only theoretician of mystical anarchism that we can halfway understand. Then there is V. Ivanov, who stands apart from the *Shipovnik* group, but influences them from afar, and like the two-faced Janus, he is also turned toward *Vesy*. The latter group is the most complex, the most varied group of modernists. Their ideology is a mixture of Bakunin, Marx, Solovyov, Maeterlinck, Nietzsche and even . . . Christ, Buddha, and Mohammed. The following group consists of Merezhkovsky, Gippius, and the publicist-critics—Filosofov and Berdyaev; then begins a group of authors who work problems of religion: Volzhsky, S. Bulgakov, Florensky, Sventsitsky, Ern. Here we encounter religious sermons, of a more or less revolutionary hue. The remarkable L. Shestov, V. V. Rozanov, and Minsky's slightly boring philosophy of *meonism* stand entirely apart. I will not deal with them here.

There remains, finally, the last group of actual Symbolists, whose central figure is Valery Bryusov; it is united around *Vesy*. This group rejects all hasty slogans about overcoming or explaining Symbolism. It realizes the tremendous responsibility that lies on the shoulders of Symbolism's theoreticians. It acknowledges that the theory of Symbolism is the result of the varied work of all of culture and that every theory of Symbolism that appears now is in the best case only a sketch of a plan, a blueprint, according to which we must construct a building. Consciousness of the construction of a theory of Symbolism, the freedom of symbolization—this is the slogan of this group.

What is the relationship of these literary groups to Symbolism?

What ideology does the group of realist writers bring us? 1) Faithfulness to reality; 2) an exact depiction of how people live; 3) serving social interests and, from this, 4) an assortment of common features of society that makes contemporary Russia appear before us, with its various social groups and their relationships (Gorky's tramps, Kuprin's "Duel," and Yushkevich's *Jews*); this or that tendency shows through everywhere, whether it's populistic, or social-democratic, or anarchical.

Well, what then?

Are all these features rejected by Symbolism? Not in the slightest; we accept Nekrasov, greatly value Tolstoy's realism, recognize the social significance of *The Inspector General* and *Dead Souls,* Verhaeren's socialism, and so on. And where Gorky is an artist, we value Gorky. We only want to protest against the idea that the task of literature is to photograph the way people live; we do not agree that art expresses class contradictions; statistics' figures and special treatises speak to us eloquently about social injustice, and we trust Mehring's *History of Social Democracy* more than Minsky's poem, "Workers of the World Unite." Reducing literature's purpose to illustrating social treatises is naive; for a person with a vital social temperament the figures are more eloquent. Reducing literature to number (the essence of the sociological method) is the "non-sense" of art. Both Gogol and Boborykin are equally reducible to numbers; then why is Gogol—Gogol, and Boborykin—Boborykin? And the sociological critics' conclusions are often devoid of sense: when mysticism, pessimism, Symbolism, and impressionism are derived from the contemporary conditions of capital and labor, we fail to understand why we meet mystics, pessimists, and Symbolists in a pre-capitalist culture. The sociologist is correct when he approaches everything with his own method, but the aesthetician is also correct when he subjects sociology's method to the criticism of the theory of knowledge at that moment when the sociologist relegates aesthetic values to numbers and clothes his cyphers in the cloaks, regal mantles, and overcoats of literary heroes. And so the indication that the *Znanie* writers express a defined social tendency cannot be accepted as an indication of their pre-eminence.

No, if anything unites the *Znanie* writers, it is the dogma of naive realism (in the spirit of Moleschott, not at all in the spirit of Avenarius); in accordance with this dogma, reality is the reality of visible objects and experience. But then where do we put the reality of experience? To reduce experience to physics and mechanics now, when all of contemporary psychology and philosophy tends to examine groups of external experiences as parts of internal experience, is impossible. It is unthinkable to fail to see the subjective limits of the external world: we need only recall our experiences with a specter, with a siren, and so on. But if the boundaries of an objectively given appearance are unstable, then we are doomed to subjectivism. Where then are the limits of subjectivity in the area of talent? In this way the certainty of naive realism disappears; realism crosses over into impressionism; Andreev changes from a realist more and more into an impressionist. Certain pages of Gorky's *Confession* are thoroughly impressionistic. Consequently, it is impossible to remain a realist in art; everything in art is *more or less real,* you cannot build the principles of a school on "more or less"; "more or less" is not aesthetics at all. Realism is only an aspect of impressionism.

But impressionism, i.e., a view of life through the prism of experience, is already a creative view of life. My experience transforms the world; by going deeper into experience, I delve more deeply into creativity; creativity is, at the same time, the creativity of experiences and the creativity of images. The laws of creativity are the only aesthetics of impressionism. But these are the aesthetics of Symbolism. Impressionism is superficial Symbolism; the theory of impressionism could use some presuppositions borrowed from the theory of Symbolism.

The theoreticians of realism should understand their own duty as a private duty; our common duty, and theirs too, is the construction of Symbolist theory; until they realize the inescapability of such a duty, we will label them narrow-minded dogmatists who are trying to fit art into a framework. A great artist who blindly submits to the dogmas of this school reminds us of a giant in Lilliputian clothes; Gorky sometimes appears in such a costume. Fortunately his tight costume of naive realism sometimes tears and before us stands an artist in the real, not the dogmatic sense.

These are the artistic precepts of the dogmatists of realism and impressionism.

Semi-impressionism, semi-realism, semi-aesthetism, semi-tendentiousness all characterize the right flank of writers grouped around *Shipovnik.* The person on the extreme left of this wing is of course L. Andreev. The left flank is comprised of open and often talented writers, even typical Symbolists. But the ideological credo of this left group is mystical anarchism.

What is mystical anarchism?

We have before us two theoreticians: G. Chulkov and V. Ivanov. I feel uncomfortable speaking about the substance of G. Chulkov's theoretical views; I'd have to say a lot of bitter things; I will only remark that Chulkov's principal slogan, "non-acceptance of the world," is indeterminate; definitions of the concepts of "non-acceptance" and "world" are lacking and prevent us from understanding this slogan. I don't know what the world is, in the sense that Chulkov uses it. I don't know how to understand "non-acceptance"; I know only that if one understands them in the broadest sense, then there is no one theory that would totally accept the world. All the further conclusions from Chulkov's "hundred-mouthed" declarations have either a hundred senses or none. What we get are snippets of at least a hundred world views, each of which has a great founder—that I don't doubt; I also do not doubt that, for Chulkov, Christ, Buddha, Goethe, Dante, Shakespeare, Newton, Copernicus, etc., are mystical anarchists. I also do not doubt that he numbers himself among his famous family of friends and chases enemies from it. I absolutely cannot say anything more about G. Chulkov's theory.

Another mystical anarchist—Meyer—has hardly expressed himself; there is cause for hope that we will finally be able to assess Chulkov's incomprehensible philosophical experiences in Meyer's transpositions.

The most interesting and serious ideologue of this movement is V. Ivanov. If mystical anarchism were not compromised by Chulkov's unfortunate dithyrambs, we would reckon more seriously with V. Ivanov's words; but G. Chulkov has discovered hidden imperfections in V. Ivanov's views.

Both Chulkov and Ivanov start out with the slogan about the freedom of creativity; both understand and value the techniques of writing; both declare that they have outlived individualism; both value Nietzsche highly; consequently, both gather ideological baggage from Symbolists at the starting point of their development. V. Ivanov brings, in his opinion, substantial improvement on the objectives stated by the older Symbolists.

What is this improvement?

V. Ivanov seeks that focus in art where the rays of artistic creativity, so to say, cross; he finds that focus in drama. Drama includes the basis for broadening art to the point where artistic creativity comes closer to life's creativity. Wilde recognized just such a role for art; only the form of Wilde's creed is different; he called the creativity of life a lie. It is not without justification that he is called the singer of falsehood. But if Wilde himself believed that the creation of an image is not a falsehood at all, that a series of images, united by unanimity, is predetermined by some law of internal creativity, he would recognize the religious essence of art; V. Ivanov is entirely correct when he affirms that there is a religious sense behind art. But by dating the moment of the transition from art to religion from the moment of the reform of the theater and the transformation of drama, he falls into error. Artistic visions are internally real for Ivanov; the connection of these visions forms a myth; the myth grows out of a symbol. Drama deals primarily with myth; consequently, the origins that will transform the forms of art are concentrated in it. He turns his attention to the classification of art forms; he compels them to follow one after the other in the direction of an ever-increasing embrace of life. Meanwhile, the forms of art, under modern conditions, are parallel; they gain profundity in parallel. Each has in it a peculiar feature that religiously deepens the given form; the theater is only one of art's forms, not at all the basic one.

According to Ivanov, contemporary Symbolism does not adequately see the religious essence of art; therefore, it is unable to inspire the masses; the Symbolism of the future will co-mingle with the people's religious element.

And so: 1) the religious essence of art is affirmed behind myth; 2) the origin of myth from symbol is affirmed; 3) the dawn of a new mytho-creation is perceived in contemporary drama; 4) a new symbolic realism is affirmed; 5) a new populism is affirmed.

But after all, every deepening and transformation of experience that comprises the true essence of its aesthetic choice presupposes the basis of that choice, i.e., the norm of creativity. Let the artist ignore this norm; it will come out in the ever-deepening stream of creativity; and the artist who experiences freedom (and is, so to say, outside the criteria of good and evil) only submits more totally to the higher order of the *same* duty. The objective of Symbolist theory consists of the establishment of certain norms; how it relates to the norms is a different matter. As a theoretician, I can only state the norms; as a practitioner, I realize that these norms are aesthetic or religious realities. In the first case, God's name is hidden from me; in the second I name that name. Theoreticians of Symbolism in art can study the processes of religious creativity as one of the forms of aesthetic creativity, if they want to remain in the area of knowledge that deals with refinement. Thus, as practitioners, they can experience the established norm either as a vital, super-individual connection (God), or as a broadened artistic symbol. The theory of artistic Symbolism neither rejects nor establishes religion; it studies it. This is a condition of the seriousness of the movement, not its drawback. And so Ivanov's attacks on the theory of Symbolism would be justified from his point of view if he fell upon the aesthetes as a candid preacher of a defined religion. He would then have to admit that art is godless, but that the freedom of investigating the processes of creation demands limitations, constrictions by determined religious requirements. But he neither abandons the ground of art, nor appears before us as a definitely religious preacher, nor does he shy away from theories of art; for us, his call for religious realism remains lifeless as preaching and dogmatic as a theory. It is impossible to demand religious practice theoretically and only theorize practically; that is not candid, not irreproachably honest. Ivanov's religious realism seems to us, as Symbolists, an attempt to cast the area of theoretical investigations into the area of dreams, or even worse, to create new dogmatics of art from dreams, even more narrowly than the dogmatists of realism and Marxism do. Believing that mystical anarchism is a religion, we fool ourselves and find no God in it; believing that mystical anarchism is a theory, we fall into dogmatic sectarianism.

As for the origin of myth from symbol, who among us will deny it or relinquish the right to experience mythical creativity religiously? We only feel that to affirm this on the basis of the theory of Symbolism is premature, for now the theory of Symbolism is entirely in the future. It is impossible to crown the foundation of a temple directly with a steeple; what do we do with the temple's walls?

There is a movement toward mystery plays in contemporary drama; but it is impossible to build a mystery play on indeterminate artistic mysticism; a mystery play is a divine service; which god will be served in the theater: Apollo or Dionysus? God have mercy, what a joke! *Apollo, Dionysus*—these are only artistic symbols; but if these symbols are religious, then give us a candid name that symbolizes God. Who is Dionysus? Christ, Mohammed, Buddha? Or Satan himself? To unite people who are connected to various divinities with a Dionysian experience means to arrange a wax museum of gods or (what's even worse) to turn religion into a spiritual seance. Fashionable ladies and gentlemen of all modes will say, "interesting, piquant," and accept mystical anarchism without reservation.

But can we Symbolists, for whom the method of answering a question of this or that direction is a question of life, we—among whom there are people who confess to the name of only one God, and not all gods together—can we relate to a theory that throws us into the embrace of surprise without feeling extreme pain and irritation? Here they accuse us of polemicizing, of vehemence; but if we were to exhibit a smiling breeziness in regard to all the questions raised, we would be "decorated coffins," without God, without duty.

V. Ivanov affirms a new Symbolist realism, forgetting that the artist for whom the artistic image is internally unreal is not an artist; only charlatans can call themselves illusionists in the literal sense of the word. For illusionists of Edgar Allen Poe's type, illusionism is a form of confession of faith. Symbolist realism is raising something to one squared; if Ivanov is able to divide true artists into realists and illusionists, then he is busying himself in vain; the square of one is one. A futile occupation!

We know that here and there a defined social program is connected with the slogan of populism; Symbolism walked the narrow line between the artist's political conviction and his creativity so that art would not cloud the area of economic struggle for us, but this latter feature would not kill the artist in the artist. When they taunt us with the multi-faceted slogan of uniting with the people in artistic creativity, it still seems to us that they just want to make us utopians in the areas of politics and aesthetic theory.

Utopianism, either here or there, is dangerous.

Symbolists know by experience all the harm that dogmatism and groundless utopianism in the sphere of artistic theory can cause. They want a sober theory; they know that only a concerted series of investigations will lead to a firm foundation for aesthetics. And if they raise a question about the theories of various artistic schools, only because these theories are predetermined by a method that does not lie within the essence of aesthetics, then of course they do not hesitate to pull the weeds of vague guessing about art that grow around them. This is the basis of their disagreement with mystical anarchism; all of its positive aspects in these theories are contained in Symbolism; everything specific is weeds, which they should pull.

They will dispute the straightforward requirement concerning the submission of Symbolist theory to religious dogmatism, but they are able to respect only those people who exhibit such a requirement in the name of a defined religion; where the confession of religious convictions is not directed against art, then we disunite and unite with that confession, depending on whether we are religious or not, depending on which religion we confess. *"Confession"* is our *"Privat-Sache,"* while we are theoreticians of art. It is obvious from these words what position we occupy in relation to the religious movement which has appeared in Russian literature, beginning with Solovyov and ending with Merezhkovsky. I personally depart from Solovyov in many areas and unite with Merezhkovsky in many ways; some of my artistic brothers-in-arms do not. This is a divergence that lies beyond the bounds of that area where we defend Symbolism.

Andrei Bely
1908

THE THEATER OF ONE WILL
F. Sologub

On the vessel there is a seal—
on the seal, a name—
only the one who has sealed it
and the initiated know
what is hidden in the vessel.

*E. C. Wiesner. The First Bride's
Silence. A Novel.*

"You're philosophizing like a poet."
Dostoevsky. *Letters.*

Out of all the things that have at any time been created by the genius of man, perhaps the lightest creation on the visible surface and the most terrifying, in the depths it can reach, is theater. The fatal steps—a game—a spectacle—mystery... High tragedy to the same degree as light comedy and coarse farce.

Tragic horror and a fool's laughter shake the dilapidated but still seductive curtains of our world before us with equally unconquerable force. The world that seems so usual and suddenly, in the vacillation of the game, so unexpected, so wierd, astounding or repulsive. Neither the tragic nor the comic mask deceives the attentive viewer in equal measure—as they did not deceive the participants in the game, enchanting him, as they will not deceive the participant in the mystery, giving him access to the secret.

Beyond the rotting masks and beyond the rouged mugs of the carnival jester, and the pale mask of the tragic actor—the one Face shines through. Terrifying, indomitably calling...

The fatal steps. We played when we were children, and we've already lost heart for the simple games, now we're curious, we come to look at the spectacles and the hour is approaching when, in the transformation of mind and body, we will come to true unity in liturgical action, in a rite of mystery...

When we were children, when we were alive—

Only the children are alive
We're dead, long dead.

—we played. We divided up the roles among ourselves and played them—until they called us to go to bed. Our theater was partly like everyday life—we were very imitative and observant—partly symbolic with an undoubted tendency toward decadence—we loved fairy tales so much and words of strange, old incantations, and all the amusing and useless—useless from the practical point of view—rites of the game. The conventionalities, the naivities, and the absurdities were so dear in our games. We were well aware that it was pretending, that it was all for fun. We didn't need a decorator or a propman. We saddled a chair and agreed:

"This will be a horse."

But if we really wanted to run a little bit more, we said:

"I'll be the horse."

We weren't exclusive or one-sided in the character of our games. There was a game for the greater public, with lots of people, noise, and uproar, in the corridors of large halls, in the garden or a field:—"a fight isn't a fight, a game isn't a game"—and there were intimate games in secluded corners, where grownups and strangers never looked. There things were merry and tiring. Here it was eerie and also merry, and our cheeks reddened more deeply than when we were running wildly and dull fires were lit in our eyes.

We played and didn't know that our games were only grownups' hand-me-downs. We replayed something old that seemed new for us. And in this replaying of someone else's game, we were infected by the heavy poison of the obsolete.

The significance of a game was not in its contents, however. The drops of burning poison mixed in with the vernal nectar of a young life. The riotousness of a new life made us dizzy with light, sweet intoxication, our legs were inspired by swift racing—the heavy burdens of a difficult earthly time burned up in the ecstasy of bright oblivion. And sharp, fleeting moments burned up, and from their ashes a new world, our world, was built. A world blazing in young ecstasy . . .

And if later we wanted something else from a game, which became only a spectacle for us—and from tragedy, from comedy? We go so willingly to the theater, especially to the premieres of famous plays—but what do we want from theater? Do we want to learn the art of living or purge ourselves of obscure experiences? To decide a moral, social, aesthetic, or still another kind of problem? To see a "reed, shaken by the wind? a person dressed in soft clothes, a prophet?"

Of course all this and lots of other things can be dragged into the theater, not without foundation and even without utility—but all of this must burn up in the true theater, as old rags burn in a fire. And no matter how different the external contents of a drama are, we always want from it—if we have still remained somewhat alive from the peaceful days of our childhood—what we wanted before from our children's games—fiery ecstasy that abducts our soul from the tight chains of a boring and meager life. Enchantment and ecstasy—this is what attracts each of us into the theater. These are the means by which the genius of tragedy draws us into participating in its mysterious intentions. But what makes up these intentions?

Either I absolutely don't know what drama is to a person, or it is only for drawing a person to Me. To carry him from the kingdom of the whimsical Aisa, from the world of strange and ridiculous accidents, from the area of comedy into the kingdom of the stern and comforting Ananke, into the world of necessity and freedom, into the area of high tragedy. To abolish the temptations of life and crown the eternal comforter, not the false one, but the one who doesn't deceive.

A theatrical spectacle, to which people come for amusement or diversion, will not long remain only a spectacle for us. And soon the viewer, tired of the alternations of spectacles alien to him will want to become a participant in a mystery play, as he was at one time a participant in a game. The person banished from Eden will soon knock on the door with a brave hand; behind the door the bridegroom is feasting with the wise virgins. He was a participant in an innocent game when he still lived in paradise, in My beautiful garden between the two rivers. And now his only way to resurrection is to become a participant in a mystery play, to join his hand with that of his brother, with the hand of his sister in a liturgical rite, to press his lips, eternally parched with thirst, to the mystery-filled cup, where *I* "mix blood with water." To do in the bright and public temple what is now only done in the catacombs.

But a theatrical spectacle is a necessary transitory condition and in our time theater, unfortunately, still cannot be anything other than only a spectacle and is often an idle spectacle. Mere spectacle—that is, unless we are speaking of the intimate theater that must be brought into being, but to speak of which—indeed, how can one speak of it? After all this is a temptation for the uniniated... really only hints and outlines.

Contemporary theater wants to be primarily a spectacle. Everything in it is set up only for spectacle. For a spectacle, there are professional actors, footlights and a curtain, cleverly painted decorations that aspire to give the illusion of reality, intelligent contrivances of the theater of everyday life, and the wise fictions of conventional theater.

If a path has already begun to show in our consciousness, however, a path along which the development of the theater must pass so that theater answers to its high calling, then the task of the theater worker—author of drama, director, actor—consists of bringing it nearer to ecumenical activity, to mystery play and liturgy, by raising theatrical spectacle to all the perfections that are only attainable for a spectacle.

It seems to me that the first obstacle that must be surmounted on this way is the actor. The actor attracts too much of the viewer's attention to himself, and by this he overshadows both the drama and the author. The more talented the actor is, the more intolerable his tyranny is for the author, and the more harmful for the tragedy. To depose this seductive, but nevertheless harmful, tyranny, there are two methods: either transfer the center of the theatrical presentation to the viewer in the audience or transfer it to the author offstage.

The first thought that might follow upon the recognition of theater as a field of ecumenical activity would be, evidently, that the footlights must be destroyed, the curtain, perhaps, removed, and the viewer made a participant in or even a creator of the presentation. Instead of two-dimensional decorations leave four adorned walls or the external space of a street, square or field. To turn the spectacle into a masquerade, which is a combination of game and spectacle. But then why get together? Only so that the "folks get their extreme unction," as one of the contemporary ditties has it? Not a bad occupation, but where does it lead?

It's true that elements of mystery are admixed to game and spectacle in masquerade. Hints about it, secrets. But this is still not sacrament. Just as the most eerie fears come at noon, when, risen to his zenith and hidden behind violet shields, the evil Dragon weaves his spells, so the deepest secret also appears only when the masks are removed.

All the meridians meet at one pole (or two, if you wish—but by the law of the identity of polar opposites, it's always sufficient to speak of only one pole)—all earthly roads invariably lead to the one eternal Rome—"always and in everything, there is only *I*, there is no Other, nor was, nor shall be." Every unity of people has significance in so far as it leads to Me—from the vain-seductive disunity to genuine unity. The pathos of a mystery play is nourished by the accidental multitude of My and only My possibilities, the totality of which creates laws but itself moves with freedom.

And thus there is only one who wills and acts in tragedy, which adds to the unities of action, place, and time the unity of the will's aspiration in the drama.

(Perhaps the transitions in thoughts here will seem rather unexpected to some—but I don't argue, and not because I can't do it, I'm only stating one thought. "I'm philosophizing, like a poet".)

The one who wills and acts in a tragedy should always be alone, not in the sense that he leads the action of the chorus, but in the sense that he is the one who expresses the inevitable, not the tragic hero, but his fate.

Contemporary theater presents a sad spectacle of a splintered will, and for this reason, disunited action. "It takes all kinds," the simple-minded playwright thinks, "to each his own." He goes to different places, notes down the conditions, mores, and everyday life, observes various people, and depicts all of it with great versimilitude. Kozmodemyansky and Nalimov and Vaksel recognize themselves and their neckties, and are very happy if the author—for friendship's sake—has flattered them, or they become angry if the author has made it understood that he doesn't like their looks or their behavior. The director is happy that he has enough material for an entertaining staging of a play. The actor is happy that he can get himself made up in a good and interesting way, and can mimic the looks and mannerisms of painter X, or poet Y, engineer A, advocate B...The public is in ecstasy—it recognizes its acquaintances and non-acquaintances, and feels at an undoubted advantage: no matter how widespread the sins dragged out onto the stage are, every viewer, except for the small number of people on display, clearly sees, nonetheless, that he is not being depicted, but someone else.

And none of this is necessary. No mores, no customs, no everyday life, only an eternal mystery is being played out. No plots or denouements; all the plots were begun long ago, and all the denouements long ago predicted—only an eternal liturgy is being performed. What are words and dialogue? There is only one eternal dialogue; the questioner answers himself and craves an answer. And what themes? Only Love, only Death.

There are no different people, there is only one person, only one *I* in the whole universe, willing, acting, suffering, burning in an unquenchable fire, and from the fury of a horrible and ugly life saved in the good and joyful embrace of the universal comforter—Death.

I put on many masks, of My own free will, but I am always and remain in everything myself—like some Chaliapin who is always the same in all his roles. And beneath the terrifying mask of the tragic hero, and beneath the ridiculous disguise of the jester, whom the comedy makes a jest of, and in the bright coveralls of multi-colored rags that dress the body of a puppet-show clown who grimaces for the amusement of the peanut gallery— beneath all these coverings, the viewer should discover Me. The theatrical spectacle must appear before him like a problem with one unknown.

If a viewer comes to the theater, as a simple-minded gawker comes to the world, "to see the sun," then I, a poet, create a drama in order to recreate the world according to My intentions. As My will alone rules in the wide world, so only one will—the will of the poet—should rule in the small circle of the theatrical spectacle.

Drama—like the universe, also a work of one design—is a work of one creative thought. Only the author presents the fate of the tragedy, the accident of comedy. Isn't his powerful will in everything? As he wishes, so it will be. By his whim, he can unite lovers or sadly separate them, exalt the hero or cast him into a gloomy abyss of despair and ruination. He can crown beauty, youth, loyalty, bravery, insane daring, selflessness—but nothing prevents him from glorifying ugliness and debauchery, and from placing the betrayer Judas above all the apostles.

> As a rebuke to the unjust day I will raise abuse
> over the world and tempting, will tempt.

But the actor is vainglorious. He has overshadowed the author by his arbitrary interpretation, by his unsuitable and disjointed social and psychological observations, and he has turned the drama itself into a collection of roles for different parts. Then the director comes and abolishes the author's directions. Then the nemisis of the dramatic action, the hollow voice of the commanding Moira, is hidden by the theater manager's order in the narrow prompter's box. And when there have been few rehearsals, then everyone on stage focuses on one point, from which an annoying voice is heard by those in the first rows. And they mercilessly garble the poet's words.

But do I really want to have my voice heard from a narrow cellar? to have windows I thought up turned into unnecessary (for my purposes) columns on the stage by the whim of a director? to have my words and stage directions realized only in the painted sets?

No, my words should sound loudly and clearly. The visitor at a theatrical spectacle should hear the poet before the actor.

This is how I imagine a theatrical spectacle: the author, or a reader who replaces him—and even better a reader, passionless and calm, and not agitated by the author's shyness before the viewers who will shout praise or approbation at him (both are equally unpleasant), and perhaps they have brought with them some latchkeys for whistling merrily—the reader will sit near the stage, somewhere to the side. On the table in front of him will be the play that is to be presented. The reader will begin, in order, at the beginning:

He reads the title of the drama. The name of the author.

If there is an epigraph, he reads it. There are interesting and useful ones. For instance, the epigraph of *The Inspector General:* "It's no use scolding the mirror if your mug's crooked. A folk saying." A coarse epigraph, as was the author—but fair and suitable for the establishment of the appropriate connection between the viewer and the action on stage.

Then the list of the dramatis personae.

The preface or the stage directions, if there are any.

The first act. The setting. The names of the people on stage.

The actors' entrances and exits, as they are noted in the text of the drama.

All the stage directions, not omitting even the slightest, even if it's just one word.

As the reader is near the stage reading, the curtain moves, is raised. The stage is revealed. The setting requested by the author is lit. The actors come out on stage, and do what is spelled out for them in the author's stage directions, just read, and they say what is stated by the text of the drama. If the actor forgets a word—and when doesn't he forget them!—the reader reads it, just as calmly, also aloud, like all the rest.

And the action unfolds before the viewer, as it unfolds before us in life itself; we go and speak according to our own wills (or so we imagine); we do what we have to do, or what comes into our heads, and try to realize our own desires (or so it seems), in so far as the laws of nature or the desires of other people do not hinder us; we see, listen, smell, touch, taste. We use all our senses and mental efforts to find out what there is in the real world, what has its own existence and laws, partly understandable to us, partly miraculous for us; we feel love for one person and hate for another, and we are aroused by still other passions, in conformity with them establish our relationships with the world and with people. And we usually don't know that we have no independent will, that our every movement and our every word are dictated and even long ago predicted in the demonic creative plan of the universal game once and for all, so that we have neither choice nor freedom, nor even ad-libbing, so dear to the actor, because it has been included in the text of the universal mystery by some unknown censor: and that world we are cognizant of is nothing other than a marvelous decoration, and beyond it there is backstage untidiness and dirt. We play the role dictated to us the best we know how, actors and at the same time viewers, alternately applauding or booing each other, sacrificing and at the same time being sacrificed.

Can the theater give us any spectacle other than that of a world too wide for our strengths and too narrow for our will? And should it? Play as you live, transfer your life to the stage, isn't that what the theater of everyday life wants?

But what will remain of the actor's playing then? After all, the actor will turn into a speaking marionette, and an actor can't like this, especially if he likes strong roles and the audience's attention turned toward him and the cries of the simple-minded in the peanut gallery, and the newspapers' clamor around his name. Such theater is unacceptable for the contemporary actor. He will say scornfully:

"That won't be a theatrical presentation, but simply a literary reading, accompanied by conversations and movements. Then it would be better to organize a marionette theater, a child's amusement. Let painted dolls move, let one person offstage speak with seven voices—speak and jerk the strings."

And why shouldn't an actor be like a marionette, however? It's not insulting for a person. Such is the unshakable law of the universal game. That a person is like a marvelously made marionette. And it's impossible for him to leave this behind, and even impossible for him to forget it.

Everyone's appointed hour will come, and everyone will turn into an immobile and lifeless doll, no longer able to play any roles...

Here it is, a worn-out doll that no one needs, lying on the canvas for the last ablution, its arms are crossed as they crossed them, its legs are extended, as they pulled them, its eyes are closed, as they closed them—a poor marionette fit for tragic play alone! Back there, in the wings, someone indifferently pulled your invisible strings, some cruel person tortured you with the fiery torment of suffering, some evil person frightened you with the pale horrors of a hateful life, you turned your grieving gaze toward some merciless person in pre-death langor. But here, in the main floor seats, your clumsy movements—caused by the jerking of the terrible strings—your confused words—the hidden prompter spoke so softly—and your useless tears and your pitiful laughter, as useless as the tears, have amused someone. Enough, all the words of your role are somehow spoken, all the author's directions have been followed fairly closely—the strings are rolled up—and your dried lips now want to say some new word in vain—they open and close mechanically—and fall silent forever. They'll hide you and dig a place for you, and forget you...

An actor, even one with great genius, is no more than a person. His role, even the strongest, is less than life and easier than it. And it is of course better for him to be a speaking marionette and to move in accordance with the intelligible and passionless voice of the reader than desperately mix up his lines, to the accompaniment of the hoarse whispering of the prompter hidden in his box.

The single, even, and passionless voice of the "man in black" leads the entire theatrical action—and in correspondence with this, everything on stage should aspire to the unity that is necessary so that the viewer's unsteady attention is not dispersed, so that nothing is distracted from what is singularly substantive in a theatrical spectacle—the exposure, by dramatic action, of My single, changeless Image, beneath the many and varied masks.

The person performing the action is never onstage by himself. Even when there are no other actors on the visible stage, the person who remains before the viewers' eyes carries on a constant dialogue with someone. The aspiration toward unity, toward Me, can originate only in that which is My polar opposite—the many, the not-I. But all streams must flow together into one sea and not be lost in the quicksand of the divided multitude. The single Image, hidden under masks, should show through to the viewers in the course of the theatrical action. From this comes the demand that there be only one hero, essentially one dramatis persona, only one point on which the viewers' attention is focused. And the rays of stage action should come together in one focus, so that the bright flame of ecstasy suddenly flares up.

The other personae in the drama should be only necessary steps in the progression toward the single Image. Their significance in the drama depends entirely on the degree of their proximity to the center of the will's aspiration in the drama, as it is revealed in the hero. Only in this kind of arrangement, on the descending scale of ranks of one and the same staircase of dramatic action, lies the basis of their individual differences, their separate characteristics, which otherwise would in no way be needed in the drama. Desdemona is significant in the tragic situation not because she has a great and touching role, not because Othello loved and destroyed her, but because she was that fatal person whose hand removed his mask and revealed only to him the fatal falsehood and ambivalence of the world.

It follows, from the fact that an actor in a tragedy should essentially be alone, that theater should be freed from play-acting. A game, with all its variety of faithfully observed and accurately reproduced gestures and intonations, with all that has entered into theatrical tradition, that is acquired by diligent training, or that is discovered again by the gifted actor's guessing and inventing, this is the game that seems normal to us, inspired or serenely deliberate, that presents a depiction of conflict and struggle of totally separate people, each of which is sufficient unto himself. But there are no such autonomous personalities on earth. Thus there are no struggles between them. There is only the appearance of a struggle, the fatal dialectics on their faces. And a struggle with fate is unthinkable, there is only a demonic game, fate's amusement with its marionettes.

The better the actor plays the role of Man, the more pathetically he cries:

"We'll bang our shields, we'll cross our swords," the more ridiculous is his irrelevant game, the more clear his incomprehension of the role. "Someone in gray" has never accepted a challenge to a duel from anyone. A little girl doesn't fight with her dolls—she tears them up and breaks them, and she laughs or cries, depending on her mood.

It becomes funny for us to see an actor being too zealous, and a grandiose declamation, and a majestic gesture, and extreme conscientiousness in transmitting particulars of everyday life—all these charming things make us feel a little uncomfortable. Uncomfortable, as when someone suddenly begins speaking loudly and excitedly and begins to gesticulate in front of a sedate gathering. It's not worth it to act very zealously. Only the people in the peanut gallery will laugh or cry at what is presented on stage— the people on the main floor smile slightly, sometimes sadly, sometimes almost gaily, always ironically. It's not worth acting for them.

Tragedy tears away the world's enchanting mask, and where it seemed to us there was harmony, predetermined or created, it opens up before us the world's eternal contradiction, the eternal identification of good and evil and other polar opposites. It affirms every contradiction and to every one of life's pretensions, correct or not, it equally and ironically says *Yes!* To neither good nor evil will it say the lyrical *No!* Tragedy is always irony; it is never lyrical. We must stage it that way.

And so there should be no acting on the stage. Only the even transmission, word by word, the calm reproduction of situations, scene by scene. And the fewer scenes there are, the slower they change, the clearer the tragic intentions emerge before the enchanted viewer. Let the tragic actor stop straining and grimacing—extreme gestures and bombastic declamation should be left to the clowns and the buffoons. The actor should be cool and calm, his every word should resound smoothly and deeply, his every movement should be slow and beautiful. The presentation of tragedy should not remind us of the flickering of pictures at a cinema. And the attentive viewer must pass along the very long path to comprehending tragedy without this annoying and useless flickering.

Furthest of all from the viewer stands the hero of the tragedy, the chief manifestation of My will—the path to understanding him is the longest of all, the viewer has to ascend a steep staircase to him, to overcome and conquer much within and without himself. And the further from the hero, the nearer to the viewer, the more comprehensible it is for him, and finally the characters come so close to the viewer that they more or less coincide with him. They begin to resemble the chorus in an ancient tragedy, saying what the people seated on the steps of the ampitheater would have said.

And so the peaceful and content bourgeois comes to the theater. How is he to accept the plot and the denouement of the drama, and what will he understand in it, if these speeches, all foreign to his notions, will ring out from the stage? Just as you do not have a Shakespearean tragedy without a jester, so contemporary drama cannot get along without these cliched mannequins, whose faces are obliterated, whose mechanisms are slightly damaged and squeak, and whose words are dull and commonplace. And if the bourgeois himself were to shudder at their intolerable flatness, then that would be good, there would be a comforting sign in this, a sign that he is nearing the comprehension of the single Image, who hides under various masks, injured but not killed by the flatness of earthly speech. In this lies the true justification of light comedy and farce, and even puppet show buffoonery.

There is also another meaning in this—because until now this has been the only means in the public theater—again I am not speaking of intimate theater, most desired and dear for us, but about which it is so difficult to speak—the only means of involving the viewer in the action. It is the only way and in many cases it is perhaps enough.

And even mystery itself, being action that is ecumenical to a great degree, still demands one performer, priest and victim, for the sacrament of self-sacrifice. Not only the highest kind of social activity, the mystery, but social accomplishment in general is at the same time completely individual. Every common deed is performed according to the thought and plan of one person, every parliament listens to one orator and doesn't raise a hubbub together, gathering together in a common, merry din. "On the vessel there is a seal, on the seal a name; only the one who sealed it and the initiated know what is hidden in the vessel." The temple is open to everyone, but the name of the builder is chiselled in stone. The person coming to the altar must leave his spite at the threshold. And so the crowd—viewers—cannot be mixed into the tragedy, except by means of burning their old and trivial words in themselves. Only passively. The person performing the action is always alone.

What can the interest for the stage be in flooding it with a multitude of people, each of whom pretends to have his own character and his separate role in the drama? Their flickering is annoying to one who understands drama, it's difficult to keep them all straight, and there's no point. It's even hard, for this reason, to read a drama—you always have to look at the dramatis personae. That's why drama isn't in favor in the book business.

Isn't it all the same to me who is fussing and bustling about on stage, Shuysky or Vorotynsky—if I know that before me a tragedy of imposture is going on, so brilliantly plotted by the genius of Russian history (and yet so insipidly outlined by the geniuses of Russian literature)! One person speaks, or another, aren't these your words, simple-minded viewer? Aren't those your dull, long ago effaced and still dear, nickels rolling on the floor of the stage, next to the ruddy gold of poetry?

It is a naive accounting—but wise and true—that as the theatergoer greedily picks up his nickels, he will take even My heavy gold with them and sell Me in exchange his soul, which, though it be of little weight, is still dear to me. But it's better, nonetheless, if less of this change is on the floor of the stage: a plea addressed to the authors of drama.

As only one in a drama has a will—the author, and only one performs the action—the actor, so should there be only one viewer. In this respect, that insane king who saw the play of his actors alone in his magnificent theater, hiding behind the thick damask in the silence and darkness of his royal loge, was right. In tragic theater every viewer should feel like this insane king who hid from everyone. And no one should see his face and no one be surprised that

> he veiled the game of
> his passions with a secret,
> at times happy at the grave
> and sad at the feast.

And if he dozes or falls deeply asleep—art is a golden dream—and why couldn't the dream be a rhythmic dream vision—no one will laugh at him, and no one will be disturbed or shocked by his sudden snoring in the most pathetic part.

And he himself should neither see nor hear anyone—neither the people artlessly reflecting on their faces all the feelings, moods, distresses, and sympathies, nor those who pretend to understand and be intelligent. Not see a handkerchief by reddened eyes, a nervously wadded glove in restless hands. Not hear those who sniff and sob, or those who laugh when they're supposed to laugh and even when they're supposed to cry. The viewer of a tragic spectacle should be in darkness, silence and solitude. Like the prompter in his narrow box. Like a theater mouse.

Not distracted by anything peripheral, a viewer should not be distracted by anything on stage that is not strictly necessary for the drama. Whether the excellently painted sets should be on the stage or only drapes hanging over or lying on it—in any case the stage should be arranged in two dimensions. This spectacle should be like a painting, so that the viewer doesn't have to look for an actor in the depths of a multidimensional stage, in that area where something can be externally hidden, at the same time when his attention should be concentrated on him who acts and wills and contemplates.

Scenery on stage is pleasant—it sets the desired mood straightaway, gives the viewer all the external hints—and why shouldn't it be there? If, in the wide, external world also:

> And suddenly it all seemed like
> flat decorations to me then—
> the dawn stretched out like a paper strip,
> a star twinkled like spangles.

But a person lost in the world of external decorations comes to the theater to find himself—to come to Me. And it's impossible to distract his gaze by an unnecessarily splendid variety of scenery. By the way, it's better, for this reason, for the drama to be performed with only one set of scenery. In any case at every given moment the viewer should know what he is supposed to be looking at, what he should be seeing and listening to on the stage. The author's directions, loudly pronounced by the reader, will of course help in this, and all the art of mechanical contrivances will help him in this too. Everything that appears to the viewer on stage should be significant, each detail of the setting should be strictly thought out, so that there is nothing superfluous, nothing beyond what is most necessary, in front of the viewer.

The lighting arrangements are perhaps appropriate and advisable along these same lines: perhaps the viewer should only be shown what he must see at a given moment, and all the rest should disappear in darkness, as everything we pay no attention to falls under the threshold of our consciousness. It exists, but at the same time it seems like it doesn't. Because for Me, only what is in Me and for Me exists—all the rest, despite its possible reality for someone else, lies only in the world of possibilities, only awaits its turn to be.

Such is the outline of the form for a theatrical spectacle. And the contents put into this form can be the tragic play of Fate with its marionettes, a spectacle of the fatal melting of all earthly masks, or a mystery of complete self-affirmation. Playing, I play with dolls and masks—and the masks and covers, visible to the world, fall away—and My single image is mysteriously revealed, and rejoicing, My single will triumphs. My fatal error ties all knots and I struggle with the constricting fetters of irresolvable, earthly contradictions—until a sharp stiletto, piercing My heart, cuts the fatal knots. I have raised worlds with a merry game—and I am victim and I am priest. Burning love is comforting, and consuming, it burns—and the final comforter is—Death.

Of course theater gravitates toward tragedy. And it should become tragic.

Every farce in our time becomes a tragedy, our laughter sounds more terrifying than our lament to the sensitive ear, and hysterics precede our ecstasy. In the old days, happy, healthy people laughed. The victors laughed and the defeated cried. Among us, the grieving and the insane laugh, Gogol laughs...My insanity has happy eyes.

Our comedy, to put it simply, is nothing more than funny and amusing tragedy. But tragedy is also funny for us.

The sorrows of young Werther? No. They're the sorrows of a conscientious high school student. It's very funny but also very serious. He could have been birched—but he shot himself. Little girls crowd around the grave dug for him, roses fall on his coffin—parents cry and sniff. They wanted to birch him, but they didn't make it in time. It's not their fault.

Around us rippling laughter pours forth like music. It is rhythmic perhaps. It calls for dances. And does only Death dance on the fresh graves? We also know how to dance. We're a terrible merry people—we dance like a family of gravediggers during a cholera epidemic...

No matter what the contents of future tragedy are it cannot manage without dance. It's not surprising that quick-witted authors of drama are now putting the cakewalk, maxixe and other kinds of nonsense in their plays.

But the dance, I hope, will be choral. And for this we must take away the footlights in the theater.

If the contemporary viewer can only participate in the theatrical spectacle in such a way that he will recognize himself in the more or less distorted mirrors placed on the stage for him, then the next step of his participation in tragic action should be his participation in tragic dance.

It's good that Isadora Duncan dances with her legs bare, inspired by the dance...

> How nice it is to know that there is
> another life with us!
> Valery Bryusov

But soon we will all become infected with this "other life," and like religious zealots, will gush onto the stage and whirl in violent zeal.

The action of the tragedy will be accompanied by and alternate with dance. Merry dancing? Perhaps. In any case more or less violent. Because dance is no more than rhythmic violence of body and soul, submerging in the tragic element of music.

If you look at a person dancing and think that as he is turning he is being bathed in sweat, and thus loves to be bathed in a tender aroma of scents, then you are mistaken, of course. He is not turning before you—the world around him revolves ever faster and faster, dying, decaying, melting in swift, free, and light movement. But you don't see this universal whirling, because you're shy and sensible, and don't dare to give yourself up to the violent rhythm of dance that dissolves the chains of everyday life. You see only the humorous—the faces too red, an arm awkwardly put out to the side or unflatteringly bent, damp locks of hair, and those disgusting little drops on young skin. You don't know that it is the world's whirling that fans sweet fire onto the frenzied body which has surrendered to the universal dance, and Eden's dew combined in itself joyous coolness and joyous heat.

A black lock beats against a white neck, the tip of a white slipper flickers from under a white dress, a happy smile on vermillion lips sparkles and is carried away, the train sweeps and brushes. Put on your gloves, invite whichever lady you want, don't be afraid—this is only a ballroom dance, and you're not at Brocken but in the dance hall of Baronness Jourfixe. The floor is waxed—"the gift of the wise bees"—but is not dangerous at all. "The Maiden Snandulia dances only with those who are worthy of being her partner" (Wedekind: *The Awakening of Spring*)—she is a well-bred maiden, although "her dress is low-cut in front and back—in back to her waist, in front to drive a man mad. She has, of course, no shift."

This ballroom dance is only a hint at what should be a tragic dance. It's true that the dancing lady's corset, gloves, and slippers partly, although only to a slight degree, correspond to the mask of the ancient tragic actor. But after all we know that we need no mask made by a theatrical propman, no matter how good it is. We always wear our own masks, and they fulfill their purposes so well that we often deceive ourselves and others with the game of the expressions.

The entire world is only scenery, behind which the creative soul hides. My soul. Every earthly face and every earthly body is only a mask, only a marionette for a single performance of the earthly tragicomedy—a marionette made for words, gestures, laughter and tears. But tragedy comes, refines the decorations and appearances, and through the decorations the world transformed by Me, the world of My soul, the fulfillment of My will, shows through—and through the masks and appearances, My single image and transformed flesh show through. Beautiful and liberated flesh.

The rhythm of liberation is the rhythm of the dance. The pathos of liberation is the joy of the beautiful, naked body.

The dancing viewers, male and female, will come to the theater, and at the threshold, they will leave their coarse, petty bourgeois clothes. And they will dart about in light dancing.

And so the crowd that came to watch will be transformed into a group dancing in a ring that has come to participate in the tragic drama.

Fyodor Sologub
1908

PEREDONOV'S LITTLE TEAR
Z. Gippius

Once, a long time ago, while discussing the subject of rhyme, we
discovered that the most profound Russian words are "solitary," un-
rhymable. *Pravda* (truth) is solitary, *istina* (truth) is solitary.

There and then Bryusov volunteered to write a poem with a rhyme for
istina and produced these lines:

> I have long not believed
> In unshakable *truth,*　　　　[*istine*
> And all seas, all *refuges,*　　　*prístani*]
> I like the same...

The poem is beautiful and remarkable in that nowhere else has
Bryusov expressed himself with such precision, vividness, and truth.
Nonetheless, the rhyme for *istina* in not an exact rhyme.

I had better luck. True, my poem was written partly in jest and not for
publication. I had forgotten it long ago, and I recall excerpts from it now
not for the sake of rhyme (albeit for the sake of truth), but because I want to
speak about Sologub, to whom the poem was dedicated:

> ...he extracted water,
> Living water from a *wall,*　　　[*iz steny*
> But he didn't see, the sage and prophet,
> His own *truth*　　　　　　*istiny*]

Perhaps—and this may even be a good thing—Sologub himself has
not laid eyes on his own hero Peredonov *(The Petty Demon)* and does not
relate to him as he should. I am not concerned here with whether this is
good or bad. I am only establishing the fact that both the author and the
public, which has been enthusiastic about *The Petty Demon,* understood
and interpreted Peredonov in exactly the same way—and further, that such
an interpretation was simple, understandable, and natural. In the foreword
to the recently released second edition of the novel, the author seems to be
arguing with his readers about Peredonov; but the essence of his argument
is the question of who is depicted in the figure of Peredonov: Fyodor
Sologub, or his contemporaries. The readers, apparently, assumed that the
author, in a penitent spirit, had presented himself in the figure of his hero;
the author clarifies this matter:

"No, my dear contemporaries, it is about *you* that I have written my
novel of the Petty Demon and his sinister *'nedotykomka,'* of Ardalion and

Varvara Peredonov...About you."

Here the offended reader might catch Sologub: "How can you write about us and not about yourself, if you yourself have many times declared that there is no such thing as 'we' but only 'I'—that is, you? This means that Peredonov is your own 'I' too, and it is about this 'I' of yours, about yourself, that you have written...Please don't deny it..."

But I am not an offended reader and have no intention of engaging in such semantic hounding of Sologub. No matter how we settle the argument of who is depicted in the figure of Peredonov, you, us, him, the central issue remains unchanged. For this argument is peripheral. *The Petty Demon* remains a "satire," a venomous tangle; it is a magic mirror *which exposes* defects...whether of all people or almost all matters little. What is important is that it *exposes*. Incidentally, the author himself mentions a mirror in his foreword.

And indeed *The Petty Demon* was accepted as an artful exposure of hidden Peredonovism. The author himself confirms that this is how he regards his Peredonov: "Look, folks, look at yourselves in this faithful mirror; shudder, be repelled, hate Peredonov and ... please repent, change yourselves if you can." True, the author is not moralizing, but that doesn't prevent anyone from turning over a new leaf.

It should be said that in no way do I deny this primary, accusatory, and repelling aspect of the novel or the mirroring quality of Peredonov. The novel supports this interpretation and may be understood in this sense. It is difficult, very difficult to pass beyond the triple line, deep into that region where even the father of Peredonov and the *nedotykomka* has not penetrated. But in the final analysis it is impossible not to go there.

I remember my first meeting with Peredonov many years ago. I remember the stack of blue student notebooks from Polyakov's store, covered with Sologub's high, clear script. There were a good many of them, but it was impossible to stop before reading through all of them. At that time the novel still contained a number of biting, sharp words, later omitted by the author; but Peredonov stood as he stands today: in his full stature. And—one must be truthful—my first impression was identical with that obtained by almost everyone who reads the novel today. I was enchanted by Ludmila and the symphony of spirits; I was horrified by the revolting truth, the living filth of Peredonov. What could be more hateful than a vulgar fool going out of his mind? Yes, yes, here is an object truly worthy of our hatred, and if, in each of us, there sits this indecent fool who will certainly go mad, then we have all the more reason to hate him. I was delighted by the author's disinterested art, excited by a sordid hatred towards the living Peredonov. And I experienced then the strong conviction that Peredonov exists, not only somewhere in ourselves, but that he is alive and actual—complete, real. If he does not exist today—he will exist tomorrow, he existed yesterday. In a word, he *can* exist.

The years passed. Peredonov "appeared" in literature several times—
The Petty Demon was first printed in a magazine, then in separate editions.
But since the time of the blue notebooks I felt no need to reread the novel. I
thought I knew Peredonov as many know him today; oh, of course, he is
the most absolute, most revolting "image of evil." How could one not hate
him?

Finally, I open the book. The author's striking foreword prepares me
for the familiar feelings. I wait for them—and I read.

Here he is, the dirty and dull Ardalion in all his obscenity, rotting and
stinking, not even going out of his mind upright, but creeping out of it. He
lies clumsily, is trivial when he plays dirty. He is hated, not only by the
reader, but by everyone who has dealings with him: Varvara deceives him,
Ludmila gaily ridicules him, the Director knits his brows and shudders . . . Nothing goes right for him, the *nedotykomka* sucks at him; he feels
that he is drowning, that everyone is against him. Why is this? is it madness
that makes him feel this? This can drive one mad, of course, but this is not
yet madness, for in actual fact everyone and everything *is* against him.

A strange, new, as yet unthinkable feeling for Peredonov stirred
within me. And the last thing it resembled was hatred. Not the printed
pages of the story about Peredonov, but Peredonov himself, with his gray,
embittered face, passed before me. And I irrestibly wished *that things had
happened differently,* that Varvara had not deceived him, that the Director
had not thrown him out, that the *nedotykomka* had been caught and killed.
It is impossible not to wish this. You can wish not to wish—but you will
wish it anyway. Why the devil do we say "satire," "embodiment of evil,"
when a loving man, yesterday's, tomorrow's Ardalion Peredonov finds
himself in such hopeless, unprecedented misery! Before his misery, all the
horrors so laboriously heaped up by Leonid Andreev are mere trifles. In
Andreev's novel, first the son of Father Fiveysky drowns, then his wife
becomes a drunkard, then an idiot is born to them, then his wife is burned
to death in a fire that destroys his home, then . . . what next? He performs
psychopathic rituals over the body of a dead peasant, flees along the road
during a storm, and dies in the dust. (Did lightning strike, or something like
that?) Apart from the fact that Fiveysky is entirely invented, that we don't
believe in him, and therefore don't give a damn about him—leaving all this
aside—can we compare Fiveysky's misery to Peredonov's? Fiveysky was
created for everyone to sympathize with and pity. Peredonov has the just
hatred and contempt of all. Ivan Karamazov suffers, but he is intelligent, he
has a luminous strength of spirit; an old woman in the country suffers, the
hanged man in his noose suffers—but surely they are guiltless, someone
loves them, wrings his heart a little for them. A child suffers, shedding
"fistfuls of tears," but he is charming, he is dear, he is holy. Dostoevsky isn't
the only one who will demand justification for the tears of this child, Ivan
Karamazov isn't the only one who will intercede for him. In all suffering

there is a gleam of hope; but in Peredonov there is none. No one will intercede for him. He is ugly, dirty, evil, and dull; he has nothing, nothing at all. And nevertheless he is created, he *is;* he is an "I" like any other "I," he matters "first to himself and is everything to himself." The gray, slowly contracting ring has seized him, is suffocating him, and he cannot do anything; he possesses nothing beyond the agony of suffocation.

The little tear of the tormented child, the troubles of Vasily Fiveysky— all this is still within the bounds of our human understanding of justice and injustice. Perhaps one might say, from this point of view, that Peredonov suffers *justly,* that he deserves his torment . . . But then it becomes clear that every human heart is broader than justice. Peredonov's misery is not just. but somehow *extremely unjust.* It is incumbent upon us to justify the "little tear of the tormented child" because we must know: for what crime? why, for what purpose? But similarly, it is incumbent, compellingly incumbent upon me to justify each of Peredonov's slobbery tears, each of his shudders at the sight of the *nedotykomka,* each blow of a heel on his physiognomy, which he "justly" receives from a good man, each of his shrieks and wails in the madhouse where he will inevitably be sent. If we continue to live in and even to love this world full of tormented children and rocks that will fall on our heads tomorrow—it is only because we say our "I do not wish it" and with stubborn, instinctive hope wait for an answer to "what for," "why?" And our "I do not wish it" stands up even more boldly before Peredonov's complete and unheard-of misery. "I do not wish it"—not in the name of justice, but in the name of that which is higher than justice, whose existence in man is indisputable, whose nature is a mystery, and which may be called Love. There are very few, however, who understand this word.

Beyond the limits of pure justice, the simple definition of guilt, of human culpability or innocence, disappears. The question "for what crime?" disappears too. We cease to judge Peredonov; we have shielded him. And, shielding him, we ask: *How did he dare* to create his creature? And how will he *answer for him?*

*   *   *

Of course, it is another matter entirely if no such person as Peredonov exists, if all this is the fabrication of a talented novelist, if, speaking plainly, Peredonov was created by Sologub. There is no point in turning to such a creator of Peredonov with the question "how did you dare" and "will you answer for him?" Clearly Sologub depicted him against his own desires, does not know him, and will in no way answer for him. The feeling of having no responsibility for his hero is very clear in Sologub's novel. *He does not love* Peredonov and confirms the fact that he did not give birth to him, but merely found him and exposed him. "I expose—and come what may! I expose—but have no desire to look myself. Who needs it?"

Thank you, nonetheless, for exposing, for remembering him who must be remembered. For, in fact, what does it mean to close one's eyes? Who dares to say, honestly, firmly, that there is not, could not be in this world a single, living Peredonov, with his complete, hopeless, Peredonovian misery, a man not only poor in spirit or in other blessings, but *poor in everything?* Who in good conscience can say, "Why, such a woe can never befall a man and has never befallen anyone"?

There are many tormented children, many innocently and guiltily suffering people such as Karamazov and Fiveysky, but the Peredonovs, suffering hopelessly, poor in everything and cursed by all, are even *more numerous.* We know this, but we think about it only rarely. And when we think—when we see and feel—we stop despising the Peredonovs, we shield them; and shielding them, we ask, "How did You, Creator of Peredonov, dare to create him? How will You answer for him? Tell us, we must know. In the name of love—tell us: we simply must know."

Zinaida Gippius
1908

ON CONTEMPORARY LYRISM
I. Annensky

I.

[...]

The new poetry?...That's no joke...just try to make some sense in that sea...no, it's not a sea...in that book depository of a bibliophile who is in no way squeamish...a week before a sale: endings, beginnings, middles...rarities and popular literature, the lives and leisures of Céladon.

It will be, I dare say, more practical to begin with those poets who have made the whole history of our Symbolism. Three names. We won't deal with the primary one, although he is the brightest. I have already said all, or almost all, that I could say about Balmont in another book.

And the main thing is that Balmont, and I hope this is clear to everyone, has already completed one very significant period in his work and as yet there is no second one beginning.

So Valery Bryusov and Fyodor Sologub remain. We'll deal with them. We only have to agree from the first on the basic terms. Symbolists? Decadents?

Wonderful words, but both came into use for the innovators of poetry comparatively recently, even in France.

According to Robert de Souza, poets were called decadents for the first time by Paul Bourde in the newspaper *Le Temps,* 6 August, 1885. And several days later Jean Moréas parried him in the newspaper *XIX siècle,* saying that if a label was so necessary, then it would be fairer to call the new poets *Symbolists*.

I don't think that after the historical information cited above it would be expedient to differentiate names or poems in the sphere of Russian poetry according to these terms, which are more like polemical nicknames. Symbolist—excellent; decadent—do me a favor. *Etymologically,* of course, there is some of the former and the latter in each of our poets.

Such serious people and refined masters as V. Bryusov and V. Ivanov print acrostics and crochet wreaths of sonnets...So have they really refused the title of decadent in addition to others, equally, if not more, deserved?

Once, still in the period of struggle for the new poetry in France, Arthur Rimbaud frightened readers (and even more non-readers) with a sonnet about vowels, where each vowel sound commandingly evoked in the poet's soul a sense of one of the colors and symbolized the different gleams and sounds of life.

And so the non-readers fiercely attacked the poet who had poured such delirium (or so it seemed) into the classical form of a sonnet.

Recently someone offered, however, a very simple solution to the riddle, trying to justify both Rimbaud and those who were at that time most interested in the sonnet, as a bold attempt to fix and unite these transitory perceptions that did not obey commonly understood schemes: it turned out that according to some old alphabet book that Rimbaud may have studied, vowel sounds were colored, and almost in the same way as the notorious sonnet. Terror turned into idyll, and the desire to shock the world—into a sentimental memory.

All that is lacking, I dare say, in Rimbaud's sonnet, is decadence, if we agree not to confuse this term with the word "Symbolism."

One can call poetic decadence (byzantism, as the French like to say) the *introduction into common literary use of various subtleties in the technique of verse-making* which have no close relation to the purposes of poetry, i.e., the intention to instill in others, through a literary, but nearly musical influence, one's own perception and understanding of the world.

If someone writes a geography textbook in verse, there would be no decadence here; there would be none in the case of all, often very instructive and interesting, scholarship about poetic technique coming into literature only in the form of scientific or scholarly material. But if there is an attempt to introduce what is admittedly not poetry into poetry itself, this is poetic decadence.

Our decadence, of course, is not Western: it has its own local color. One must see, for example, how major and serious poets exchange acrostics and printed inscriptions like Brother and Friend, and behind are the fledglings, although they are generally less expansive than the old swans.

And who has not heard of the rhymes of Bryusov's sonnet that Vyacheslav Ivanov guessed?

You can also follow, leafing through the collections of the last few years, the course of the competitions in versifying these prettily addressed themes:

The angel of beneficient silence
(V. Bryusov and F. Sologub)

The Lord's propitious summer
(Vyach. Ivanov and M. Kuzmin)

And all this stuff gets printed. And it all wants to be poetry.

Aren't these competitions really decadence?

It's not a sport; no.

It's more like monks on a summer Sunday between vespers and midnight mass—in sight of the white graveyard wall, busy skipping round stones on a smooth lake—to see who can make more momentary rings, farthest from the shore. For whom is it a secret, however, that an especially perceptible stream of byzantism (the French do not differentiate now between the words *décadentisme* and *byzantisme*) passes through our literature?

The *word,* meanwhile, has essentially been in a cabal and has been treated despotically for a long time. It's no wonder that, having finally felt its strength and value, and how people are proud of it and love it and dress it up—it, the word, now demands that yesterday's Padishahs be just a little coquettish with it!

And the passion for decoration that has exhausted us for more than a decade should have been expressed here. Is it so far from vignettes, or ornamental drawings to a flowery name for a collection, and from there to an acrostic? And who is guilty if Pushkin's frisky and sharp-eyed rhymes turned out to be a refined odalisque in Max Voloshin's poetry? Or who will take on the task of defining the border between the artist's work, when he is searching for freer, more flexible, more spacious verse, and the whim of a wordy tightrope walker, who shows us how to play with rhymes of five and six syllables?

Symbolism is a slightly unclear appellation. There is a certain ambiguity in it.

Is it possible to call Valery Bryusov's ballads, e.g., "Peplos," Symbolist? Yes and no.

In poetics the *symbol* is usually opposed to the *image.*

Poetic image is an old and positively unfortunate expression. It compels us to suppose the existence of poetry not only outside rhythm, but also outside the word, because in *words* there can be no *image* and in general nothing *cut off.*

Words are open, transparent; words not only flow, they shine. There is only a glimmering possibility of an image in words. Trying to interpret a word with images, the illustration and scene always bring along something of their own and new, and they don't so much convey Ophelia, the enchantment of whom is inseparable from the immortal illusion of words, as they stress all her intranslatability. On the other hand, music approaches poetry, but no closer. No matter how fluid it is, like a word, or how separate—*music* lives only by *absolutes,* and even Wagner could not go farther than an operatic compromise of music with poetry and the inclusion of speech in the orchestra.

In *poetry* there is only *relativity,* only *proximity*—because it has never been other than symbolic, and cannot be otherwise.

Everything rests with how imposing the *image* lying within us, but always outside poetry, is.

There are several forces that prevent words from breaking away into superficial symbolism. The first is contained in a cult legend. Aphrodite forgets the mystical distance of her symbol Ashtoreth, and the Greek boatmen force her to rise from the Aegean foam as an already formed Greek girl, Kupris (Cyprus), the daughter of Zeus or Chronos, it's not important. Here is an image that replaces a symbol.

And here is another example of the same thing. In Greece, the god Sabazius receives a peristyle and part of a bull's hip, but for this he must forget that, in his native Phrygia, he was only a prayerful appeal, less than a word, an interjection, a shout, "saboy, saboy!"

An heroic legend, romantic self-adoration, love for a woman, for God, the stage, idols—all these forces in their turn commandingly brought and are bringing the word closer to image, forcing the poet to forget about the exclusive and true force of his material, of the *words* and their most noble purpose—to join the "I" and "not-I" through a sieve of symbols, proudly and sorrowfully realizing that he is the go-between, and the only one between these two worlds. It is more fair, in my opinion, to call Symbolists those poets who do not worry so much about the expression "I" or depicting "not-I" as they try to assimilate and reflect their eternally changing mutual positions.

Here is an elementary Symbolist piece. Its author, Blok, is a rare example of a born Symbolist. Blok's perceptions are vague, his words elastic, and his verses, it seems, cannot help but be Symbolic.

> He sleeps while the sunset is scarlet
> And his armour grows sleepily pinker,
> And with a quiet whistle through the mist
> The serpent, trampled by the hoof, looks at his reflection.

> Dense, dark nights will descend.
> The serpent will uncoil above the houses.
> In Peter's outstretched hand
> The flame of a torch will dance.

> Threads of street lights will be lit,
> Store windows and sidewalks will glisten.
> Couples will stretch out in rows
> In the twinkling of dull city squares.

> Gloom will wrap everyone in its cloaks.
> A glance drown in a beckoning glance.
> Let innocence from a corner
> Keep begging for mercy,

> There, on the cliff, the merry Tsar
> Has waved a foul-smelling incense burner,
> And the city's fumes have
> Clouded the beckoning lamp with its robe.

> Everyone, answer the call, to the hunt!
> To the crossroads of moonlit streets!
> The whole city is full of voices,
> Male—clamorous, female—shrill.

He will protect his city,
And, turning crimson before dawn,
A sword flares up in his outstretched hand
Over a capital calming down.

I chose this transparent poem on purpose. It won't trouble anyone
with its pedantry or secret writing. But in order to like the piece, one must
still refuse, when reading it, to draw *direct analogies with reality*.

"The merry Tsar waves a foul-smelling incense burner"—as an image,
i.e., a reflection of reality, is of course absurd. But remember our definition.
Life and thought have crossed. And we are so used to the idea that Peter the
Great on Senate Square seems to *rule,* that the thought that all these shifts
in Petersburg illuminations and noises also depend on him, on his pointing
and powerful hand—well, the poet simply *couldn't* help separating this
thought from the intersected glimmerings of perception and reflection.
Submit yourself for a moment to this shift—nothing will tease, fool or
offend you—give a little, let yourself be hypnotized a tiny bit. Otherwise it's
impossible. The very fluency and music of the stanzas demand it. The
whole poem consists of "fourth paeons," i.e., each fourth wave splashes
evenly. Only in the concluding verses of all stanzas, except the last one (the
last line should close the entire piece, corresponding in this way to the first
line of the first stanza), the splashes double, and the fourth even yields a
little to the second in the beginning paeons:

And drawiling it begs...
The beck'ning lamplight...

Okay—but why does the serpent whistle? After all a bronze serpent
cannot whistle! That's true—but it is no less true that *this* one whistled,
using the horseman's drowsiness at sunset. Everything rests on the fact that
the whistle here is a symbol of a crushed life. From here the desire to "see
one's reflection" through the fog arises. The serpent gives a signal to its
allies with this whistle, it examines them, although it is still a captive under
the horse's hoof.

The serpent and the Tsar have not ended their primordial struggle.
And in the pink, overcast evening the examination and treason are felt to be
even more inevitable. But then the serpent grows. The serpent has used the
denseness of the guard that has descended from the tower to shift places
with the drowsy Peter, and it has "uncoiled" over the houses. This is, and is
not, its life now. The flame that has blazed up, meanwhile, reveals one of
Peter's hands. And the serpent down under the hoof, where a crushed part
remains, still continues to create. That is why:

Innocence from a corner
Keeps begging for mercy.

But the moon that has appeared fills the streets and squares of Petersburg with new life, and it now seems that the whole city has become even more spectral, that it has become a joining and separation of nighttime voices. Therefore everything genuine, everything present from everyday life, has gone into one mighty Keeper of granite; the dawn itself, when it finally replaces night, seems to the poet like a sword blazing in the same hand of the bronze horseman that has invariably fettered his tired eyes to it.

* * *

I pass on now to the portraits.

Valery Bryusov is a Muscovite. He began publishing in 1892. The basic collection which contains everything that the poet retained from his previous poetry is called *Roads and Crossroads* (two volumes, the second appeared in 1908). It includes, for example, almost all of *Urbi et Orbi* (1903) and *Stephanos* (1906). The last book of poems (many of which are new) appeared in 1909 and is called *All Melodies*. It gives something of today, but signifies more of the future Bryusov, so we will use mainly it for this essay.

Bryusov's poetry is clothed in Parnassian robes, but at the same time it is full of attempts, trials, and accomplishments—and only a careless reader would fail to see how often these searches have been painful, difficult for the poet, and even agonizing.

Bryusov's work is not something in which we can search for his personal experiences of life (as in Pushkin, Heine, or Stecchetti)—real or fantasized (it's all the same). No, Bryusov's poetry is an annal of unbroken apprenticeship and self-examination, but not of events—of work, not of life. Or, has all its personal side been concealed?

How Valery Bryusov has *lived,* however, doesn't matter.

The waters of Lake Mälar, or an English keepsake, a date with a woman, or a childhood memory—all of these are only shadows for Bryusov—everything is a stage for future creation—at first, then evaluations and distillations. Valery Bryusov stores colors and tastes, what is his own and what is foreign, tenderness that has suddenly flared up, and even fatigue from concentrated work, and filters these in thoughts in order to clothe them, if they can be of use, with the metaphor and music of verse in the stillness of his laboratory—there, where his poetry passes through and real life is created. No one can show better than Valery Bryusov through the cold beauty of words and the delicate, often alarmed, waves of rhythms the whole *repugnant uselessness of life,* the whole trial of exacting passions. [. . .]

I am afraid of resurrecting words from his preface to *Urbi et Orbi;* there are none preceding his second volume, *Roads and Crossroads.* But at that time Valery Bryusov still *imagined verses detached from poetry.*

For the *distant* future (I don't really believe that for a poet any sort of future has seemed exactly distant) he has seen verse in the capacity of a "perfect form of speech," displacing prose "most of all in philosophy."

If he has been thinking such thoughts until now, that explains a lot, of course, in *All Melodies,* and even throws light on the title of the collection. And Valery Bryusov's apprenticeship, decadence, and pedantry are dated for us in this way by the given degree of his understanding of the world. Listen, Bryusov, can verse really be *speech,* i.e., a feature of everyday life?

Because it's really laughable to project a sort of hieratics of styles in the future with an academy in Cheboksary.

Each field of knowledge seeks precisely to free itself from the way of the metaphor, from the mythological nets of speech—of course not for any refinement of style, but to escape into terminology, into silence, into writing, into the alphabet of the Morse Code. What will it do, tell me, with verse, this singing genius of myth, which assures it of Proteus' eternity and the immortality of a legend that is forever being created?

And who will need philosophy without a system, and even more, verse that has refused to be personal, irrational, divinely unexpected?

It is easier, however, to guess than to judge, and criticism is, I dare say, more *a priori* than an affirmation... I protest against one thing in Bryusov's words—"doubtlessly," and it's good that he wrote this word six years ago and now, perhaps, he has already forgotten it!

In any case his verse bore, at one time, and not without reason, not only a philosophical dream but also a philosophical doctrine. Our elegies until now have tended toward "philosophicality." [...]

There are, however, poets in Russia for whom *philosophicality* has become a sort of integral part of their being. One cannot, of course, call their poetry *philosophy.* This is not the philosophical poetry of Sully-Prudhomme; the atmosphere in which the sparks of this poetry are born is necessary for such poets' creativity—it is densely saturated with mystical fog: there are particles of theosophical coke, of that most bourgeois aspect of the Anti-mortalists; it's possible to discover even some steam of Khlystic zeal in it—a mildewed page of Schopenhauer glimmers through it, the yellow cover of the Light of Asia—Zarathustra raved about the Apocalypse in this fog.

Oh, I am far from wanting to draw a caricature. I am speaking about *our soul,* about the *ailing and sensitive soul* of our times.

And you have already guessed that I am speaking about a poet and novelist, for whom the *Petty Demon* and "The Disappointed Bride" would be enough for his name to remain an immortal expression of the time, which we, as does every other generation, tend to consider timeless because we have no perspective for that.

* * *

Fyodor Sologub is from Petersburg.

The last of his books of verse that I know of is referred to as his eighth one (published in 1908, Moscow).

Two things are most foreign to Sologub's poetry, as far as I have managed to learn: 1) spontaneity (although where are our Francis Jammeses? perhaps our sly Blok?), 2) inability or lack of desire to stand outside his verse. In this regard he is in striking contrast to Valery Bryusov who cannot—and I don't know if he even wants to—stand inside his verse, and also with Vyacheslav Ivanov, who even seems to boast that he can step back from his creations, to any distance he wants. (Try to find, for example, V. Ivanov in *Tantalus*. No, stop looking, he was never there.)

Sologub, no matter how strange it seems, is best characterized for me by his unity of these two opposingly formulated traits.

As a poet he can breathe only in his own atmosphere, but his *verses crystallize themselves;* he does not build them. [...]

Sologub is a whimsical and capricious poet, not at all an erudite pedant. There is more often even something revealing and pedagogically clear in his works.

But Sologub also has *word-tics,* and in garnishing his verses, they give it an individual color, like incorrect speech habits that *consequently* mark the speech of the majority of us.

People have found in Henri de Régnier's works recently exactly such word-tics—*or* and *mort.* Sologub abuses the word *ill* and *evil.* Everything is ill for him: children, lilies, dreams, and even valleys. Then Sologub the lyric poet has eccentricities in his perceptions. *Naked female legs,* for example, seem somehow especially affectionate and sinful in his verse—but they mainly seem immeasurably corporeal.

Sometimes sounds soothe Sologub. But he is not V. Ivanov, the visionary of the Middle Ages, who has experienced the Renaissance in order to become one of the most sensitive of our contemporaries. When V. Ivanov filters, mangles, and presses *words* for that faience mortar where he will prepare—as an alchemist—his *blinding Yes,* he first of all arouses an intellectual feeling, an interest, even an excitement, I dare say, for his knowledge and art. [...]

I omit the portrait of V. Ivanov (who made his debute with *Guiding Stars* in 1901 and then *Transparence* in 1904) from the space next to Bryusov and Sologub, since the collection, on the basis of which such a portrait could be done *(Cor Ardens),* has not appeared yet. But in speaking more about art, I will have much to say about V. Ivanov's poetry.

II.

Symbolism in poetry is a child of the city. It is cultivated and grows, filling out creativity to the degree that life itself becomes more artificial and even fictive. Symbols are born where there are no myths yet, but where there is no longer any faith. Symbols can play spaciously between straight stone lines, in the noise of the street, in the magic of gas lamps, and the lunar decorations. They soon get accustomed not only to the anxiety of the stock market and of green cloth, but also to the fearsome routine of some Paris morgue, and even to the repugnant, because of their excessive lifelikeness, wax figures in a museum.

Symbols which are forever being created have nothing to do in that space where, eternally and calmly alternating to the fullest, the day darkens and the night melts; where groves are full of druids and satyrs, and brooks with nymphs, where Life and Death, Lightning or a Hurricane are already overgrown with metaphors of joy and anger, horror and conflict...

Therefore, Myth is free to propagate its own gods and demons there. Call them what you want. It will doubtlessly seem to you that the *poetry of spaces,* reflecting this world finished once and for all, cannot and *should not add anything to it.*

Of course the city didn't start inspiring poets yesterday:

> The cast-iron design of your fences,
> The transparent twilight, the moonless luster
> Of your pensive nights.

Pushkin not only wrote "The Bronze Horseman" but also "The Queen of Spades." But there are probably two million people now living in Petersburg. And Pushkin's Petersburg needs filling out, like the pictures of Aleksandr Benois. "Peter's creation" has become a legend, and this wonderful "city" is already somewhere over us with its coloring of tender and beautiful reflection. Now we dream of new symbols, we are besieged by still unformed and different agitations, because we have passed through Gogol, and Dostoevsky has tortured us.

Aleksandr Blok, for example, gives us a different, enigmatic, white night in a new way.

The first poet of the *contemporary* city, the city that is the father of symbols, was Baudelaire, after him came Verlaine, Arthur Rimbaud, Tristan Corbière, Rollinat, Verhaeren, just to name the major ones.

Paris was, however, God knows when, Lutetia. And sometimes the silhouette of a poet, in Martial's style, glimmers in its ironic temptation.

What do we need the French for? There is still too much of the steppe, the Scythian love for space, in us. The Byzantine bucolic with its gardens, pastures, lady's tears, and gilded ornaments, is just a stratum—also ancient—over the Scythian soul.

And this is probably the deepest cultural layer of our soul.

The king of our poetry is Balmont, who before he managed to get tired of being in Mexico, under the same sun, and even under a bird in the same air, made an incursion against the stone houses, the free prisons for people. It was proud... Stuffed-shirts love and now declaim this Balmont, but how distant they are from our dear nomad of those years.

Bryusov penetrated the melancholy of the city even more intimately and magically, and he is the first—the new Orpheus—to make cobblestones cry.

> There will be light from the lamp in the window...
> I'll distinguish her earrings...
> Suddenly the quiet light will go out,
> *I'll sigh in response to it.*
> I'll wait till dawn in the square...
> She'll come out that door.
> There'll be a flower on her breast,
> A dark blue cornflower...

or this:

> And every night, regularly,
> I stand under a window.
> *And my heart is grateful*
> *That it sees your lamp.*

The special colors here are not exciting, but the city, another soul, wounded in another way, sorrowful and yielding in another way, excites us because it firmly knows its own market value.

Let another—the old, wise, greedy, alert soul of the poet—look into it, this still poor, this still new soul. But weren't they both tightly driven into the stone? And perhaps even born by this stone? Balmont struggled with this city. He hated it. But there are exotic souls, who cannot be ruled in such a sense even by the stones that gave birth to them. The city is not in Ivanov's poems. I know of six lines dedicated to Paris, and a sonnet about stones with talons, that were dropped at one time on our Academy. In order to love the city, V. Ivanov needs the height of a bird's eye view, and in order to merge with its white night—a hieratic symbol. [...]

The more that city life develops, the more that souls themselves become inevitably crucified, adapting to the stones, museums and signboards.

The wonderful mosaics of icons, which no one prays to, the pretty river's waves (hiding repugnant death), love, grace, and beauty offstage in the golden powder and under the electric light; a secret at a spiritual seance—and freedom in red rags—these are the conditions among which the young poets grow up.

Their "Shipka" is Ilovaysky's textbook, and when Tolstoy wrote *The Power of Darkness,* they were still biting their nurse's breast. The majority of them write a lot and quickly. And the early epigones print such a mass of stuff in all possible anthologies and formats that every two or three years some glimmering name seems to be already invested with a bright individuality; meanwhile only a pose, if not a masquerade costume, expertly fitted by Leifert according to an old customer parades beneath it.

From the time when poetry, and art in general, lost its "power over our hearts"—and it will hardly resurrect that power soon—our Romanticism sort of disintegrated.

And one of its pieces became fearsome and tragic. The ones before— the Romantics—only knew how to believe and perish, they sacrificed even the last flowers of youth, the beauty of a daydream, to their God. But contemporary poets, or our young artists of the word in general, are not at all like that. And if this is a Bohemia, then it is a bourgeois Bohemia. New writers symbolize the instinct for self-preservation, traditions, and the slow prospering of culture in society. Their justification is in art and nothing else. If the same Jehovah, the only one, was above the first Romantics, then the later ones have planted a whole host of gods in the garden. And poets' legends, I dare say, stick together, but not one legend emerges from these contemporary poets' names. This can almost be stated with certainty. Cyrano de Bergerac, or at least Gérard de Nerval? Pushkin? Shevchenko?

Stop, please.

And here the disintegration is too noticeable. The non-aesthetic Romantics, on the contrary, depict no legends, but they themselves are legends. And the split is old, and no one can fix the boundaries. All aestheticians suddenly imagine themselves as *tragic,* as if that meant the same thing as writing tragedies.

* * *

The champion of our young poets is undoubtedly Aleksandr Blok.

He is, in the full sense of the word and without the slightest irony, the beauty of the rising poetry. What beauty?—rather, its enchantment.

He is not only a real, born Symbolist, he is himself a symbol. His picture postcard features appear to us like those of an elegant androgyne, and his voice, coquettishly, intentionally dispassionate, white, hides of course the most tender and sensitive modulations.

An androgynous mask—but under it in the poetry itself lies the most brightly expressed male type of love, a love that can deceptively captivate, and when necessary, when a woman desires, can conquer and merrily fertilize.

But I especially like Blok when he is not speaking about love in his verse at all. For love somehow suits him less. I like him when he walks around love not with art—what is art?—but with a strange magic, one hint, one langorous gleam in his eyes, one barely audible, but already enchanting melody, where the word love is not included. [...]

* * *

Now a direct transition from a poet who has fallen silent [Sergei Makovsky] to a singer who cannot stop. Although this new singer has not yet seen his thirtieth spring, Andrei Bely (the pseudonym of B. N. Bugaev, revealed by the author himself), has already published three collections of verse and two of them are quite large.

A richly gifted nature, Bely simply doesn't know which one of his muses will smile at him once again. Kant is jealous of his poetry. Poetry of music. A bumpy road of an Indian symbol. Valery Bryusov wants to exchange staffs with him, and Zinaida Nikolaevna Gippius herself has resolved the theme of his Fourth Symphony. Criticism and the theory of creativity (articles about Symbolism) go along—on the side. And you admire that youthful-audacious building of a life. And sometimes it's scary for Andrei Bely. Lord, when does this person think? And when does he find time to burn and crush his creations?

My task is not concerned with Bely's Symphonies and other prose, but I somehow don't even understand his poems, although, God knows, I have studied them diligently. Much is likable ... but it's impossible not to see a certain perplexity in the poet, and then ... that unfortunate telegraphist with a wife, whose "side hurts ... " A vital, responsive, fiery heart, that tries so hard to get out that his tears boil (read "Through the Window of the Train" in *Ashes*, p. 21). You feel sorry for him, you like him as a person, but as a poet ... sometimes it's a pity. [...]

* * *

The results are as follows:

Among the new lyric poets there are four names that symbolize completely formed types of lyrism: Balmont, Bryusov, V. Ivanov, Sologub.

Contemporary poetry is alien to large-scale designs, the intimacy and enchantment of the lyric poets of Pushkin's school are rarely felt.

But it knows how to convey a mood more exactly and with greater variety than our classical poetry. This depends on the flexibility that rhythms have discovered in it, and also on the aspiration of the majority of poets to give their pieces a peculiar coloring. Of course, an aspiration for novelty has also been detectable.

The life of a big city, getting even more complicated, is reflected in our lyricism. As a result of a faster pace of life and other conditions of recent time—contemporary lyrics seem sometimes either neurasthenic or oppressed.

The strong influence of French poetry—lately Verhaeren and Heredia especially—is noticeable among the modernists.

Sometimes attempts at Slavonic-Byzantine stylization arise, a freakish return to the past.

III.

Among the concluding theses of the last chapter, one was missing. I thought that it would be more appropriate as the beginnning of this third chapter, as a clamp between both of them. This is the thesis.

Lyrics by females are one of the achievements of that cultural labor which will be bequeathed by modernism to history.

Now we have women writing verse. Women work on the problems of Russian lyrism with the same unconquerable fervor that they devote to science. I think that this phenomenon is determined to a significant degree by the traits of that lyrism which I tried to characterize in the first chapter.

But for the explanation of this thought, we need to divert ourselves for a minute from contemporary times.

In older Russian poetry, when a song didn't yet have letters, there were two definite types of lyrism—one was masculine, the other feminine. We don't know the authors of these songs, the singers are all the same for us. The authors are replaced for us so to say by lyric personae. This is the *he* and *she* that are strictly isolated in their lyrical types. *He* is a conqueror of life. *She* only accepts life.

He threatens or steadfastly thinks; *he* sneers and sometimes repents. *She* only cries quietly and submissively; *she* affectionately remembers. A man's irony in a folk song often seems to be only suppressed spite. [...]

Love more often goes from the freely lyrical sphere into the world of fortune-telling, wizardry, and love potions. Like a caress from the sun, she hides bashfully from song, and the spell-bound secret of love is closer to the folk soul than its beauty and joy.

Amorousness, like lyrism, like the written form, came to us from the West, together with books and assemblies.

But no one led love for a woman to adoration, to apotheosis, like Pushkin, in whom genius has so maddeningly beautifully combined the temperament of a black and the lyrical style of an Italian.

No one's genius passed more freely from revealing confessions (like the well-known piece of 19 January 1825) to almost mystical verse, at least in our perception, no longer sensitive to its conventionality:

> My soul has been awakened,
> And you have appeared again.
> Like a passing vision,
> Like a genius of pure beauty.

The woman "deified" by Pushkin ascended so high in his lyrics that her voice was no longer audible from there.

The "genius of pure beauty" has left a heavy trace on our literature.

How many Ophelias, how many mad, martyred women, how many pure, extremely beautiful women and girls have passed before us on the pages of novels, in lyric poems, and on the pavement—between *Evgeny Onegin* and the "Kreutzer Sonata," with its dishonored, its deformed conqueror of what probably seemed at one time to him the "genius of our beauty." I don't want to name those names, too close to our time, Artsybashev's *Sanin* and Andreev's *Anfisa*.

After Pushkin's period, a light current of George Sandism, let's say, passed through Russian lyrics.

He sang then:

> Give me a woman, a wild woman!

And *she* confessed:

> No fiery young rascal
> Has captured my inexperienced gaze;
> I met a Circassian in the mountains
> And from that time I gave myself to him.

But these voices have somehow not been sung to their fullest extent among us.

There is no longer a deified woman in contemporary poetry. The vicious circle of Pushkin's lyrics has been broken, most probably, forever.

Our chosen ones have different central tasks for lyricism, other justifications for life.

In Sologub's poetry the desire to believe in a metempsychosis is central, and this motif, combined with the perspicacious genius of the poet, is the source of deeply interesting and often captivating motifs.

Valery Bryusov seeks a magical secret in words and rhythms. And if he has not yet found the key that can master our hearts, then he has often compelled us to believe, together with him, that such a key is precisely in words...

V. Ivanov—a sharply imperative, almost categorical, mind—is hobbled by dualism, which the centuries of culture have imposed on him as a scholar with all its weight... As a poet, he has surrounded us with a forest of symbols and demands that we believe, with the same fervor that he himself would like to believe, in the proximity of the blossoming little meadow of myth. V. Ivanov's genius is proud, but it is almost an agonizing pride.

But Balmont? No, Balmont does not deify Her either. He loves only love, like he does the sun, air, freedom, not Her at all. Blok the poet of the Beautiful Lady, has also strayed far from Pushkinianism, and even more from Turgenevism. His Lady dons captivating clothes, but she herself is only a symbol with, moreover, a philosophical hue.

But who then? The word-sculptor Makovsky, worn out by the melodious ease of his verse and the non-literary precision of what he expresses lyrically? No, irony has led him away from Pushkinianism. Gorodetsky, with the frightening breadth and sincerity of his confessions, or Andrei Bely, in the boundlessness of his horizons, gifts, ideas, beginnings—a responsive, tremulous, almost mirage-like, but after all, still a *future* person?

Or Kuzmin, tender, full of nuances, of the fearful beauty of his unjustified beliefs? I have not named all the names that are crowded in the hollow of my pen. But there are enough of them not only to justify female lyrism but also to demand its appearance.

Lyrics have become so individual and foreign to the commonplace, that it now *needs* types of female musicalities. Perhaps she will reveal even new lyric horizons to us, this woman, no longer an idol, condemned to silence, but our comrade in shared, free, and endlessly varied work on Russian lyrics.

* * *

Two completely defined women's names naturally open our examination. Do we need to guess them? Zinaida Gippius and Allegro—Poliksena Solovyova. Z. N. Gippius is a poetess of the first calling. All the fifteen-year history of our lyrical modernism is in her works. I don't want, however, treating the theme of my article pedantically, to condemn myself to an analysis of Hippius' latest poems.

Her *Collected Poems,* 1904, remains the canonical collection. I like this book for its melodious abstractness. [. . .] Gippius' abstractness is not schematic at all in its essence, more exactly, her anxiety, or what is unsaid, or the agonizing swaying of a pendulum in her heart, always shows through in her diagrams. [. . .]

I perceive all the confessions in Gippius' book, no matter how much they might seem to contradict each other at times, as lyrically sincere; there is in them, for me at least, a certain absolute instantaneousness, a certain persistent, burning need to convey rhythmically the "full feeling of each minute," and their force and charm are in this. [. . .]

Gippius' favorite guise is indifference, apathy, and fatigue. [...] Her symbols are spiders, leeches, stopped clocks, Charon's boat, a stony sky, "heavy waters...like lead," thoughts that are gray birds. It doesn't matter for Gippius that the world has so many sounds, that it is so grossly varicolored! [...]

The poetess has not only arranged her pieces in a book that consists of letters alone with great tact, but she has also not given it one of the names that lyric poets so often think up to decorate their collected verse: *Collected Poems*—and that's all. For Z. Gippius, as far as I have understood her "prayers," the external beauty of impressions does not exist as something of worth by itself; all this obtrusive glimmering, shining, covering—and falling snow, lamplight, and a "thorny, gloomy orchard"—these things only keep her from praying, in my opinion. But, alas, there is nothing for her to pray about, there is nothing *above* her—and that is why it is so frightening for her, a lyrical person, in her life—and what would she pray to—in a word, that which she so painfully knows: *It must be (debet esse).*

For Z. Gippius there is only an immeasurable *I* in her lyrics, not her *I* of course, not Ego at all. It is the world and it is God; in it and only in it is the whole horror of fatal dualism; in it is all the justification of our doomed thought; in it is all the beauty of Z. Gippius' lyrism. [...]

Among all the types of our lyricism, I don't know any braver, even audacious, lyricism than that of Z. Gippius. But her thoughts and feelings are so serious, her lyric reflections are so absolutely true, and the consuming and decaying irony of our old soul are so foreign to her, that the male mask of this amazing lyrism (Z. Gippius always writes about herself exclusively in the masculine gender) has hardly fooled even one attentlve reader [...]

Without any special effort, I could find among masculine lyrism parallels to the feminine type mentioned. But it would be cheerless work. If the reader wants, he or she can do it. Hardly anyone will want to...I will limit myself to indicating the most characteristic features of the dissimilarity between *oní* and *oné* (male and female lyric poets).

The women are more *intimate,* and despite their *tenderness,* they are more *audacious* because their lyrism is almost always more *typical* than the masculine type.

But the men have cut down more of the forest and are still busy with the brushwood around themselves. They are more persistent...for now. Then they reflect life certainly more sensitively because life lies on them as a heavier yoke—the men are more responsible for life.

The female lyric poet suffers more softly. The male lyric poet grieves more deeply and with more concentration.

Innokenty Annensky
1909

THE PRECEPTS OF SYMBOLISM
V. Ivanov

I.

Any thought that is uttered is a lie. With this paradox-confession Tyutchev, unintentionally revealing the Symbolic nature of his lyrics, bares the root of the new Symbolism: a contradiction painfully experienced by the contemporary soul—the need to "express oneself" and the impossibility of doing it.

Thus the commanding world of "secretly-magical" thoughts in Tyutchev's poetry is not made definitively *communicative* for its listeners, it only markedly *incorporates* them in its first secrets. Breaking the rule of "cloaked" language, because of a desire to disclose and reveal, is avenged by the distortion of what is revealed, by the disappearance of what has been disclosed, by the lie of the "uttered thought . . . ."

> Breaking out, you muddy the springs,
> Live by them and be silent . . .

And this is no conceited zeal, no dreamy pride or pretense—but the realization of the common truth about the discrepancy that has arisen between an individual's spiritual growth and the external means of communication: the word is no longer equivalent to the contents of internal experience. The attempt to "utter" it—is to destroy it, and the listener does not receive life in his soul but the dead covers of a life that has flown away.

Because it is impossible to explain this discrepancy with examples of a purely psychological sort, we will examine an abstract concept—the concept of "existence," for example—as expression and expressible. Independently of the gnoseological point of view of "existence," as one of the cognitive forms, it is hardly possible to negate the inequality of the internal experiences expressed by it. A notion of existence in one's conciousness can be presented in such a variety of ways that the person who feels that the "mystical" sense of life has been revealed to him will sense the verbal attribute of this sign to objects of contemplative conceivability in the everyday meaning of the common word—as an "uttered lie"—sensing, at the same time, the lie and its negation of what language has marked as a symbol of "existence." It is absurd—this contemplator will say—to affirm that the world exists and that God exists—if the word "exist" means the same thing in both cases.

What should we think about the attempts at a verbal construction not only of judgments but also syllogisms from such ambiguous terms? *Quaternio terminorum* will unswervingly accompany the efforts logically to use the data of supersensible experience. And is the formal logic of word-concepts, after all, applicable to the material of concept-symbols? Meanwhile our living language is a mirror of eternal empiric cognition, and its culture is expressed by the force of its logical element, at the expense of purely symbolic, or mythologic, energy, woven at one time from its most delicate natural fabrics—and now the only thing capable of restoring the truth of the "uttered thought."

II

Russian Symbolism is created first in Tyutchev's poetry as a consistently applicable method, and is internally defined as dual vision and thus—a demand for another poetic language.

The poet experiences a certain dualism—a splitting, or rather a doubling, of his spiritual person—equally in consciousness and in creativity.

> O my prophetic soul!
> O heart filled with anxiety!
> How you beat on the threshold
> Of a dual existence!...
>
> So, you are the dwelling of two worlds.
> Your day is painful and passionate,
> Your dreams are prophetically vague,
> Like the revelation of spirits.

Such is self-consciousness. Creativity is also divided between the "external," "daily" world that "grips" us in the "full brilliance" of its "displays"—and the "unresolved, nighttime" world that frightens us but also attracts us because it is our own innermost essence and "family inheritance," the "incorporeal, audible, invisible" world, woven, perhaps, from "thoughts freed by dreams..."

This same dualism of day and night, of the world of perceptible "phenomena" and the world of supersensible revelations is found in Novalis. Tyutchev, like Novalis, breathes more freely in the nighttime world, which spontaneously joins a person to the "divine-universal life."

But both worlds are not divided by the final difference; it is bestowed only in an earthly, personal, imperfect consciousness:

> Are they not inimical?
> Or is the sun not the same for them,
> And, dividing them by motionless means,
> Doesn't it unite them too?

They are together in poetry. Now we call them Apollo and Dionysus, we know their infusibility and inseparability, and we sense in every true creation of art their effective dual unity. But Dionysus is mightier than Apollo in Tyutchev's soul, and the poet must escape from his spells to the altar of Apollo:

> He tears away from a mortal breast
> And craves fusion with infinity.

In order to preserve his individuality a man *limits* his craving for fusion with "infinity," his aspiration for "self-oblivion," "destruction," "merging with the slumbering world," and the artist turns to the brightest forms of daytime existence, to the patterns of the "cover woven from gold," that was thrown over the "world of secret spirits, the nameless abyss," by the gods—i.e., the abyss that cannot find its name in the language of daytime consciousness and external experience...And still the most valuable moment in our experience and the most prophetic in creativity is delving into that contemplative ecstasy, where "there is no barrier" between us and the "uncovered abyss," which opens into—Silence.

> There is a certain hour of universal silence,
> And at that hour of appearances and miracles
> The vital chariot of the universe
> Rolls openly in the the sky's temple.

Then, with this noumenal openness, a creativity that we call Symbolic becomes possible: everything that remained in the consciousness of the phenomenal "is suppressed by the unconsciousness"—

> The gods agitate only the virgin soul
> Of the Muse in prophetic dreams.

Such is the nature of this true poetry—of a somnambulist, marching through the world of essences under the cover of night.

> Night falls, and the elements beat
> Against its beach with noisy waves...
> Then its voice: it compels us and begs us.
> A magic boat has come to life again in the harbor...

In the midst of dark "immeasurability," dual vision is revealed in a poet. "Like deaf and dumb demons," the Macrocosm and the Microcosm wink at each other with their lights. "What is above is also below."

> The heavenly vault, burning with a starry glory,
> Glances secretly from the depths;

> And we swim, surrounded on all sides
> By a fiery abyss.

The same notion about poetry, as about the reflection of a dual secret—of the world of phenomena and the world of essences, we find under the symbol of the "Swan:"

> It fondles your all-seeing dream
> Between a dual abyss,
> And you are surrounded on all sides
> By a firmament full of starry glory.

And so, poetry should provide the "all-seeing dream" and the "full glory" of the world, reflecting the "dual abyss" of its external, phenomenal and its internal, noumenal achievement. A poet would want another, special language to explain this last feature.

> How can the heart express itself?
> How can another understand you?
> Will he understand how you live?

But there is no such language; there are only hints, and even the charms of a harmony that can inculcate the listener with an experience similar to something that cannot be expressed with words.

> The game and sacrifice of a private life,
> Come and overthrow the deceit of senses
> And plunge, vigorous and autocratic,
> Into that life-giving ocean!
> Come and wash your martyred breast
> With its ethereal stream,
> And commune at least for a moment
> With divine-universal life.

The word-symbol becomes a magical suggestion that *joins* the listener with the mysteries of poetry. So for Baratynsky "sacred poetry" is the "secret power of harmony," and a person's soul is its "communicant..." How far this view is from the views of the eighteenth century, which are still very much alive in Pushkin, about the adequacy of the word, about its sufficiency for *reason,* about the direct communicability of "beautiful clarity," which could be always transparent when it didn't prefer to dissemble!

III.

Symbolism in the new poetry seems like the first, vague reminiscence about the sacred language of the priests and magi, who at one time gave the words of national language a special, secret significance, which could be revealed only to them because of the correspondences that only they knew between the world of the secret and the boundaries of popular experience. They knew the other names of the gods and demons, people and things, not the ones people normally use, and they based their power over nature on the knowledge of the true names. They taught the people to appease terrible forces with tender and flattering appeals, to call the left side the "best," the furies "sweet goddesses," subterranean rulers "bearers of riches and all sorts of abundance." But they kept for themselves the continuity of other names and verbal signs, and only they understood that a "mixing bowl" (a crater) means the soul, and a "lyre"—the world, and a "cave"—birth, and "Asteria"—the island of Delos, "Scamandrius"—the youth Astyanax, Hector's son, and long before the Eleatics and Heraclitus, of course, that "to die" means "to be born," and "to be born"—"to die," and that "to be" means "to truly be," that is, "to be, like the gods are," and that "you are" means "there is divinity in you," but the unabsolute "to be" of popular usage and world view (*doxa*) related to the illusion of real or potential existence (*meon*).

Rickert's teaching about the hidden presence in every logical judgment of a third normative element, in addition to the subject and predicate (a certain "yes" or "so be it"), with which the will affirms the truth as a moral value, helps us to understand the religious-psychological moment in the history of language, expressed, in the use of the concept of "existence" for establishing the connection between subject and predicate that has first brought the whole structure of a grammatical sentence to fruition *(pater est bonus)*. The words of primeval, natural speech are joined together, like cyclopic blocks; the emergence of their cementing copula seems like the beginning of the artificial elaboration of the word. And since the verb "to be" had, in ancient times, the sacred sense of divine existence, then it is permissible to suppose that the sages and theurgists of those days introduced this symbol into every judgment that was uttered in order to consecrate it with all future cognition and to nourish—or only to sow—the sense of truth as a religious and moral norm in people.

Thus the eternal "pastors of the people" controlled the speech that the Hellenes called the "language of the gods"; and the transfer of this notion and the definition as the poetic language marked the religious-symbolic character of the sung, "inspired" word. The new realization of poetry as "Symbolism" by the poets themselves was the recollection of the ancient "language of the gods." For at that time, when the poet, delayed (if we are to believe Schiller) in Olympian castles, saw, when he returned to earth, not only that the material world had been divided without him and that there was no allotment for a singer in the earthly part, but (and Schiller still doesn't know this) that all the words of his ancestral language had been usurped—it was now possessed by the landlords of life—and used every day for ordinary needs—nothing more remained for the poet than to recall the dialect that had been given to him to chat with the sky-dwellers—and through this be unintelligible to the masses, especially at first.

Symbolism seems like a premonition of that hypothetically conceivable, properly religious epoch of language, when it will embrace two different types of speech: discourse about empirical objects and relations, and discourse about things and relationships of another order, revealed in internal experience—the hieratic discourse of prophecy. The first discourse, now the only one that is customary for us, will be the discourse of logic—the one whose basic inner form is analytic judgment; the second, now accidentally mixed with the first, winding sacred mistletoe around the oaks of poetry that are friendly with it and deafening the nurseries of science with parasitical growth, rising in thick ears of native cereal grains in pastures of inspired contemplation and foreign weeds in the field plowed by exact thought—will be mythological speech, whose basic form will serve "myth," understood as a synthetic judgment, where the subject is a concept-symbol, and the predicate is a verb; for a myth is the dynamic mode *(modus)* of the symbol—the symbol, seen as movement and motive power, as action and active force.

IV.

Symbolism seems like poetry's reminiscence about the original, primordial ends and means.

In the poem "The Poet and the Crowd," Pushkin depicts the Poet as an intermediary between the gods and the people:

> We are born for inspiration,
> For sweet sounds and prayers.

The gods "inspire" the messenger of their revelations to the people; the people also pass their prayers to the gods through him; "the sweet sounds"—the language of poetry—is the "language of the gods." The dispute is not between the worshipers of an abstract outside-of-life beauty and those people who recognize only the "useful" in life, but between the "priest" and the crowd that no longer understands the "language of the gods," now dead and thus useless. The crowd, demanding earthly language from the Poet, has wasted or forgotten religion, and is left with only a utilitarian moral. The Poet is always religious because he is always a poet;

but now he only strums the precious strings with an "absent-minded hand," seeing that no one around him is paying any attention.

People have wrongly seen in this poem, which was written in the austerely restrained style of antiquity, for which the formula "art for art's sake" was unknown, the proclamation of the artist's right to creativity that has no purpose in life and that shuts him in his own detached world. Pushkin's poet remembers his calling—to be a religious organizer of life, an interpreter and consolidator of the divine connection of the existing, a theurgist. When Pushkin speaks about Greece, he perceives the world as the Hellenes did, not as the contemporary Hellenizing aesthetes do: the words about the divinity of the Belvedere marble are not an irresponsible literary affirmation of some "cult" of beauty in the godless world, but a confession of faith in the vital engine of universe-building harmony, and not a rhetorical metaphor—the expulsion of the "uninitiated."

The purpose of poetry was the conjuring magic of rhythmical speech, mediating between the world of divine beings and man. The melodic word forced the will of higher kings to kneel, secured for the clan and tribe the subterranean help of the hero promised by the poet, warned about the inevitable regulations of fate, sealed in unwavering expressions (*remata*), god-given laws of morality and legal organization, and, affirming worship of gods by people, affirmed the world order of vital forces. Truly, the stones in the city walls were formed by lyres' spells and, without any allegory, illnesses of the body and soul were cured by rhythms, victories were won, civil strife was quieted. Such were the direct duties of ancient poetry, elegiac, epic, and hymnal. The "language of the gods" served as the means, as the system of enchanting symbolism of the word with its musical and orchestral accompaniment, from whose elements the body of the original, "syncretic" ritualistic art was formed.

Symbolism's recollection about this historically almost immemorial but unforgettable, because of the elemental force of its native heritage, time of poetry is expressed in the following phenomena:
1) in the new discovery of the symbolic energy of the word, prompted by the new requirements of the individual, not subjugated through long centuries of service to external experience, thanks to religious tradition and people's conservatism;
2) in representations of poetry as the source of intuitive cognition, and of symbols as the means of realizing that cognition;
3) in the significant self-definition of a poet not only as an artist but also as an individual—a bearer of the inner word, an organ of the universal soul, a celebrant of the secret connection of the existing, a seer of secrets and secret creator of life.

It's no wonder that the cosmic themes became the chief contents of poetry, that fleeting and barely perceptible experiences acquired the echo of "Weltschmerz," that refinement of external susceptibility and internal sensibility, bequeathed by aestheticism, served the aims of experience in the search for new world-attainments, and illusionism itself was experienced as the universal tragedy of a solitary individual.

V.

The evaluation of Russian "Symbolism" depends on the correctness of the notion about the international community of this literary phenomenon and about the nature of Western influence on the newest of our poets, who began their activities with an oath of allegiance to the poly-semantic, but multi-meaningful slogan heard in the West. Closer studies of our "Symbolist school" will later show how superficial this influence was, how immaturely thought out, and basically how little the borrowing and imitation produced, and how deeply the roots of everything genuine and viable in our poetry of the last one and a half decades go into the native soil.

The brief interval of pure aestheticism, nihilistic in its contemplation of the world, eclectic in its tastes and psychologically ailing, separates the emergence of the so-called "school of Symbolists" from the epoch of great representatives of the religious reaction of our national genius against the wave of iconoclastic materialism. Not examining the works of Dostoevsky, which long determined the path of our spirit, because they are not germane to the sphere of the rhythmical word, we remind the reader of the dear names of Vladimir Solovyov and the singer of the *Evening Lights*—two lyric poets who are preceded in the suggestion of the Symbolist tradition of our poetry, according to mental designs and artistic method, by Tyutchev, the true father of our true Symbolism.

Tyutchev was not alone as the originator of the school, destined--we believe to show in the future the precious sanctuary of our people's soul. He was surrounded, after Zhukovsky, on whose lyre the Russian Muse first found the airy harmony of mystical spirituality, by Pushkin, whose genius, like a diamond of the rarest purity and sparkle, could not help but refract, in his facets, where all of life was reflected, even the broken but blinding rays of inner experience; Baratynsky, whose pensive and hollowly triumphant melody seems like the voice of a dark memory about some knowledge long ago vital, which revealed once to the Poet's seeing gaze the secret book of the universal soul; Gogol, who knew the anxiety and rapture of second sight given to the "lyric poet," and condemned to being only a frightened spy on life, which in order to hide from his wise soul the last sense of his own symbolism, surrounded everything before him with a magical-swaying veil of freakish myth; finally the seraphic (as they said in the middle ages) and at the same time demonic (as Goethe loved to say) Lermontov, who was equally tormented by a "strange desire," in angry revolt and prayerful affection, by a longing for a secret meeting and other songs than the "boring songs of Earth," Lermontov, the first Russian poet to be excited by the premonition of the symbol of symbols—the Eternal Feminine, the mystical flesh of the Word born in eternity.

But it would be incorrect to call these poets Symbolists, like Tyutchev, in the narrowest sense of the word, on the basis of the motifs of their lyrics observed above, inasmuch as the distinguishing features of pure Symbolist art are, in our view:

1) a parallelism, consciously expressed by the artist, of the phenomenal and noumenal; a harmonically-found consonance of what art depicts as external reality *(realia)* and what it sees in the external, as internal and higher reality *(realiora);* a commemoration of the correspondences and interrelationships between appearance ("only a resemblance," nur ein Gleichnis") and its essence, which can be comprehended by the mind or perceived mystically, which casts off its shadow of visible events;

2) a sign, properly peculiar to Symbolist art and in those cases of so-called "unconscious" creation, which does not comprehend the metaphysical connection of what is depicted—a special intuition and energy of the word, which is directly sensed by the poet as cryptography of the unspoken, that absorbs in its sound many echoes of native subterranean keys, which resound from unknown places and serve in this way, together with a boundary and an exit into the "beyond," as letters (commonly understood patterns) of external experience and hieroglyphs (hieratic transcription) of internal experience.

The historical purpose of the newest Symbolist school was to reveal the nature of the word as a symbol and the nature of poetry as the Symbolism of true realities. There can be no doubt that this school has in no way fulfilled its twofold purpose. But it would be unfair to negate certain of its first achievements, primarily in the bounds of the first part of the problem, and especially the significance of the Symbolist pathos in the universal shift, experienced by all of us, of the system of the spiritual values that make up culture as a world view.

VI.

Within the bounds of the evolution of our newest Symbolism, generalizing study easily differentiates two successive moments, the characteristics of which allow us to mutually contrast them, like a thesis and antithesis, and postulate a third, synthetic moment, that can include the described period with certain definitive realizations in a series of the closest of selected goals.

The pathos of the first movement consisted of the cognition, suddenly revealed to the artist, that the world was not narrow, flat, or poor, not measured out or counted, that there is much in it that yesterday's wise men did not dream of, that there are passages and openings into its secret from the labyrinth of man's soul, if only—(it seemed to the first heralds, that everything was said by this)—man learned to dare to "be like the sun," forgetting the difference, suggested to him, between the permissible and the impermissible—that the world is magical and man is free. This optimistic moment of Symbolism is characterized by confidence in the world, as something given: harmonious correspondences *(correspondances)* were revealed in it, and others, even more enigmatic and captivating, awaited the new Argonauts of the spirit, for to know them meant to rule them—and the teaching of Vl. Solovyov about the theurgic sense and purpose of poetry, still not fully understood, already sounded in the poet's soul like an imperative appeal, like Faust's vow—"to aspire continually to the highest existence" ("zum höchsten Dasein immerfort zu streben"). The word-symbol vowed to become the sacred revelation or the miracle-working "mantra," that would lift the spell from the Earth. Artists were faced with the task of wholly incarnating in their lives and in their works (and certainly in life's exploits as well as creative feats) the world view of mystical realism—or in Novalis' words—the world view of "magical realism"; but they must have earlier endured the religio-moral test of the "antithesis": and the discord, if not the disintegration, of the former phalanx in our time clearly shows how difficult this conquest was and how many losses it cost ... The world of your glorious, suffering shadow, immortal Vrubel!

It follows from every line written above that Symbolism neither wanted to be nor could be "only art." If Symbolists were not able to experience, with Russia, the crisis of war and the liberation movement, they would be resounding brass and crashing cymbals. But to suffer the common ailment meant a lot to them; for the people's soul ached, and they had to turn the finest poisons of this ailment into their own vigilant and reckless soul. The world did not seem henceforth to be a Golconda of magical miracles, a sunny lyre, awaiting the fingers of the lyricist-enchanter—but a mound of "ashes," watched by the Gorgon's petrifying gaze. In the works of Z. N. Gippius, Fyodor Sologub, Aleksandr Blok, Andrei Bely, cries of final desperation were heard. A free man, resembling the sun, turned out to be a worm, ruined by chaos' "given," weakly persisting in affirming the god denied by reality in himself. The Beautiful Lady seemed like a "cardboard bride" to her paladin. The image of the expected Woman began to double and be confused with the apparent image of a whore. In the name of a religious acceptance of the imperishable Earth beneath its decay, the religious non-acceptance of "this world" was proclaimed; and these "non-accepters" of the world, with all the pain of its decay, were angry because of what was called by name the most painful. People began to be jealous of suffering and, seized by panic, to fear pronouncing words that burned the soul in silence. Positive religious feeling persuaded them that the "uncompromising No" is the necessary path to the unmasking of the "blinding Yes," and recent artists, shaking the dust from their feet in testimony against the temptations of art, aspired to religious actions in a different field—like Aleksandr Dobrolyubov and D. S. Merezhkovsky.

What confronted those who remained artists? All delay in the "antithesis" was equal, for artistic creation, to the refusal of its theurgical ideal and the affirmation of its Romantic origin. Recollection of the former radiant visions had to be strengthened in the soul only as recollection, losing the vitality of a real presence—to soothe the aching soul with dreamy melodies about the distant and the unrealizable; the contradiction of daydream and reality—to cultivate Romantic humor. And it was even possible, following Leonid Andreev's example, to threaten someone and curse something; but it would no longer be art, and would soon lose all efficiency and consistency, even with Byronic forces.

It was easier and more feasible to leave the vicious circle of the "antithesis" by renouncing the practice of flights above the clouds and feelings outside the individual—by capitulating before the present "given" of things. This process of wing-clipping regularly leads more mature Romantics to Naturalism, which, while it is still on the border of Romanticism, is usually colored with genre-description humor, and in the area of "poetry" proper—leads to delicacies of polishers' and jewelers' skills, raising with love to a "pearl of creation" everything that is not "beautiful" in this, in all probability , most literary of worlds. The trade just mentioned promises a pleasant flowering among us; and at this time, such a vital study of the poetic canon will doubtlessly be a useful service...

"Parnassianism" would have had, however, full rights to existence if it had not distorted—too often—the natural qualities of poetry, especially the lyrical; it is too prone to forgetting that lyrical poetry by its nature is not at all fine art, like the plastic arts and painting, but, like music, is a motive art; not contemplative, but active, and in the final analysis, not icon-creating but life-creating.

VII.

An appeal to the canon of form, generally productive—not under school-dogmatic conditions, but the genetic study of traditional forms—and harmful only with the tendency to lifeless-academic ideology and epigonism, has a special purpose in relation to the purposes of Symbolism: it exerts a purgative influence on art; it reveals the inelegance and internal falseness of unjustified innovations; it sweeps away everything casual, temporary, superficial; it cultivates a strict taste, an artistic severity, a sense of responsibility and a careful restraint in dealing with old and new: to put the poet-Symbolist face to face with his true and ultimate goals—finally, it develops in him an awareness of the vital succession and internal connection with past generations, makes him truly free, for the first time, in the hierarchical subordination of creative efforts, gives experience to his audacity and consciousness to his aspirations.

But the external canon is fruitless, as is any norm, if there are no vital forces, in the elemental agitation of which it bears the origin of order, and is feebly tyrannical, as is any norm, if its organizing principle does not enter into an organic union—if not even a marriage—with the element that seeks order, but forcibly coerces and subjugates the element. The further paths of Symbolism are conditioned—in our view—by the victory and rule of that origin in the artist's soul which we would call the "internal canon."

By "internal canon" we mean: in the experience of the artist—the free and entire recognition of a hierarchical order of real values that form, in their agreement, a divine unity of the final Realities, in creativity—a vital connection of the correspondingly subordinated symbols, from which the artist weaves a priceless cover for the Soul of the World, as if creating a second nature, more spiritual and transparent than the varicolored peplos of nature. Only when forms are correctly united and subordinated does art immediately become vital and significant: it turns into a commemorative secret sight of innate (to the form) correlations with higher essences and into a sacred secret action of love, conquering the division of forms, into the theurgical, transfiguring "Fiat." Its mirror, turned toward the mirrors of smashed consciousness, restores the original truth of what is reflected, correcting the fault in the first reflection that distorted the truth. Art is made with the "speculum speculorum"—the "mirror of mirrors," everything—in its very mirroring—is one set of symbols of the one common existence, where every cell of live, fragrant tissue creates and praises its petal and every petal radiates and praises the shining center of the unconfessable flower—the symbol of symbols—the Word's Flesh.

Symbolism still contemplates symbols in the distinctions of accidentally manifested correlations, which seem to have been torn from the bond of the whole; it still has not perceived to the end and "sees passing people as trees." In the symbolic system of the final attainments, the way to which leads through the "internal canon," there are no longer any symbolic forms; there is only one form, one image, as a symbol, and the justification of all forms is in it. Fet, "looking straight from time into eternity," sang his swan song, which "floats and melts," about it, perceiving the "Sun of the world:"

> And motionless on fiery roses
> The living altar of the universe smokes;
> In its smoke, as in creative dreams,
> All power trembles, and all eternity is dreamed.

> And everything that rushes along ether's abysses,
> And every ray, corporeal and incorporeal—

Is only your reflection, O Sun of the world,
And only a dream—only a passing dream...

Only the person who has managed to be spun in the Dionysian whirlwind can mix Dionysianism with internal anarchism and amorphism. When a maenad loses herself in her god, she stops with her hand outstretched, ready to take and carry whatever her god gives her—a torch or a thyrsus with the head of her son, a sword or a flower—totally and selflessly obedient to someone else's will. Her unuttered word: "Veniat! Fiat!"—"And so you, my heart, greeting god—stand! stand, my heart! ...At the final threshold, my heart, stand, my heart..."

The "internal canon" signifies the internal feat of *obedience* in the name of that to which the poet says "yes," to which he is betrothed with the golden ring of a symbol:

A wedding band fell
Onto the purple bottom:
Stormy confusion, in the azure,
O Face! Appear!

And whence has the Soul of the World come? from the bluing crystal of untold distances? from the light blue nimbus of unuttered proximity?— the poet answers:

I wear a ring
And my face is—
The meek ray of
The mysterious "Yes..."

The fate of the Symbolist poet depends on this uniting act of his totally surrendering will and the religious system of his entire being. That is how Symbolism obligates us.

Until now Symbolism has complicated life and complicated art. From now on, if it is destined to *be*—it will simplify. Before, symbols were isolated and scattered, like a shower of precious stones (and hence arose the preeminence of lyric poetry); from now on Symbolists' creations will resemble symbol-monoliths. Before there was "symbolization"; from now on there will be *Symbolism*. It will be revealed in the poet's whole world view, whole and unified. The poet will discover religion in himself, if he finds a *bond* in himself, and the "bond" is "duty."

In the terminology of aesthetics, the bond of subordination means: "*high style*." Generic, hereditary forms of the "high style" in poetry are epic poetry, tragedy, and mystery plays: three forms of the same tragic essence. If Symbolist tragedy turns out to be possible, it will mean that the "antithesis" has been overcome: epopee is the negative affirmation of the individual, through the renouncement of the individual, and the positive affirmation of the common origin; tragedy is its coronation and celebration by passing through the gates of death; mystery is victory over death, the positive affirmation of the individual, its resurrection. Tragedy is always realism, always a myth. Mystery is the abolition of the symbol as a likeness and of myth as reflected action; it is the restoration of the symbol as incarnated reality and of myth as the realized "fiat . . . "

In conclusion—some words to young poets. Everything in poetry that has poetic spirituality is good. It is not necessary to want to be a "Symbolist"; it is possible to discover the Symbolist in yourself by yourself—and then it is better to try to hide it from people, Symbolism binds. The school's old cliches have been erased. Nothing new can be purchased at any price other than by the inner deed of the individual. One should remember the precept about a symbol: "Do not accept it in vain." And even a person who does not accept a symbol in vain must work on it for six days, as if he were an artist who knows nothing about *"realiora"*— and create his things in these six days, so that he can reserve the seventh day of the week, in the more highly interpreted, solemn sense:

> for inspiration,
> For sweet sounds and prayers.

Vyacheslav Ivanov
March, 1910

ON THE PRESENT STATUS OF RUSSIAN SYMBOLISM
A. Blok

The direct duty of an artist is to indicate, not to argue. Approaching my reply to Vyacheslav I. Ivanov's lecture, I must say that I am deviating from the artist's direst duties, but the present position of Russian belles-lettres obviously indicates that we Russian Symbolists have passed a fair distance along our path and we are now confronted with new problems. In such cases, when the transitional moment is so fixed, as it is in our time, we appeal to recollection for help and guided by its thread, establish and point to—perhaps more for ourselves than for other people—our origin, to that land from where we came. It is as if we are in an immense ocean of life and art, already far from the shore where we climbed to the deck of a ship. We still cannot make out the other shore, toward which our dream, our creative will draws us. There are few of us; we are surrounded by enemies. At the time of the Great Noon we recognize each other more clearly; we exchange handshakes with cooling hands and raise the flag of our homeland.

At issue is something that every artist dreams about—to "express his heart without words," as Fet says; because for the fulfillment of the difficult task I have taken on—to give an account of how far we have come and to guess about the future—I am compelled to choose conventional language. And, since I am in agreement with V. Ivanov's basic positions, as well as the method he chose for ease of formulation—I call my language the language of *illustration*. My goal is to express in concrete form what V. Ivanov says, to disclose his terminology, to paint illustrations for his text; because I belong to those people who know what sort of reality is hidden behind his words, which seem abstract at first glance. I beg you to treat my words according to their subordinate role, as you would a Baedeker, which a tourist uses by necessity. I cannot state anything more definite than what I will say; there is no self-confidence in my words when I say that for those who find my guidebook vague—our lands will also remain shrouded in mist. Whoever wants to understand will understand; once I have stated what has gone on before and have established the internal connection of events, I consider it my duty to be silent.

Before proceeding with the description of the thesis and antithesis of Russian Symbolism, I must state one more reservation: the history of Russian Symbolism, of course, is not at issue. It is impossible to establish a precise chronology when we are talking about events that have taken and are taking place in definitely real worlds.

Thesis: "You are free in this magical world, which is full of correspondences." Create what you want, for *this world belongs to you.* "Realize, understand, all secrets are in us, twilight and dawn are in us" (Bryusov). "I am the god of the mysterious world, the whole world exists only in my dreams" (Sologub). You are the lonely possessor of a treasure, but nearby there are others who know about this treasure (or it only seems like they know, but for now it doesn't matter). This is where we—the few cognoscenti, the Symbolists—come from.

From the moment when these principles are found in the souls of a few people, Symbolism is conceived, a school emerges. This is the first youth, the childlike novelty of first discoveries. Here no one knows yet where, in what world, another person is located, doesn't even know that about himself. Everyone just "winks," agreeing on the point that a schism lies between this world and "other worlds," united forces go off to battle for these "other," still unknown worlds.

An impudent and inexperienced heart whispers: "You are free in the magical worlds"; but the blade of a mysterious sword is already leaning on your chest. A Symbolist from the very beginning is a *theurgist,* that is, a possessor of secret knowledge, behind which secret action stands. But he looks upon this secret, which only later turns out to be universal, as his own; in it, he sees a treasure, on top of which the flower of a fern blooms in the middle of a June night and in this blue midnight, he wants to pluck this "blue flower."

In the azure of Someone's radiant gaze, the theurgist abides; this gaze pierces all worlds like a sword: "seas and rivers, and the distant forest, and the peaks of snowy mountains"—and it comes to him at the beginning, through all the worlds—only as the radiance of someone's calm smile.

> Just doze off during the day, or wake up at midnight,
> Someone is here. There are two of us,—
> Radiant eyes look straight into your soul
> Day and dark night.
> Ice melts, the heart's blizzards die down,
> Flowers bloom.
> *The Radiant Friend has only one name.*
> *Will you guess it?*
> (Vl. Solovyov)

The worlds that appear in the light of the radiant sword become more and more appealing; melancholic musical sounds, appeals, whispers, almost *words,* already float from their depths. At the same time they begin to acquire *color* (here the first deep knowledge about colors emerges); finally, that color which I find easiest to call purple-violet (although this name is perhaps not quite precise) becomes predominant.

The golden sword, cutting the purple of violet worlds, blazes up blindingly—and pierces the theurgist's heart. A face begins to appear among the heavenly roses; a voice is distinguishable; a *dialogue* arises, similar to the one described in Vl. Solovyov's "Three Meetings." He says: "Have you not revealed yourself thrice to the eyes of a mortal? Your face has appeared, but I want to see all of You." The voice says: "Be in Egypt."

Such is the end of the "thesis." now the miracle of lonely transformation begins.

Then, with a clear premonition of an alteration in the figure, as if feeling the touch of someone's countless hands on his shoulders in the violet-purple twilight, which begins to ooze into the gold, foreseeing the approach of some huge funeral, the theurgist answers the calls:

> It's obvious that we can't remain together
> In this golden-purple night;
> Through the heaven's roses
> I caught something restrained, but storming, in your eyes.

The storm has already touched the Radiant image, it is almost incarnate, i.e.,—*the Name has almost been guessed*. Everything has been foreseen except for one thing: *the dead point of triumph*. This is the most complex moment of the transition from the thesis to the antithesis, which is determined *a posteriori* and which I know how to relate only by introducing the fiction of someone's outside interference (I don't know the person). The whole picture of experiences changes substantively; now begins the "antithesis," the "alteration of the figure," which was already felt at the very beginning of the "thesis." The events that testify to this are the following.

As if jealous of the lonely theurgist's Dawn-like clarity, someone suddenly cuts through the golden thread of the blossoming miracles; the blade of the radiant sword darkens and is no longer felt in the heart. The worlds that were pierced by the golden light lose their purple tinge; as if through a breached dam, the dark blue-violet worldwide twilight (the best depiction of all these colors is in Vrubel's paintings) bursts through, to the heart-rending accompaniment of violins and melodies similar to gypsy songs. If I were to paint a picture, I would depict the experience of this moment as follows: in the violet twilight of an immense world a huge white catafalque sways, and on it lies a dead doll with a face that is vaguely reminiscent of the one that appeared through the heavenly roses.

Characteristic for this moment are an unusual sharpness, clarity, and diversity of experiences. In the violet twilight of intruding worlds, everything is already filled with correspondences, although their laws are completely different from before because there is no longer a golden sword. Now, against the background of a whole orchestra's deafening wail, exalted weeping responds the loudest: "The world is beautiful, the world is magical, you are free."

The person who experiences this is no longer alone; he is full of many demons (otherwise called "doubles") from which his creative will arbitrarily creates constantly changing groups of conspirators. Every moment he hides, with the aid of these conspiracies, some part of his soul from himself. Thanks to this net of deceptions—the more magical the surrounding violet twilight is, the more adroit they are—he is able to turn each of these demons into a weapon, to bind each double to a contract. They all rove in the violet worlds and, subservient to his will, extract the best gems for him—whatever he wants; one wants a cloud brought to him, another a sigh from the sea, a third an amethyst, a fourth a sacred scarab, a winged eye. Their master throws them into the crucible of his *artistic creativity* and finally, with the help of incantations, he obtains what he is seeking—a pretty doll for his wonder and amusement.

And so, it has happened: my own magical world has become the arena of my personal actions, my "anatomical theater," or *puppet show,* where I myself play a role alongside my amazing dolls *(ecce homo!).* The golden sword has been extinguished, the violet worlds have intruded into my heart. The ocean is my heart, in it everything is equally magical: I don't differentiate between life, dreams, or death, this world or other worlds (O moment, halt!). In other words, I have already made my own life art (a tendency that clearly goes through all European *decadence*). Life has become art, I have brought forth an incantation and before me has finally arisen what I (personally) call the "Stranger": the pretty doll, the blue specter, the earthly miracle.

This is the crown of the antithesis. And light, winged ecstasy remains for a long time in front of its creation. Violins praise it in their language.

The Stranger. This is surely not simply a lady in a black dress with ostrich feathers in her hat. It is the devil's alloy of many worlds, primarily dark blue and violet. If I had Vrubel's capabilities, I could create a Demon; but everyone does what is designated for him to do.

What is created in such a manner—by the conjuring will of the artist and with the help of many petty demons, which every artist has at his disposal—has neither beginning nor end; it is neither alive nor dead.

> The train of a dress, sprinkled with stars,
> A blue, blue, blue gaze.
> Twixt earth and skies
> A fire whipped up by a whirlwind.
> *The Earth in Snow*

> There, in the night's howling cold,
> I looked for a ring in a field of stars.
> Then a face emerges from the lace,
> From the lace emerges a face.
> Then her stormy trills swim up,
> Dragging bright stars like a train,

And the rising tambourine of a storm
Jingles restlessly, like bells.
Unexpected Joy

This is the creation of art. For me it is an accomplished fact. I stand in front of the creation of my own art and I don't know what to do. In other words, what to do with these worlds, what to do with my life, which henceforth has become art, for next to me my creation *lives*—neither dead nor alive, a blue specter. I see clearly "the sheet lightning between the clouds' brows" of Bacchus (V. Ivanov's *Eros*), clearly distinguish the wings' mother-of-pearl (Vrubel's Demon and Swan-Princess) or hear the swishing of silk ("The Stranger"). But all of this is a specter.

In this state of affairs, questions arose about the damnation of art, about the "return to life," about "the people and the intelligentsia," about "social service," about the church. This is a perfectly natural phenomenon, of course, which lies within the bounds of Symbolism, because this search for the lost golden sword, which will again pierce the clouds, organizes and pacifies the raging violet worlds.

The value of these searches is in the fact that they even discover, evidently, the *objectivity and reality* of "those worlds"; here it is positively confirmed that all the worlds we visit and all the events that take place in them are not at all "our notions," i.e., that the "thesis" and "antithesis" have more than a personal meaning. Thus, for example, in the period of this searching the *Russian Revolution* is evaluated according to its essence, that is, it stops being conceived of as *semi-reality,* and all its historical, economic and similar partial causes receive their own higher sanction. Counterbalancing the judgment of vulgar criticism that "We were gripped by the revolution," we propose the reverse judgment: the revolution took place not only in this world but also in other worlds. It was one of the manifestations of the gold's darkening and the triumph of the violet twilight, i.e., of those events which we witnessed in our own souls. As something tore loose in us, so something tore loose in Russia. As the blue specter, created by it, stood before the people's soul, so it stood before us. And Russia herself turned out to be our own soul in the rays of this new type of citizenship (not at all Nekrasovian; only connected with the tradition of Nekrasov).

At this moment the situation is as follows: the violet worlds' rebellion is calming down. The violins that praised the specter are discovering at last their true nature; they even know how to weep loudly, to weep in spite of the will of the one who sent them; but their loud, triumphant shriek, turning at first into weeping (this is the world's soul, grieving in the fields) almost totally calms down. Only somewhere beyond the horizon, muffled, sad notes are heard now. The violet twilight disperses; an empty plain opens up—the soul devastated by a feast. The deserted, distant plain and above it—the last warning—a star with a tail. And in the rarified air the bitter smell of almonds (for a somewhat different interpretation of this— see *my* play, *The Song of Fate*).

The reality I have described is the only one which, for me, gives sense to life, art, and the world. Perhaps these worlds exist, perhaps not. For those who say "no," we will remain simply "decadents," authors of unseen sensations, and we talk about death now only because we're tired.

Personally, I can say for myself that if I ever had the desire to convince anyone of the existence of something beyond, something higher than myself, I have completely lost that desire. I even dare to add that I would most humbly beg the venerable critics and public not to waste time on the incomprehensibility of my poems, for my poems are only a detailed and consistent description of what I say in this article, and I can only send those who want to get better acquainted with the experiences described to the poems.

If "yes," that is, if these worlds exist, and everything described could and has happened (and it's not possible that I don't know it), then it would be strange to see us in a different state than the one we're now in. They suggest that we drink, be merry, and come to life, but our faces are burned and mutilated by the violet twilight. It is permissible to ask those who exalt us as "apostles of dreams and death" where they were during the epoch of "thesis" and "antithesis." Or maybe they weren't born yet and simply don't suspect anything? Have they had *these* views or not, are they Symbolists or not?

Symbolists are not made, they're born; from here arises all the external and vulgar obscurantism to which the so-called "realists," who are trying with all their might to become Symbolists, are so devoted. Their efforts are as understandable as they are pitiful. The sun of naive realism has set; to conceive of anything beyond Symbolism is impossible. Thus writers, even with great talent, cannot do anything with art if they have not been baptized by the "fire and spirit" of Symbolism. To indulge in puzzling fictions does not mean that one is an artist, but to be an artist means that one must endure the wind from the worlds of art that do not resemble our world at all, only influence it terribly. In these worlds there are no causes or effects, time or space, corporeal or incorporeal, and these worlds cannot be counted: Vrubel saw forty different heads for his Demon, but in actuality they are innumerable.

Art is *Hell*. Not without reason, Bryusov has instructed the artist: "Like Dante, a subterranean flame should burn your cheeks." Only a person who has a companion, a teacher and a guiding dream about the One who leads, where the teacher dares not go, can pass along the endless circles of Hell without perishing.

What happened with us during the period of "antithesis?" Why did the golden sword darken, violet-blue worlds intrude on and merge with this world, creating chaos, making life into art, dispatching the blue specter from its bowels and devastating one's soul with it?

This is what happened: we were "prophets" and wanted to become "poets." In the stern language of my teacher, Vl. Solovyov, this is how it is stated:

> He replaced the soul's delight with a circumspect deception,
> The living language of the gods with servile speech,
> And the muses' shrine with a noisy puppet show,
> And he deceived the fools.

Yes, all of it is true. We have entered into deceitful conspiracies with obliging doubles; with the power of a slave's audacity we have turned the world into a Puppet Show. We have sworn against the demons—not the beautiful oaths, only the pretty ones (after all, the prettiest things in the world are slaves who surrender but don't take anything), and finally, we *deceived the fools,* for our "literary notoriety" (which isn't worth a cent) visited us just when we betrayed the "Muses' shrine," when we believed more in the specter of "antithesis" (which we created) than in the real data of "thesis."

Is what happened with us correctable or not? This question, as a matter of fact, leads to another question: "Is there a future for Russian Symbolism?"

Simple pessimism, or simple optimism, or even a confession—all this is just a digression from the posited question. Our sin (both personal and collective) is too great. There are a lot of horrible ways out from this position we are in now. One way or another, the violet worlds intruded on Lermontov, who submitted to the pistol by his own free will, and on Gogol, who burned himself while floundering in the clutches of a spider; even more significant is what happened before our very eyes: Vrubel's madness and Komissarzhevskaya's death. That's how it is with artists everywhere, because art is a splendid and monsterous Hell. The artist draws his images out from the darkness of this Hell; thus Leonardo prepares a black background beforehand to have the outlines of Demons and Madonnas step out into it later; thus Rembrandt draws his dreams out of the black-red shadows, and Carrière, from the gray, net-like mist. Thus Andrei Bely, in the beginning of his brilliant novel *(The Silver Dove),* throws out the question: "And the sky? And its pale air, at first pale, but if you stare at it, completely black air?... Hey, don't be afraid, you're not in the air..."

But the artist who perceives other worlds is in just this black air of Hell. And when the golden sword fades, extended straight toward the heart by someone's Unseen Hand—through all the multicolored skies and hollow air of the other worlds—then a mixing of the worlds takes place, and in the solitary midnight of art the artist goes and perishes.

But in the *thesis,* where a premonition of the antithesis' twilight has been given, what was given first of all was a golden sword:

> I already sense you. Years pass by.
> I imagine you always in one form.
> The whole horizon is fiery and intolerably bright.
> And I wait silently—longing and loving.
> The whole horizon is fiery and your appearance is near.
> *But I'm afraid: you'll change your form...etc.*
> *(Verses about the Beautiful Lady)*

We have lived through the madness of other worlds, demanding a miracle too soon; the same thing has happened with the people's soul: it demanded a miracle before one was due, and the violet worlds of revolution burned it to ashes. But there is something ineradicable in one's soul—there, where it is an infant. At one point in the funeral address for infants the deacon stops begging and says simply: "You made a *true promise,* that the *blessed infants* will be in *Your Kingdom."*

A promise was made to us in our first youth. We should say simply, with a courageous voice: "May they rise to Heaven," about the people's soul and our own, which has also been burned to ashes with it. Perhaps we will die, but the dawn of that *first* love will remain.

It is as if we were all raised up to a high mountain, from where the kingdoms of the world in an unprecedented radiance of a violet sunset appeared to us. We surrendered to the sunset, we were pretty as queens but not as beautiful as kings, and we ran away from our deed. Thus it was easy for the uninitiated to rush after us; thus Symbolism became suspect.

We dissolved a "Pearl of love" in the world. But Cleopatra was the *Basilis Basileon* only until that time when passion forced her to put the asp to her breast. Either death in submission or a feat of courage. The golden sword was provided so that we might strike with it.

The feat of courage should begin with *obedience*. Descending from the high mountain, we should emulate the prisoner of the Reading Gaol:

> I never saw a man who looked
> With such a wistful eye
> Upon that little tent of blue
> Which prisoners call the sky,
> And at every drifting cloud that went
> With sails of silver by.

Staring into the heights, will we find a trace of the darkened gold in this empty sky? Or is our destiny that death about which artists sometimes dream with terror? This is the death from a "play of fate"; it seems that all the paths have been traveled, prayers for forgiveness of all the sins have been spoken, when, unexpectedly, in a remote alley, a heavy brick falls from an unfamiliar house straight onto a person's head. Lermontov lived by this lyric of fate:

Like a shot, a horse carried its rider
To freedom from the battle,
But an Ossetian's evil bullet
Caught up with him in the darkness.

My conclusion is as follows: the path to the deed that demands our service is, first of all, an apprenticeship, self-absorption, a persevering gaze, and a spiritual diet. We should learn again from the world and that infant who still lives in our burned soul.

The artist must be anxious in his very audacity, knowing what it costs to mix art with life, and remaining a simple person in his own life. We are obligated, as artists, to clearly contemplate all the holy conversations *("santa conversazione")* and the overthrow of the Antichrist, like Bellini and Beato. We must keep Signorelli and his dear pilgrimage in mind, and recall that when he arrived in the foreign, rocky Orvieto in the twilight of his years, he humbly begged the citizens to allow him to paint frescoes in the new chapel.

Aleksandr Blok
April, 1910

ABOUT "SERVILE SPEECH," IN DEFENSE OF POETRY
V. Bryusov

For me, like the majority of people, it seems useful for each object to serve a definite purpose. A hammer is used for driving nails, not for painting pictures. It's better to shoot with a gun than to drink liqueur from it. A cookbook should teach the preparation of various foods. A book of poetry... What should a book of poetry give us?

Grandpa Krylov warns us against those singers whose chief merit is that they "never touch spirits." Together with Krylov, I also demand that singers most of all be good. Their attitude toward alcoholic drinks is, it's true, a matter of secondary importance. Similarly, I expect poets to be most of all poets.

Mr. Vyacheslav Ivanov and Mr. Aleksandr Blok, in their mutually complimentary articles printed in the eighth issue of *Apollon,* evidently do not share my (I must confess, rather "banal") views. Both of them strive to demonstrate that a poet should not be a poet, and a book of poetry not a book of poetry. They say, it's true: "a book, not of poetry, but of something higher than poetry," and "not a poet, but something greater than a poet." But Krylov's hero, who had such a praiseworthy aversion to intoxicants, was probably certain that his singers were "higher" than simple singers.

Summarizing his article, Vyacheslav Ivanov writes: "From every line of what has been posited above it follows that Symbolism did not want to be and could not be only art." A. Blok, calling himself V. Ivanov's Baedeker, develops this thought in a repentant article, in which he confesses his sin, that he, A. Blok, was a "prophet" and lowered himself to the point where he became a "poet." This, in the stern language of A. Blok's teacher, Vl. Solovyov, seems to mean: "He replaced the soul's delight with a circumspect deception, the living language of the gods with servile speech, and the muses' shrine with a noisy puppet show."

I very much doubt that the verses of Vl. Solovyov quoted in the article had exactly the same sense that A. Blok wants to give them. It would be amazing if Vl. Solovyov, given his well-known attitude toward poetry, the language of "poets," i.e., the language of poetry, would have called it "servile speech." But for A. Blok (and for V. Ivanov?) this is so. Poetry is "servile speech," a "deception," a "puppet show." Whence the conclusion: don't be a poet, be something higher than a poet, or as the "Baedeker," A. Blok, says: "be a theurgist."

I think that after reading these statements, very many people, together with me, will decisively stand up in defense of poetry, although V. Ivanov and A. Blok have declared it to be "servile speech." To be a theurgist, of course, is not a bad thing at all. But why does it follow from this that to be a poet is something to be ashamed of? In my opinion, for example, it is honorable to be an astronomer. But will I really abuse some historian with these words: "Deceiver, slave, puppeteer, aren't you ashamed to study history and not astronomy?"

It's true that both V. Ivanov and A. Blok are not talking about poetry in general, but exclusively about Symbolist poetry, about Symbolism. How do they understand this appellation, however?

Do they understand the word "Symbolism" in a broad sense, in accordance with the notion that Aeschylus and Goethe can and should be called Symbolists (for Symbolism is the natural language of any art)? But then the concept "Symbolist poetry" coincides with the concept of poetry in general. Or do V. Ivanov and A. Blok have in mind just the artistic movement of the last decades? Evidently, the last supposition is the fairest, since V. Ivanov speaks of Tyutchev as the first Russian Symbolist, speaks of the "common, international character of this phenomenon," about the "essence of Western influence on the most recent Russian poets," etc. Then... Well, then one must reckon somewhat with history.

No matter how much I respect V. Ivanov's artistic gifts and energy of thought, I still cannot agree that whatever he likes should be called "Symbolism." "Symbolism," like "Romanticism," is a defined historical phenomenon, connected with definite dates and names. The "Symbolist" movement arose as a literary school in France (not without some influence from England) at the end of the nineteenth century and found followers in all the literatures of Europe, impregnated other arts with its ideas, and could not help reflecting on the epoch's world view. But it always developed exclusively in the field of art. V. Ivanov can point to whichever future goals of Symbolism he likes, and his Baedeker—the paths to these goals, but they have neither the right nor the power to change the past. No matter how disappointing this is for them, "Symbolism" *wanted to be* and always *was only art.*

The "Symbolists'" books, thank God, still haven't perished because of some elemental catastrophe; you can obtain them in any library. Many "Symbolists," leaders of the movement, are still among us. Ask Verhaeren and Vielé-Griffin, George and Hofmannsthal, and here, Balmont, and I'm certain that they will all say, unanimously, that they wanted one thing: to serve art. They saw (and see) their greatest pride and highest honor in the name "artist," and "poet." How could they suddenly announce: "Symbolism did not want to be and could not be only art?" With such an attitude toward historical facts, who will stop V. Ivanov from announcing tomorrow that: "Romanticism always was and could only be an original geological theory!"

Symbolism is a *method* of art, realized in that school which got the name "Symbolist." By this method, art is distinguished from rationalistic cognition of the world in science, and from attempts at non-rational penetration into its secrets in mysticism. Art is autonomous; it has its method and its own purposes. When will it be possible not to repeat this truth, which long ago should have been considered a truism? Really, after it was forced to serve science and society, now they compel it to serve religion! Give it some freedom finally!

There are, of course, no reasons for limiting a person's field of activities. Goethe is twice as dear to us because he was not only the greatest poet of the nineteenth century but also a powerful scientific mind in his time. In Dante Gabriel Rossetti, the harmonic combination of a poet's gifts and an artist's colors enchants us. Why can't a poet also be a chemist or a politician, or if he prefers, a theurgist? But to insist that all poets necessarily be theurgists is as absurd as insisting that they all be members of the State Duma. And to demand that poets stop being poets in order to become theurgists is even more absurd.

As Blok, at the end of his article, asks: "Is what happened with us correctable or not?" In other words: "is it possible to stop being a 'poet' and again become a 'theurgist'?" It seems already sufficiently clear that this question does not relate to Symbolism in general. Not wishing at all to condemn this path of spiritual development, which, in easily interpreted allegories, A. Blok depicted in his article, it is in no way possible to accept this path as typical for the contemporary poet. Those sins, which A. Blok confesses, "Symbolism" does not accept as its own, and there is nothing that needs to be "corrected." Symbolists will remain poets, as they always have been.

But, in so far as we are talking about V. Ivanov and A. Blok, their aspiration to "correct" something, and with the most radical means, this can lead us into some apprehension. And what if these corrections turned out to be like those of many Russian municipal councils, who often find it necessary to raze this or that building because it is "not pretty," and then because of a lack of funds, leave a vacant lot in its place? V. Ivanov and A. Blok are wonderful poets; they have shown us that. But whether they will make simply "good," and I don't even say great, theurgists, is a matter of completely permissible doubt. For some reason, I have a hard time believing in their theurgical calling.

I am calmed by the consideration that V. Ivanov's and A. Blok's theories have not yet prevented them from becoming true artists. And A. Blok slanders himself when he says that his most recent verses are "servile speeches." Fortunately for us, and everyone for whom art is dear, this is genuine and, at times, wonderful poetry. In regard to V. Ivanov's call, and that of his interpreter, which leads the whole development of contemporary Symbolism to a new road, i.e., shifts poetry from the path it has followed for not less than ten millenia, this is less a cause for apprehension, I think. Alexander the Great had sufficient strength to pull the Pythian, against her will, onto the tripod; but I don't see Alexander's strength here, only a much more difficult undertaking!

Valery Bryusov
1910

A WREATH OR A CROWN
A. Bely

> Let the poet create not
> his books, but his own life.
>
> Grief awaits the person who
> exchanges a crown for a wreath.
> Valery Bryusov

The exchange of opinions about the destinies and purposes of Symbolism which has taken place on the pages of *Apollon* prompts me to say a few words.

Radically disagreeing with V. Ya. Bryusov's article "About Servile Speech, in Defense of Poetry," I unwillingly quote V. Ya. Bryusov's words from his article "A Holy Sacrifice" (*Vesy*, No. 1, 1905). Here are these words:

> We demand from a poet that he tirelessly bring his "holy sacrifices," not only with his verses, but with every hour of his life, with every feeling—his love, his hate, accomplishments, and failures.

And I subscribe to every word . . . In his beautiful, deeply felt article, A. Blok says essentially this: he sort of asks himself and us if we will bring our "holy sacrifices" with every feeling, every hour of our lives. On the other hand, V. Ivanov definitely expressed the thought that Symbolism is not only a school of art. It seems that Bryusov, who spoke several years ago on behalf of Russian Symbolist poetry with his credo, would only rejoice at the coincidence of V. Ivanov's declaration with his own.

"Symbolism neither wanted to be, nor could it be, 'only art,'" V. Ivanov confesses.

"We demand from a poet that he tirelessly bring his 'holy sacrifices,' not only with his verses," V. Ya. Bryusov confessed in 1905.

Both slogans openly declare that Symbolism is something greater than a literary school; in the current type, formed in France as a literary school and in Germany as a new world view (even Nietzsche numbered himself among the Symbolists), something greater than arguing about coining verse should and must be present. French Symbolism, it's true, was created as a literary school, but German Symbolism was formed not only within the bounds of the history of literature. And what is important for us is not how Symbolism was formed historically, but what is important is—What is Symbolism, reflected here as a school, and there as the propagation of a new attitude. The declaration of two of the most important representatives of Russian Symbolism that Symbolism is not only a literary school does not at all indicate a betrayal of the precepts of Symbolist art, but points out the character of Russian Symbolism as it was originally expressed.

Bryusov, who in 1905 gave the same definition of the artist's task as Ivanov and Blok in 1910, takes exception to Ivanov and Blok with the following humorous, but entirely unconvincing words:

> A hammer is used for driving nails, not for painting pictures.
> It's better to shoot with a gun than to drink liqueur from it...
> Grandpa Krylov warns us against those singers whose chief merit
> is that they "never touch spirits."
> (*Apollon*, No. 9, p. 3)

It doesn't follow, from the notion that a hammer is used for driving nails, that if I were attacked by robbers and had no weapon other than the hammer, that I would let myself be killed and not defend myself with the hammer simply because it is used for driving nails. It is true that people don't drink liqueur from a rifle, but in an army a rifle fulfills two essentially divergent purposes: 1) people shoot with it, 2) a bayonet is attached to it and people use it as cold steel. Of course the beauty of a singer is not that he doesn't touch alcohol; but this doesn't mean at all that a singer shouldn't dare worry about his sobriety; as we know, wine weakens creativity. What does V. Ya. Bryusov want? Does he want people not to defend themselves with a hammer, even when there is no other weapon; and soldiers who have used all their bullets and see the enemy attacking the fortress, is it better for them to throw down their rifles and be taken prisoner than to fix their bayonets? Or doesn't he want poets to fight against alcoholism? Of course V. Ya. Bryusov would deny such a clear application of Tolstoy's principle of non-resistance to evil in relation to his beloved art, but it comes out in this case that such non-resistance is what he is preaching.

Art has been symbolic from time immemorial; no one can argue against the symbolism of any kind of art; this symbolism comes nearer to us when we ascend to the snowy heights of the creative Olympus. The symbolism of Goethe, Dante, and Shakespeare is aristocratic not only in the figurative sense, but also in the literary, and genuine science and genuine philosophy are aristocratic as well.

Since the middle of the nineteenth century, the democraticization of knowledge and philosophy has grown; whole strata which had nothing to do with art until now are more and more the legislators of its fate; in our present epoch the circles of aesthetically educated people are not the active participants in the life of art; the democratic masses have been actively concerned with art, the line of art's development has been displaced; art is in jeopardy.

The development of the Symbolist school in art, as well as Ibsen's and Nietzsche's propagation of Symbolism, appeared as an answer to the spreading vulgarization of art; the aristocratic depths of eternal Symbolism appeared before the masses in its clear propagatory form: the Symbolist school in poetry summed up individual slogans of artists (confessed as a *Privat-Sache*), with the proclamation of these slogans as paragraphs of an artistic platform; the propagation of Symbolism began in democratic taverns, not on the heights of academic Olympianism. The first Symbolists stepped forth both as theoreticians and as artists: they threw the "elusive" aspect of every symbol over the surface of an image. In the Symbolism of the French school, the "secret" of each image, outwardly distinct, became "evident," a mist—an image. Goethe is outwardly clear; and only under the clarity of form, somewhere in the depths, the endless corridors of the "elusive" meet us; Verlaine is outwardly hazy; but under the hazy cover a simple and clear thought often shows through in his works. The former is an aristocrat, the latter a democrat.

If the question about the origin of the mystical smoke of what lies beyond the limit that is based on art does not arise with persistence in the classically finished forms of Goethe's symbolism, then in the exaggeratedly clamorous stressing of this smoke among the latest Symbolists this question does arise; together with it the question about the aim, about the sense of Artistic Creativity, about its place in the hierarchy of knowledge and creativity (for example, of something religious) arises anew. This question now agitates not only the theoretician, it agitates the artist as well; to understand the purposes and aims of art, independent of its historically established forms, this is now a question of conscience for an artist, especially a Symbolist artist, who by the strength of his position emphasizes much of what had been previously kept silent, and clearly displays before us, like a slogan, the individual announcements of the artists of the past. The *laurel wreath* that shamefully covered the *priestly crown* has been torn off by the Symbolists in the persons of Ibsen and Nietzsche; the religious searching of Baudelaire, Verlaine, Wilde, Huysmans, Strindberg, V. Ivanov, and Blok is not stifled by the questionnaires about free verse; in the torments of conscience, in the struggle for the distant horizons of life, not only a love for art has been manifested among contemporary Symbolist poets; "Only a priest's knife, cutting our breasts, gives us the right to be called a poet," Bryusov himself wrote. The wreath was exchanged for a crown. Bryusov exchanged his own wreath for a crown, the one who had stated quite clearly:

> Grief awaits the person who
> Exchanges a crown for a wreath.

But in his article in *Apollon*, No. 9, he precisely trades his crown for a wreath: one doesn't want to reply to him with his own words: Grief...

We perceive the introduction of the aim dictated for art in the propagatory note that appeared in the works of the greatest Symbolists of our time, Ibsen and Nietzsche, in the fact that they recognize the creator of life in the artist: a new life and the salvation of humanity proceed from art. This is the bayonet that the artist-conqueror fixes to his rifle; the religious creativity of life itself, which defines cognition itself, is in art; the development of the major courses of contemporary psychology and the theory of knowledge answers as follows: the bayonet is given to the artist by the philosopher; the bayonet is necessary; but Bryusov at the critical moment ridicules the use of a bayonet with his lame comparison of a bayonet with liqueur. Acting thus, he chops off the branch he's sitting on, he renounces his own words: "We throw ourselves on the altar of our divinity."

V. Ivanov and Blok, as literary figures, throw their activities on the altar of their divinity, believing in the magical power of creativity, as the origin of the transformation of life; they live up to Bryusov's precepts; we believe that because of this the flame of their aritstic creativity only flares up even more: V. Ivanov will give us even more accomplished sonnets, Blok, dramas. But Bryusov laughs at their worshipful attitude towards art.

I will not answer him with his words: Grief...

I fashioned this reply to Bryusov on the continuation and development of his joke about the rifle and liqueur. Apart from this joke V. Ya. Bryusov refutes Ivanov's reference to the fact that Symbolism is a definite historical phenomenon; Bryusov proposes that we remain contemporary Symbolists on that theoretical ground that the French Symbolists had beneath them. But we confess: they had no theoretical ground to stand on; the very interest in verse, the very discussions about form are only good when we know what art, form, and verses are; Symbolists' slogans demand philosophical justification and exposure, it is impossible to remain on the grounds of history, to regret that contemporary Russian Symbolists went beyond the circle of interests of the French Symbolists means the same as regretting that mankind went beyond the primitive state. And, moreover, to ascribe Symbolism to France is too narrow; after all, Nietzsche definitely declared himself a Symbolist, and the circles of his themes cannot be compared with those worked out in France. Symbolism is a phenomenon of worldwide, historical significance; it is still entirely in the future, to hammer it into France and measure it by a decade is cruel; nothing of Symbolism will remain. "Ask Verhaeren and Vielé-Griffin," Bryusov exclaims, "and I'm certain that they will all say, unanimously, that they wanted one thing..." It would be offensive for Symbolism if its fate were to be decided by the personal opinions of Verhaeren and Vielé-Griffin. I hope that Symbolism is something greater than Vielé-Griffin...

The Symbolist's aspiration is not to destroy millenia of art in the past, but to illuminate and deepen these millenia with the light of the future. This belief in the future moves all of us, and we declare openly that the fate of Russian Symbolism does not depend on the definitions taught in schools.

Otherwise Bryusov would have to agree with the fierce criticism of French Symbolists printed in the same issue of *Apollon*, in the article "Parisian Dialogue." This is what the author of the dialogue writes: "Consistent Symbolists will not leave behind any creations or will leave what in a hundred years will be read only for the sake of curiosity." Symbolism, understood as the method of a literary school, is doomed to perish; that's clear. Does Bryusov really want to see the demise of Symbolism? But there are two Bryusovs.

"Let the poet create not his books, but his own life," he writes in 1905.

"Symbolism wanted to be and always was only art," he writes in 1910.

> Grief awaits the one who
> Exchanges a crown for a wreath.
> Val. Bryusov.

A wreath or a crown?

Andrei Bely
1910

SYMBOLISM AND THE FUTURE
Ellis

We will now pass on to the summation of the development of Russian Symbolism examined by us in the persons of three typical representatives of three of its most important facets, in order to have the possibility and right to make final conclusions, on the basis of these summations, about the present crisis of Symbolism and about the great future of the Symbolist movement in Russia.

We won't repeat here the detailed comparative characteristics of the three typical representatives of Russian Symbolism, K. Balmont, V. Bryusov, and A. Bely, who successively expressed three stages of Symbolism, one after the other: the romantic stage, with its cult of the aloof daydream, the classical or "symbolic, in the full sense of the term," stage, with its method of "correspondences" and craving for contemplative attainment of the world, and finally the last stage, which we call the ecstatic or "Symbolism of clairvoyance," which turns the Symbolism of "aesthetics" into a world view, trying to crystallize the free compilation of artistic symbols into a unified, systematically hierarchical, inner-active Symbolism. Sketching the succession of these three waves, we have tried to explain its internal, logical necessity and to place it in connection with an approximately analogous logicality in the school of Europe's "Symbolist movement."

Here we will limit ourselves simply to reducing everything we've said on this question to one, approximate, graphic scheme [see the following page].

This scheme, despite its approximateness, gives us a chance not only to survey, all at once, what is essential in the writings and personalities of each of the three Symbolists we have studied, or to compare them among themselves, but also to analyze, while defining, other representatives of Russian Symbolism that were not subjected to our special analysis. F. Sologub's solipsism, Blok's chaotic combination of the elements of extreme Romanticism with realism, V. Ivanov's very deep synthesism, the newest epigones' Parnassianism and "clarism," and many other things that are contained in the depths of the broad current which became the Symbolist movement in present day Russia—all of this can be analyzed and classified with the aid of our scheme, which directly encompasses only a part of the material. There is a close connection between all the links of Symbolism and a strict, typical correspondence between these links. This allows us to make general conclusions on the basis of only a few, essentially typical phenomena.

General Scheme of the Development of Russian Symbolism

	K. Balmont	V. Bryusov	A. Bely
Representatives:	K. Balmont	V. Bryusov	A. Bely
Form of Symbolism:	Romantic	Aesthetic in the strict sense of the term	Symbolism of clairvoyance
Mode of Symbolism:	Aloof daydreaming	Concentrated, contemplative attainment	Ecstatic merging
Transformation of res through	Dream	Insight	Vision
Method of Symbolization:	Contrast of res to realiora	Seeing realoria in res	Merging with realiora and raising to Ens realissimum
General character of creativity:	Illusionistic idealism	Ideo-realism	Theurgic symbolics
Formal-artistic delineation:	Aestheticism of reflections and pure lyrics of shadows	Rhythmics of correspondences and symbolics of polarities	Mysticism of All-unity
Beginning point of world view	Extreme impressionism (philosophy of the moment, immoralism)	Aspiration for differentiation, Objectivism, specialization	Craving for central synthesis
Philosophical reference point:	Pluralism	Dualism	Monism
Ethical self-definition:	Ideal of beautiful infatuation	Ideal of sacrificial attainment	Cult of holy love
Predominant spiritual side:	Feeling	Intellect	Will
Central aspiration of creativity	Lyrism of femininity and sensual bliss	Eroticism and cult of passion	Religious pathos of Eternal Femininity
Primary goal:	Aloofness	Contemplation	Evocation (and craving for action)
Relationship to society:	Egotism	Individualism	Ecumenism
Supreme ideal:	Beauty	Truth	Perfection
Form of development of creative "I":	Complete transformation of "I"	Organic evolution	Chaotic dynamism of forms, with stability of central idea
General definition of creativity.	Exclusively poetic creativity	Poetics, merging with metaphysics of self-definition and scientific method	All-encompassing, synthesizing creativity (poetics, philosophy, science, mysticism)
Main poetic means:	Rhyme	Epithet	Rhythm
Historic place in development of Symbolism:	Symbolism's past	Present	Future

What do these general conclusions lead us to?

The thing that strikes us first of all is the exact parallelism in the development of Russian Symbolism and Western Symbolism. Not only are the basic tendencies the same—the successive sequence of forms and the chief stages of development essentially coincide. The basic tendency of Symbolism—the *unlimited self-absorption in the process of development,* successively changing it from the "craving for new forms" into a "reappraisal of all values," from a school of aesthetics into a new, synthetic world view, into the premonition of a new, cultural epoch, from the creation of "free verse" into the self-definition of "free spirit"—was equally felt in every step of both currents. The Russian to the same degree as the West European.

The basic stages are the repudiation and the chaotic, daring and revolutionary principle that recognizes itself *a contrario* (Ibsen, Schopenhauer, Wagner, Nietzsche [*Birth of Tragedy*], Poe, Baudelaire, Verlaine), the further development of the basic tendencies to their final conquest through self-denial (Nietzsche's cruel optimism, Huysmans' synthetic and mystical searches, Mallarmé, the Catholic tendency in French Symbolism), and finally, the state of Symbolism's present crisis, when this crisis seems to be the final "decadence of decadence," and the death-agony, to one person, and another, only the temporary slack time before the new path of ascent.

The same three periods (revolutionary period, period of self-broadening and external hegemony, and the period of crisis) are found in the development of Russian Symbolism; the names Balmont and Bryusov serve as the most vivid slogans of its first stage; their later works initiate the second stage; in them, together with Bely's things, Russian Symbolism reached its apogee; in the works of Bely, the maximum tension of Symbolist ideas appears; it becomes the idea of theurgism and universal synthesis, and finds a correspondence for itself in V. Ivanov's teachings about myth and symbolics. The contemporary epoch of crisis captures only the last works of Bryusov, which complete the first full cycle of his creativity, and all the most versatile and valuable works by Bely, in the center of which stand *The Silver Dove* and his synthetic theory of Symbolism, which is only now being developed for the first time in detail. The epoch of crisis in Russian Symbolism is marked by the swiftly growing and deepening creativity of V. Ivanov, who has decisively overcome the last remnants of aestheticism and illusionism and aspires to tie a great knot between Symbolist art and hierarchical mysticism, to combine teaching about artistic creativity with the idea of symbolics, to analyze the path on which the idea of the primary symbol moves, successively developing itself in teachings about mytho-creation. V. Ivanov's theoretical views, peculiarly logical and original, although they are often paradoxical, have been collected in his book *By the Stars.* In it, he has much in common with Bely's most cherished dreams and constructs. Both of them, down to their last word, are zealous pupils of Nietzsche—and this essentially brings their synthesizing searches together. Beyond the work of these two seekers, the picture of contemporary Symbolism is a really dreary sight. The more fruitless the whole general background of contemporary artistic literature is, almost exclusively epigonistic, self-satisfied, formal, alien more and more to the precepts of the great teachers and the first harbingers of Symbolism, equally as well as the impudences of the great, distinctive searches, which come down exclusively to the search for compromise between the forms that are opposed to each other, to the one-sided cult of style techniques, and to the "stylization" which has at all times been the truest and most ominous symptom of decadence, the more painfully we feel F. Sologub's shallowing of creativity, which has essentially come down to common realism and solipsism, the darkening of Blok's romantic ideal and his inability to seek different paths, which has compelled him essentially to retrace the way of self-negation that K. Balmont passed through.

We should state our definite opinion about the *crisis of Symbolism*, considering this phenomenon in all its significance and not ignoring the fact that several symptoms compel us to look upon it as a worldwide phenomenon. In Russia, of course, a number of specific reasons especially intensify and aggravate this phenomenon. The great political and general moral crisis of 1905-06, which evoked a common hesitation and an unprecedented collapse, the widespread, non-ideological, purely mercantile speculation in the area of book publishing, which grow out of this collapse, the uncertainty and instability of literary and general ideological groupings in our culturally too young society, the victory, too quick and easy, of Russian Symbolism, and the absence of seriously cohesive opposing tendencies, which ultimately are reduced to indecent and unconscientious badgering in the newspapers, and which are unable to evoke, *a contrario*, the cohesiveness of the Symbolist school, the excessive chaos and individuality of the main leaders, generally characteristic of undisciplined Russian life—all these phenomena aggravated the crisis of Russian Symbolism. However, the internal and main reason does not lie in these phenomena, but much deeper, where the inevitability of the "crisis of Symbolism" generally had its roots. This inevitability is contained in the instability of the general form by which Symbolism itself has been shaped from the very beginning. The reason is within it, though it essentially touches only its form, and not its very essence. Every evolution is a contemporary and rhythmic succession of forms that corresponds to the growth of the internal nucleus of every phenomenon; the reasons for this are always beyond the boundaries of this world, in so far as it is not revealed; they are innermost, it's only possible to sense them vaguely, to guess them intuitively. An inopportune succession of forms, a contradiction, in which it becomes an obsolete form that has broken with its internally broadened content too late—this is the usual form of a crisis that differentiates it from the final degeneration of a given process. What is the "crisis of contemporary Symbolism"? A temporary self-contradiction or a degeneration? A convulsion or an agony?

We definitely declare that it is precisely a comprehensible, inevitably temporary and entirely conventional self-contradiction. As a recovery from an illness is inevitably preceded by a crisis, the rebirth of Symbolism presupposes conquering this internal contradiction to the utmost.

Unnoticed even by themselves, the very enemies of Symbolism point to this by calling the crisis of Symbolism the "decadence of decadence"; however, if Symbolism itself were only the decline of something, then the "decadence of decadence" is already the restoration of something valuable and healthy.

But where is it, this thing that has fallen away from Symbolism and with its decline has revived? Where is it?

We assume that outside of Symbolism there are no paths to the future, and there were none until Symbolism toppled the already rotten barriers of old forms and teachings; consequently, there can be no talk of the possibility of returning to the old. The reason for the crisis is in Symbolism itself, the reason and the necessity of a future revival are also in it. Every destruction, either from without or within, is conceivable. But outside itself, Symbolism has nothing to fear! Its internal agony and death could be equivalent to the death of all culture and the cessation of all ideological life in general, which is inconceivable. Consequently, contemporary Symbolism alone must overcome itself, move precisely, overcome something in itself! It must cast off its *dual form,* which it accepted from the very beginning under the revolutionary negation of the old; this narrow form from the beginning became narrower and tighter with its every further step, externally victorious and internally deepening. Finally the moment arrived when it had to be broken no matter what! If our hands had to do this, then it is our supreme vocation, our duty and our feat! . . . Otherwise the old form would smother the new that was already breathing and throbbing inside it . . .

Where is, however, this self-contradiction of contemporary Symbolism? Where do we find the narrowness of its obsolete forms?

We have frequently stressed the dualistic character of the "Symbolist movement," conventionally and approximately distinguishing the two waves in it: the "purely aesthetic" and the "ideological," i.e., the synthetic. We have even noted the essential difference between Symbolism as a "school of new art" and Symbolism as a "new world view," and the search for new, primary criteria of culture that have inevitably turned into seeking and even touching, united with premonition, some new secret, a new inner, internal world that is coming into being, the vague premonition of a new religion.

Now, abandoning the objective grounds of research, we would like to say more definitively that these two different sides of the organically and genetically united ideological movement, from the very beginning, capriciously and diversely conflicting, and combining with each other, created a whole cycle of very profound contradictions in Symbolism, a whole complex network of fissures and rough spots. One main gaping fissure passed through its very heart, lay like a fatal curse on its every manifestation, appeared to be the primary reason for the contemporary crisis. With every step forward this contradiction of Symbolism became greater, gripped it tighter and restricted its every movement, smothered it, tormented it, and finally blocked its path threateningly. After Nietzsche it became too clear that we weren't talking about the same form of something private and self-contained, but about the inescapable reconstruction of the whole edifice of culture... And from that time our contemporary culture has been valuable only in its appeal to the future. For us, our culture is only a bridge, thrown across the abysses, about which we hadn't even thought previously, with one end resting on the historical method (only after Nietzsche did we understand the horror of this) of all our concepts and feelings, and the other fleeing into the distance, about which it was even difficult and terrifying to speak. On the one hand, each of us has felt himself to be a little history and encyclopedia of the whole universe, some Ahasuerus of culture; on the other hand—we all turned out to be ridiculous, helpless, and naive, like little children in front of what the greatest of us saw in the paroxysms of holy insanity. Thus we were all brought out of Egypt, but no one saw with his own eyes the land of Canaan! Thus began our wandering in the desert... but in this wandering we were given a fiery pillar, leading and threatening, and now we know its name. *It is Symbolism!* The best among us have already perished in the desert; those who are now moving forward will inevitably perish, perhaps tomorrow, but the pillar will never die out... [...]

Ellis
1910

THOUGHTS ABOUT SYMBOLISM
V. Ivanov

I met a shepherd mid deserted mountains
Who trumpeted on an Alpine horn.
His song was pleasing; but his sonorous horn
Was only used to rouse a hidden echo in the mountains.
Each time the shepherd waited for its coming,
Having rung out his own brief melody,
Such an indescribably sweet harmony
Came amid the gorges that it seemed
An unseen chorus of spirits,
On instruments not of this world,
Was translating the languages of earth
Into the language of heaven.
And I thought: "O genius! like this horn
You sing earth's song to rouse in our hearts
Another song. Blessed is he who hears!"
From beyond the mountains a voice responded:
"Nature is a symbol, like this horn,
It sounds for the echo—the echo is God!
Blessed is he who hears both song and echo!"

If, as a poet, I know how to *paint* with the word (poetry is similar to painting—"*Ut pictura poësis*"—classical poetics stated, through Horace, after ancient Simonides), to *paint* so that the imagination of the listener reproduces what I depict with the clear visual quality of what is seen, and things which I name present themselves to his soul prominent in their tangibility and graphic in their picturesqueness, darkened or illuminated, moving or frozen, according to the nature of their visual manifestation;

if as a poet, I know how to *sing* with a magical power (for "it is not sufficient that verses be beautiful: let them also be delightful and willfully lead the soul of the listener"—"*non satis est pulchra esse poëmata, dulcia sunto et quocumque volent animum auditoris agunto*"—as classical poetry stated, through Horace, concerning this tender constraint), if I know how to *sing* so powerfully and sweetly that the soul, entranced by the sounds, follows submissively after my pipes, longs with my desires, grieves with my grief, is enflamed with my ecstasy, and the listener replies with a harmonious beating of his heart to all the tremblings of the musical wave bearing the melodious poem;

if, as a poet and sage, I possess the knowledge of things, and delighting the heart of the listener, I edify his intellect and educate his will;

but, if crowned with the triple crown of melodious power, I, as a poet, do not know how, with all this threefold enchantment, to force the soul of the listener to sing together with me in another voice than mine, not in unison with its psychological superficiality, but in the counterpoint of its hidden depth—to sing about that which is deeper than the depths revealed by me, and higher than the heights revealed by me—if my listener is only a mirror, only an echo, only one who receives, only one who absorbs—if the ray of my *word* does not betroth my *silence* to his silence through the *rainbow* of a mysterious precept:

then I am not a *Symbolist* poet.

II.

If art is in general one of the mightiest means of uniting humanity, one could say of Symbolist art that the principle of its activity is, above all, union, union in the direct and most profound sense of this word. In truth, not only does it unite, it also combines. Two are combined by a third, the highest. The symbol, this third, resembles a rainbow that has burst into flames between the ray of the word and the moisture of the soul which reflected the ray... And in every work of genuinely symbolic art is the beginning of Jacob's ladder.

Symbolism combines consciousnesses in such a way that they jointly give birth "in beauty." The purpose of love, according to Plato, is "birth in beauty." Plato's depiction of the paths of love is a definition of Symbolism. From enamorment of the beautiful body, the soul, growing forth, aspires to the love of God. When the aesthetic is experienced erotically, artistic creation becomes symbolic. The enjoyment of beauty is similar to enamorment of beautiful flesh and proves to be the initial step in erotic ascent. The meaning of artistic creation as that which has been experienced is itself inexhaustible. The symbol is the creative principle of love, Eros the leader. Between the two lives—that one incarnated in creation and the other creatively joined to it (*creatively* because Symbolism is that art which transforms whoever accepts it into a *co-participant* in creation)—is accomplished what is spoken of in the ancient, naive profundity of an Italian song, where two lovers arrange a rendezvous on the condition that a third person will also appear together with them at the appointed hour— the god of love himself:

Pur che il terzo sia presente,
E quel terzo sia l'Amor.

III.

L'Amór | che muove il Sóle | e l'altre Stélle—"The Love that moves the Sun and the other Stars . . . " In this concluding verse of Dante's *Paradiso,* images are composed into myth and music teaches it wisdom.

Let us examine the musical structure of this melodic line of verse. In it there are three rhythmic waves, brought forth by the caesuras, pushing forward the words: *Amor, Sole, Stelle*—for on them rests the *ictus.* The radiant images of the god of Love, the Sun and the Stars seem blinding as a consequence of this word arrangement. They are separated by the low points in the rhythm, the obscure and dark *muove* (moves) and *altre* (others). Night gapes in the intervals between the radiant outlines of those three ideas. Music is embodied in a visual manifestation: the Apollonian vision emerges above the gloom of the Dionysian frenzy: indivisible and yet not combined is the Pythian dyad, the soul. But the soul, as the beholder (epopt) of the mysteries, is not abandoned without some instructive direction clarifying that which is perceived by consciousness. Some hierophant standing over it intones: "Wisdom! you see the movement of the radiant heavenly vault, you hear its harmony: know then that it is Love. Love moves the Sun and other Stars." This sacred word of the hierophant *ieros logos* is the word as *logos.*

Thus Dante is crowned with that triple crown of melodious power. But this is not yet all that he achieves. The shaken soul not only accepts, not only echoes the prophetic word: it discovers within itself and out of the mysterious depths painlessly gives birth to its fulfilling inner word. The mighty magnet has magnetized it: it too becomes a magnet. The universe is revealed within itself. What it espies in the heights above gapes in it here below. And within it is Love; for after all it already loves. *"Amor"* . . . at this sound which affirms the magnetism of the living universe its molecules arrange themselves magnetically. And within it are the sun and the stars and the harmonious tumult of the spheres moved by the might of the divine Mover. It sings in harmony with the cosmos its own melody of love that it sang in the soul of the poet when he prophesied his cosmic words— Beatrice's melody. The line of verse under discussion (which is examined not merely as the object of pure aesthetics, but in relation to the subject, as the perpetrator of spiritual experience and inner experience) proves to be not only filled with an external musical sweetness and an inner musical energy, but is polyphonic as well, the consequence of the fulfilling musical vibrations summoned forth by it and the awakening of overtones clearly perceived by us. This is why it is not only an artistically perfect verse, but a *symbolic* verse as well. This is why it is divinely poetic. Being composed, moreover, of symbolic elements insofar as its separate words are pronounced so powerfully in the given connection and the given combinations that they appear as symbols in themselves, it represents in itself a synthetic judgment in which for the subjective symbol (Love) the poet's mytho-creating intuition finds the effective word (moves the Sun and the Stars). And thus before us is the *mytho-creating* crowning of Symbolism. For the myth is the synthetic judgment where the predicate verb is joined to the symbol-subject. The sacred word, *ieros logos,* is transformed into the word as *mythos.*

If we dared to give an evaluation of the above-mentioned effect of the concluding words of the Divine Comedy from the point of view of the hierarchy of values of a religio-metaphysical order, we would have to recognize this effect as *theurgic.* And with this example we could test the already frequently pronounced identification of the genuine and exalted Symbolism (in the above-mentioned category of examination, by no means, incidentally, unnecessary for the aesthetics of Symbolist art)—with theurgy.

IV.

And thus I am not a Symbolist if I do not arouse in the heart of the listener a subtle hint or influence those incommunicable sensations which at times resemble some primeval rememberance ("and for a long time on earth the soul languished, filled with a wondrous desire, and the monotonous songs of earth could not replace for it the heavenly sounds"), at times a distant, vague premonition, at times a trembling at someone's familiar and long-desired approach—whereby this rememberance and this premonition or presence we experience as the incomprehensible expansion of our individual personality and empirically restricted self-consciousness.

I am not a Symbolist if my words do not evoke in the listener feelings of the connection between that which is his "ego" and that which he calls his "*non*-ego,"—the connection of things which are empirically separated; if my words do not convince him immediately of the existence of a hidden life where his intellect had not suspected life; if my words do not move in him the energy of love towards that which he was previously unable to love because his love did not know of the many abodes it possessed.

I am not a Symbolist if my words are not equal to themselves, if they are not the echo of other sounds about which you know nothing, as about the Spirit, where they come from and where they go—and if they do not arouse the echo in the labyrinths of souls.

V.

I am not a Symbolist, then, for my listener. For Symbolism signifies a relationship, and the Symbolist work in itself, as an object removed from the subject, cannot exist.

Abstract aesthetic theory and formal poetics examine an artistic work in itself; in this regard they have no knowledge of Symbolism. One can speak about Symbolism only by studying the work in relationship to the perceiving subject and to the creating subject as undivided personalities. Hence the following conclusions:

1) Symbolism lies outside all aesthetic categories.

2) Every artistic work is subordinated to evaluation from the point of view of Symbolism.

3) Symbolism is connected with the wholeness of both the individual as the artist himself, as well as the one who experiences the artistic revelation.

Obviously the Symbolist-artisan is inconceivable; just as inconceivable is the Symbolist-aesthete. Symbolism deals with man. Thus it resurrects the word "poet" in the old meaning—of the poet as a person *(poëtae nascuntur)*—in contrast to the everyday use of the word in our time which strives to lower the value of this elevated name to the meaning of "a recognized artist-versifier, gifted and clever in his technical area."

VI.

Is the symbolic element required in the organic composition of a perfect creation? Must a work of art be symbolically effective in order for us to consider it perfect?

The demand of symbolic effectiveness is just as non-obligatory as the demands of *"ut pictura"* or *"dulcia sunto ... "* What formal characteristic is at all unconditionally necessary in order that a work be considered artistic? Since this characteristic has not been named, even in our day, there is no formal aesthetic in our time.

To make up for it there are schools. And the one is distinguished from the other by those particular seemingly super-obligatory demands which it voluntarily imposes on itself as the rules and vows of its artistic order. And thus the Symbolist school demands more of itself than of others.

It is clear that these very same demands can be realized unconsciously, outside of all rules and vows. Each work of art can be tested from the point of view of Symbolism.

Since Symbolism designates the relationship of the artistic object to the two-fold subject, creating and receiving, then whether the given work appears for us to be symbolic or not essentially depends on our reception. We can, for instance, accept in a symbolic sense the words of Lermontov: "From beneath the mysterious, cold demi-mask I heard your voice ... "

Although in all probability, for the author of these verses, the foregoing words were equivalent to themselves in their logical extent and content and he had in mind simply an encounter at a masquerade.

On the other hand, examining the relationship of the work to the integral personality of its creator we can, independent of the actual reception itself, establish the symbolic character of the work. In any case Lermontov's confession appears this way to us:

> You will not meet the answer
> Amid the noise of this world.
> Out of flame and light
> The word is born.

The effort of the poet to express in the external word the inner word is clear, as is his despairing of the accessibility of this latter word to reception by listeners, which nonetheless is necessary lest the flaming word, the radiant word be enveloped by darkness.

Symbolism is magnetism. The magnet attracts only iron. The normal state of molecules of iron is potentially magnetic. And that which is attracted by the magnet becomes magnetized ...

And thus we Symbolists do not exist if there are no Symbolist listeners. For Symbolism is not merely the creative act alone, but the creative reciprocal action, not merely the artistic objectivization of the creative subject, but also the creative subjectivization of the artistic object.

"Is Symbolism dead?" contemporaries ask. "Of course it's dead!" others reply. It's better for them to know whether Symbolism has perished for them. But we who have perished bear witness, whispering in the ears of those celebrating at our funeral feast, that there is no death.

VII.

But if Symbolism has not died, then how it has grown! It is not the might of its standard bearers that has waxed strong and grown—I wish to say—but the sacred branch of laurel in their hands, the gift of the Muses of Helikon that commanded Hesiod to prophesy only the truth—their living banner.

Not long ago many took Symbolism as a device of poetic depiction, related to Impressionism, formally capable of being carried over into the category of stylistics concerning tropes and figures. After the definition of the metaphor (it seems that I am reading a fully realizable but not realized fashionable textbook on the theory of philology)—under the paragraph concerning the metaphor I envisage an example for grammar school pupils: "If the metaphor consists not of a single part of speech but is developed into an entire poem, then it is acceptable to call such a poem symbolic."

We have come a long way from the Symbolism of poetic rebuses, of that literary device (again only a device!) that consisted in the art of evoking a series of notions capable of arousing associations, the sum total of which forces one to guess and, with a special power, to perceive the subject or experience, purposely obscured, not expressed by direct meaning, but having to be deciphered. This kind, beloved in the period after Baudelaire by the French Symbolists (with whom we have neither a historical nor ideological reason for joining forces) does not belong in the circle of Symbolism outlined by us. Not only because this is merely device; the reason lies deeper. The goal of the poet becomes in this case—to give the lyrical ideal an illusion of a great compass, in order, little by little, to decrease the compass, to condense and give substance to its content. We were about to abandon ourselves to dreams about "dentelle" and "jeu suprême" and so on,—but Mallarmé only wants our thought, having described wide circles, to alight on a single point designated by him. For us Symbolism is, on the contrary, energy liberating us from the bounds of the given, lending the soul the movement of a broadening spiral.

We want, in opposition to those who call themselves "Symbolists," to be true to the purpose of art, which takes something small and makes it great, and not vice-versa. For such is the humility of an art that loves the small. It is more characteristic for genuine Symbolism to depict the earthly than the heavenly: the power of the sound is not important to it, but rather the might of the echo. *A realibus ad realiora. Per realia ad realiora.* Genuine Symbolism does not tear itself away from the earth; it wants to combine roots and stars and grow like a starry flower out of the nearby, native roots. It does not replace things, and when speaking of the sea, means the earthly sea, and snowy heights ("and what age gleams whitely there, on the snowy heights, but the dawn, and now sows fresh roses on them,"—Tyutchev) are understood as the peaks of earthly mountains. It strives, like art, towards one thing: the elasticity of the image, its inner vitality and extensiveness in the soul, where it falls like a seed and must give rise to a seed-pod. Symbolism in this sense is the affirmation of the extensiveness of the word and of art. This extensive energy does not seek or avoid intersection with spheres that are heteronomous to art, for example with religious systems. Symbolism, as we affirm it, does not fear a Babylonian Captivity in any of these spheres; it alone realizes the real freedom of art; it alone believes in its real might.

Those who have called themselves Symbolists, but did not know (as at one time Goethe, the distant father of our Symbolism, knew) that Symbolism speaks of the universal and the collective—they led us by the path of symbols through the radiant valleys in order to return to our prison, to the cramped cell of the insignificant "ego." Illusionists, they did not believe in the divine expanse and knew only the expanse of fantasy and the enchantment of slumberous daydream out of which we awoke to find ourselves in a prison. Genuine Symbolism sets a completely different goal for itself: the liberation of the soul (*katharsis*) as a development of inner experience.

Vyacheslav Ivanov
1912

A SPEECH ABOUT SYMBOLISM
F. Sologub

In opening the present discussion about contemporary literature, I permit myself a few short prefatory remarks as an introduction to our discussion.

Questions about art, as we all know, often recede into the background in the face of questions of a more practical nature, so that, for example, discussing the laws of printing is of course easier and much more interesting than talking about printing itself or about literature.

But meanwhile, if there is any value on earth that people can't really get along without, it is of course, art, or to use a more general term, creativity. A person has to busy himself with many other matters because of necessity, because of practical considerations, a person does a lot of things because he is forced to, unwillingly, almost with revulsion; he comes to art only because art comforts and gladdens him; he always comes to it freely, in no way is he driven to do it. And it is impossible to approach art if obscure and serious passions and feelings control one's soul. A person puts his whole soul into art and thus the person's spiritual world, that "which men live by," leaves an impression nowhere else than in art. When we wish to make a judgment about a person from one epoch or another, then our only reliable guidance in this regard can be the art of that race, that time, or more precisely the attitude of those people to art.

Thus it would be strange to look at art only as a means of depicting a chosen moment of life in a pretty or expressive way. Art is not just a mirror, placed before the vagaries of life, it does not want to be that kind of mirror. This is uninteresting, boring for it. It's a boring job—reflecting the accidents of life, retelling barely amusing anecdotes; it's not at all possible to put a living soul into this. A person's living soul always craves a vital deed, vital creativity, craves the creation of a world within itself, similar to the world of external objects, but a real, a created world. The vital life of the soul flows not only in the observation of objects, in the assignment of their names, but also in the constant aspiration to understand their vital connection and to place everything that appears before our consciousness in some common, universal blueprint.

In this way objects appear (for our consciousness) not only as separate accidental existences, but also in their general interrelationships. And so, depending on the complexity of the connection of these relationships in our consciousness, all the complex things of the world that we perceive reduce to the least possible number of common origins, and each object is perceived in its relation to the most common thing that can be thought of.

So, in this relationship, all objects become only a perspicuous mirror of certain common relationships, only a multiform manifestation of a certain world-size commonality. Life itself stops seeming like a series of accidents and anecdotes; it appears in our consciousness like a part of the world process, directed by a single will. All of the phenomena's similarities and dissimilarities appear to be the exposure of diverse possibilities, the bearer of which the world becomes. Not one of the objects of objectified reality has any self-contained value. Everything in the world is relative; this is recognized in our time by science in regard to time and space.

The Symbolists' understanding of the world, however, abolishes this universal relativity of phenomena so that, while accepting this relativity of objects and phenomena in the world of objects, at the same time it recognizes something unified, to which all objects and phenomena are related. Only in regard to this unity does everything that appears and exists in the objective world get its sense. And so, only this world view has always given, up to the present time, a basis for high, great art; when art is no longer at the stage of idle amusement, it always becomes an expression of the most general world view of a given time. Art only seems to be always an appeal to something concrete and private, only seems to be scattering, brightly colored combinations of casual anecdotes; in essence, art always seems to express the deepest and most general thoughts of contemporaneity, thoughts directed toward a world view by a person in a society. The very figurativeness that is characteristic of a creation of high art depends on the fact that for art at its high stages the images of the objective world only open a window into limitlessness. They are one of the means of understanding the world. A high external perfection of images in art corresponds to their purpose, always elevated and significant. Thus in high art the image strives to be a *symbol,* i.e., aspires to accommodate within itself highly significant contents, aspires to a point where the contents of the image in the process of perception by a viewer or reader can reveal its deep meaning more and more.

The secret of the external existence of high works of art lies only in this capacity of the image for its endless disclosure. A work of art, completely explicated, totally interpreted, quickly dies; there is no reason for it to live any longer. It has fulfilled its minor, temporary duty, has faded and gone out. Thus the useful lights of fires die out when they fulfill their purpose—but the stars high in the sky continue to shine.

In order to have the possibility of making a symbol the eternally opening window into infinity, the image must have a dual exactitude. It must itself be an exact depiction, lest it be an accidental and futilely concocted image—you cannot discover any depth behind futile fabrications. Besides this, the image must be taken in its exact relationship to other objects in the objective world, it must be put in its appropriate place in the blueprint of the world. Only then will it contribute to the expression of the most general world view at a given time. From this it follows, of course, that the most legitimate form of Symbolist art is *realism,* and this is almost always how it has really been.

If we take even folk tales, made up by the people, then we distinguish in them, on the one hand, an expression of the most common world view of those people who created the tales, and on the other hand, an amazing exactitude of details from everyday life, interwoven with fantastic fabrications. A tale is not, of course, a mechanical depiction of life, it arbitrarily combines its basic elements, remains art, in this sense free from life, but it doesn't fool a person steeped in its mythological significances, who wants only to search for a depiction of people's everyday life.

This characteristic of Symbolist art has appeared repeatedly in our time. Those who dislike the new art have said that it constantly turns away from life and turns people away from life. This is a mistake, of course! We find nothing like this if we become more closely acquainted with the new art. If we pick up a novel by a persistently rejected poet like Rukavishnikov, the novel *Iron Family,* we won't find any mistakes in depicting everyday life. We see exactly the same depiction of life and living in the novels of Andrei Bely, in the contemporary and historical stories and tales of Valery Bryusov, and other participants in the new school of poetry.

Of course it cannot be otherwise. Symbolist art is not tendentious, not at all interested in whether to depict life in one way or another—it is only interested in speaking its truth about the world. Such art has no motive for an inexact use of its models, which for it are all objects in the objective world. It happens in the history of literature that realism forgets its true purpose of serving as a form of that art which expresses a Symbolist world view—then art turns to simply copying reality, and sometimes this copying becomes a task with a publicistic nature. Then realism—high and marvelous art—degenerates and falls to the level of naive naturalism. Russian literature has existed in this naive naturalism, which replaced the high art of Pushkin, Lermontov, Turgenev, and Lev Tolstoy, almost until the end of the nineteenth century.

Then, twenty years ago, that literary movement arose which was greeted so disapprovingly, with such ill will, the one that was called "decadence," "modernism," and perhaps some other names. The representatives of this new current have been and are quite distinguishable from each other, and they do not represent one literary school, but the aspiration to return to poetry its true purpose, to express the most general world view, has united all of them, i.e., it is characteristic for all these poets to aspire to restore the rights of Symbolism, and on the other hand, to revitalize realism as the legitimate form of Symbolist art. This has been done in the last twenty years, has been done with such vigor and authority, that now art's return to naive naturalism seems quite impossible. In the course of this last period of approximately twenty years, the new art has not remained stationary, of course. The common law of replaceability has touched it.

It's possible to distinguish three stages in the movement, but it is also necessary to note that there is no precise chronological sequence here, and the boundaries of these stages are blurred. I would call them: 1) Cosmic Symbolism, 2) Individual Symbolism, and 3) Democratic Symbolism.

The first stage of Symbolist art represents meditation about the world, about the sense of universal life, and about the one will, which rules in the world, if this is accepted, or about the wills that rule the world, if several deities governing the world are accepted. On the path of these elevated inspirations, our predecessor was the great poet Tyutchev. Among the contemporary poets it is fair to point to Vyacheslav Ivanov, the author of exquisite poems and thorough theoretical articles. Perhaps this poet is the representative of the deepest thoughts about the universe, although he does not believe in a world-directing will because wisdom does not always agree with faith.

This cosmic aspiration toward Symbolism, however, was not a sharp break in literary life. The individualistic verse of Russian modernists seemed particularly unpleasant to Russian critics and caused mostly censure. The individualism of the Russian modernists was interpreted as an anti-social tendency, which was of course false. Individualism can never be an anti-social phenomenon. Sociality itself has a value only when it is supported by the clearly expressed consciousness of separate personalities. After all, it is only worth uniting with other people to preserve one's own face, own soul, one's right to life. It's not without reason that the precept of the strongest society is the saying: "My house is my castle." In part, the individualism of Russian modernists directed its sting not against society, but in precisely the opposite direction. We retreated into ourselves, into our own wastelands, in order to find our place in the external world, in the great kingdom of the one will. If the one will forms the world, then what is my will? If the whole world lies in the chains of necessity, then what is my freedom? I also perceive my own freedom, after all, as a necessary law of my existence, and I cannot live without freedom at all.

Our individualism was not a mutiny against society, but an uprising against mechanical necessity. In our individualism, we sought not an egoistic separation from other people, but freedom, self-confirmation, on the paths to ecstasy, to searching for a miracle, or on some other paths. Before us stood the question of what a person is, and what his relationship to the one will is. If everything in the world is bound by the chains of necessity, then I have borne, and every day bear, the whole weight of an evil act perpetrated at one time and all the exultation of concommitant good deeds done at any time by anyone. Each of us is ultimately responsible for all of our acts. The yoke of all-embracing responsibility for the sinfulness of all the world lies on our own weak shoulders, on mine and on all of yours.

This gives us, at the same time, the elevating possibility of finding our wills, like powerful poetics, the universal will.

And so this mood of the soul led us to an elevated perception of man-godhood through haughty solipsism and egocentrism. The merging of our individualism with the one will was the basis of the religious-philosophical aspiration of Russian poetry of recent times. By itself, this poetry was only a transition to the third moment of the movement of art, to Democratic Symbolism, which craves ecumenism and collegiality.

Russian Symbolism is presently at this last stage. Here it meets that demand which never confronted life or art in previous ages, a demand which sounds strange and displeases many. This demand is to love life. Evidently it is not worth demanding because who does not normally love himself, his own little separate life, in which there are some great and small joys? But in our age, when the spontaneous feeling for life has become so weak, this demand has taken on a special tragic character. We demand that people love life sort of because we feel a lack of the ability to love in ourselves. Meanwhile, what does the demand to love life mean? There is much that is wonderful in life, but there is also much that is ugly and repulsive, that one must hate with all the force of one's soul. To love life in general, life, no matter what, is of course absurd because this means loving the executioner and the victim. One has to choose, of course, to love one and hate the other. Do not love life as it is because contemporary life in its general direction is not worth it at all. Life demands transformation in a creative will. In this craving for transformation, art should go before life because it shows wonderful ideals to life, by which life can be transformed, if it wants to be, but if it doesn't to, then it will stagnate.

Fyodor Sologub
1914

SYMBOLIST JOURNALS
Introduction

For the section of this book devoted to the main journals of Symbolism, four programmatic articles have been chosen. These editorial statements represent the views of the authors whose essays appear here, and of others as well. The journals were selected because they were central to the Symbolist movement and forums specifically created to expose Symbolist views in criticism and belles-lettres. Individual Symbolist authors obviously published elsewhere, but these four journals, especially the first three, which were published during the time of Symbolism's greatest prominence, are recognized as the leading journals of this movement.

The first, *Vesy,* was without question the most important journal of the Symbolists. *Vesy* is sometimes known by its French title, *La Balance,* and is often translated as *The Scales,* but this English designation does not convey the full sense of the title, which is taken from the zodiacal sign we call Libra. The astrological aspect of the title was evident in the initial pages, with their illustrations of the zodiac taken from medieval French miniatures.

Vesy, which was published in Moscow from 1904 through 1909, was conceived as Russia's counterpart to literary journals in Western Europe. Though Bryusov often tried to downplay the significance of his role in *Vesy*'s operations, his editorial and organizational activities provided the main impetus for the journal's existence, and without his active involvement the last year it was published, the journal came to a rather quick demise.

As the reader can see from its editorial statement in 1904, the intention was to devote the journal solely to criticism and a chronicle of cultural activities. This emphasis was later altered, and poetry, drama, and prose fiction were published. The list of contributors includes all the leading Symbolists and many others; traditional and non-traditional areas (e.g., esoterism, Theosophy) were covered, and *Vesy* had correspondents sending contributions from Europe and India. At the end of this introductory piece, the journal tips its hat to its "older brothers," which were in fact soon replaced by *Vesy.*

Zolotoe runo began publication in Moscow in January 1906; it was an artistic, literary, and critical journal. It was originally published in Russian with parallel French translations, but later in 1906, the French translations were dropped. The journal was richly illustrated with color reproductions and black and white drawings.

At first, Blok, Bryusov, Bely, Ivanov, Merezhkovsky, Sologub, and others were actively involved in its publication, but later Bryusov, Bely, and Merezhkovsky left in a highly publicized break. They and others at *Vesy* then frequently attacked *Zolotoe runo* and its main contributors, Ivanov, Blok, and Chulkov.

The name of the journal, in English *The Golden Fleece,* also known by its French title, *Toison d'Or,* was evidently taken from Bely's poetry and prose of 1901-4 and the Moscow group of Symbolists called the Argonauts. Bely wrote of a journal called *Zolotoe runo* in a lyrical fragment in prose called "Argonavty" (Argonauts, 1904), and later claimed that the publisher, N. P. Ryabushinsky, had taken the name of the journal from his works.

The journal's program sounds rather pompous to us now, but seen in its historical context, the call for eternal, free, symbolic, indivisible art had a strong appeal. Three years later, however, emotions had cooled somewhat, and the journal ceased publication with the December issue of 1909.

The third Symbolist journal of this period, *Pereval,* began publication in Moscow in November of 1906 and lasted through only twelve issues, i.e., until the October issue of 1907. The journal was edited by Sergei Sokolov and was devoted to "free thought," as the subtitle of the journal and the editorial statement make clear. As in the case of *Zolotoe runo,* the editors of *Pereval* saw a bright future ahead, and encouraged people to follow the roads to the City of the Sun. Though political parties are specifically shunned, a political radicalism is forthrightly proclaimed, and artistic and literary considerations are pushed somewhat into the background.

The name, *The Divide* or *The Watershed,* is taken from the notion that Russian society was at that time balanced on a critical point between the past, perceived as oppressive, and the future, which many hoped would be new and free. One author who actively supported this view of Russian culture being at the divide was Bely, who came to work for *Pereval* after his break with *Zolotoe runo.* Some of the other authors who also contributed to *Pereval* were leading Symbolists, like Blok and Sologub.

The last journal represented here, *Trudy i dni,* was published in Moscow after Symbolism's high point, from 1912 through 1916. It was edited by Bely and E. Medtner, and first appeared as a bimonthly during 1912; later issues appeared very infrequently.

The journal was largely a product of the Second Wave of Symbolism; Bely and especially Ivanov were major contributors, though Bryusov and Ellis also participated. As is evident from the editorial statement, the journal's intentions were grandiose indeed. It was devoted specifically to elucidating true, pure Symbolism, and coordinating true culture, and somehow revealing the "Universal Truth."

Blok, for one, felt the journal's scope was somewhat too broad and found room for disagreement with Ivanov's "Thoughts on Symbolism," published in *Works and Days*. Bely, in addition, helped to lessen the journal's importance by departing for Europe at the time the journal was starting out; he was in fact, not an ideal editor. But clearly the journal was not right for the time; other movements, chiefly Acmeism and Futurism, were coming into favor, and Symbolism itself was fragmented, with its authors following their own creative paths.

VESY
To the Readers

Vesy wants to create a critical journal in Russia. It selects from its foreign models such publications as the English *Athenaeum,* the French *Mercure de France,* the German *Litterarische Echo,* and the Italian *Marzocco.* Poems, stories, all works of belles-lettres are consciously excluded from *Vesy's* program. There is a place for such works in a separate book or in an anthology.

Vesy wishes to be impartial in its critical judgments, to evaluate artistic creations independent of its agreement or disagreement with the author's ideas. But *Vesy* cannot help devoting most of its attention to that important movement which, under the name of "decadence," "Symbolism," "the new art," has penetrated all fields of human activity. *Vesy* is convinced that the "new art" is the last point reached by humanity on its path until now, that precisely in the "new art" all the best forces of the earth's spiritual life are concentrated, that in bypassing it people have no other way forward to the new, even higher ideals.

Every issue of *Vesy* will be divided into two sections. In the first, there will be general articles about questions of art, science, and literature. In addition to theoretical articles about the purposes and means of art, testimonials about the creativity of leading artists, their biographies, and articles about the history of literature, etc., will come in at this point. From the field of science, *Vesy* will primarily deal with those questions which have some relation to literature and art. The second section of *Vesy* is devoted to a chronicle of literary and artistic life. Here there will be critical and bibliographical notes about new books that have appeared in Russian and other languages. There will also be lists of new books, Russian and foreign. Here there will be accounts of theatrical presentations, musical performances, and picture exhibitions. *Vesy* has invited correspondents in various cities in Europe and Asia to contribute. *Vesy* hopes to significantly increase the number of these correspondents. In the first section of *Vesy,* the following people will take part: K. Balmont, Ju. Baltrušaitis, Valery Bryusov, Andrei Bely, Max Voloshin, I. Dosekin, Vyacheslav Ivanov, Mark Krinitsky, D. Merezhkovsky, N. Minsky, P. Pertsov, V. Rozanov, M. Semyonov, F. Sologub, and others.

In the bibliographic and artistic chronicle section, in addition to the above, the following will take part: L. Batyushkov (Theosophy), A. Blok, V. Vladimirov (artistic exhibits), V. Kallash (history of Russian literature), K. Korovin (artistic exhibits), N. Lerner, A. Miropolsky (esoterism and spiritualism), S. A. Polyakov (linguistics), G. Popov (mathematics), S.

Rafalovich (theater), V. Rebikov (music), A. Remizov, I. Rachinsky (music), and others.

The following people have promised their correspondence: M. Voloshin (France), Franz Evers (Germany), René Ghil (France), H. Kasperowicz (Poland), Dagny Kristensen (Norway), A. Leman (India), A. Madelung (Denmark), William R. Morfill (England), Léon Rouané (Spain), M. Semyonov (Italy), Maximilian Schick (Germany), and others.

In conclusion, *Vesy* is pleased to express its gratitude to D. V. Filosofov, who greeted the new journal (see *Novyi put,* January, 1904, p. 224ff.) and correctly pointed out its relation to its older brothers, *Mir Iskusstva* and *Novyi put.*

ZOLOTOE RUNO

At this stormy time, we set our course.

All around, renewing life seethes like a violent whirlpool. In the roar of the struggle, amid the pressing questions that each day raises, and the bloody answers that our Russian reality gives to them, for many people the Eternal grows dimmer and recedes into the distance.

We sympathize with everyone who works for the renewal of life, we do not deny any of the contemporary tasks, but we firmly believe that it is impossible to live without Beauty, and together with free institutions we have to win for our descendents a free, bright creativity, lit by the sun, drawn on by tireless searching, and preserve for them the Eternal values forged by many generations. And in the name of that new, future life, we, the seekers of the golden fleece, unfurl our flag:

Art is—eternal, because it is based on the immutable, on that which cannot be rejected.

Art is—indivisible, because its only source is the soul.

Art is—symbolic, because it bears within itself a symbol—the reflection of the Eternal in the temporal.

Art is—free, because it arises from a free, creative impulse.

PEREVAL
From the Editors

In undertaking this endeavor, the editorial staff cannot ignore the difficulty of its task—the unification of free art and free society.

When the principle of art as a free manifestation of the individual creative "I" was first enunciated in Russian literature, the protesting voices of the representatives of the ruling school (until now) of the utilitarian understanding of art rang out because they saw the distraction of efforts from serving the uses and demands of life in the affirmation of individual creativity.

The natural result of these attacks on the defenders of the individualistic movement is the aspiration to shut oneself up in a circle of purely personal experiences. Their aspiration to defend themselves even externally from the too straightforward servants of life has frequently turned into distancing oneself from life itself with its eternally throbbing pulse of society.

Both the conscious enemies of an individualistic understanding of art and those who didn't like it because they didn't understand it have used this period of reticence to cast aspersions about politically reactionary views on the bearers of the new art.

Their withdrawal from life was explained by a lack of sympathy with its progress, their silence as enmity.

For a number of years, Russian society has lived under the yoke of these prejudiced directions. But the critics' anathemas did not bother that, in which the grain of undying truth was concealed, from doing its own thing. The new conception of creativity blazed a path for itself and captured a firm and irremovable position in the history of Russian thought.

With its reorganization this time, society left the critics behind. Life, in its victorious march, turned out to be stronger than people. The fog of mutual alienation and mutual prejudice is dispersing little by little, and beyond it the consciousness that all who have risen in the name of the future are brothers is becoming more and more clear, be these brothers political activists, or destroyers of harmonious bourgeois morals, or defenders of the rights of free creativity in its struggle with civic tradition and congealed academism, or, finally, the romantic seekers of ultimate freedom outside all compulsory social forms. All roads lead to the City of the Sun, if their starting point is hatred of chains.

An elemental volcanic process has stirred Russian life to its very depths, and in a delirious onslaught all its creative forces, breaking and undermining the barriers, are making their way through, chest first.

But many stone walls and many granite idols stand in the way of freedom. Some of them suppress the development of life's forms, others defeat and mortify its very sources.

By coming out in support of the overthrow of the former, we consider unceasing work on the renewal of life's contents necessary. When the rotted forms collapse, people will remain, as before, petty bourgeois, if they continue to live in the circle of old ideas and old morality. An organic connection between the forms and contents of life exists, and for that reason, the bourgeois morality would return people to the previous yoke and render the matter of revolution null and void.

* * *

There is no enemy more cunning than despotism under all its guises; there is no struggle more difficult than against the power of dogmas. Often, too often, a fighter for freedom, without noticing it, turns out to be entangled in the nets of the sly enemy who has succeeded in stealthily surrounding him—has changed his mask—he has pretended to be other than what he is. And then the person who thought he was breaking the ancient chains becomes a forger of new chains and again the desired appearance of freedom recedes into the distance.

* * *

We will define *Pereval's* attitude toward all progressive political parties.

We consider the presence of parties advisable and necessary, except for the parties of the past, in the affairs of political construction. But recognizing the usefulness of party *work,* we reject the possibility of a party *world view.* On this level, from where every political system should represent only a step to the future, party spirit, no matter how imbued it is with noble incentives, is always a yoke and chains. The ideal of absolute ("estranged") freedom is an ideal that *rises above parties.*

* * *

In the area of social content articles, as well as in other areas, we will not place any prohibitions or boundaries for ourselves. We note only one limit for our activities—the idea that not serving the creative principle is unthinkable. Beyond this limit we will leave everything that comes from despotism.

* * *

And so, let our activity be imbued by the principle of freedom. We want to go all the way on the paths of freedom. And let our triple motto be: Philosophical, aesthetic, and social radicalism!

TRUDY I DNI
From the Editors

Trudy i dni posits a dual goal for itself. The first, *special* purpose of the journal is to facilitate the disclosure and affirmation of the principles of genuine Symbolism in the field of artistic creativity.

Its other more *general* purpose is to serve as the interpreter of the ideological connection that joins the multifaceted efforts of groups of artists and thinkers, united under the banner of *Musaget.*

In accordance with this dual goal, the journal consists of two parts.

In the first section, theoretical and critical articles devoted to general questions and separate phenomena of artistic creativity will find their place.

In the second—problems of contemporary and religio-moral consciousness, as well as aesthetical themes, studied in a general philosophical connection, will be worked out.

The object of the first section is the development and deepening of those artistic quests which, independent of *all* phenomena of so-called "modernism," first distinguish themselves as the *Symbolist* school of art, in the true meaning of this word, not binding itself in a relationship of subordination, not by affirmation of preeminence by formulas or slogans elaborated in the last decades of the past century. Conscious of itself as primarily *Russian,* this Symbolist school stresses not the partial and only formal connection of our newest artistic creativity with its contemporary Western currents, but its internal, organic connection with the primordial precepts of our original poetry that have not been understood or have been only superficially interpreted in their time.

The object of the second, general section is the selection of materials that serve to coordinate the different aspirations of art, scientific thought, and religious consciousness, and to define the points of intersection of these aspirations in the ideal of true culture, as an organic integrity of world view and life-creation—of culture as a realized synthesis. Since *Musaget* affirms in culture not a system of only relative values, but seeks its basis in absolute reality and in the goals of such a basis, systematically grouping conclusions of artistic self-determination, philosophical, historic, and religious thought—the second section of *Trudy i dni* is for it an organ of synthesizing review and summarizing—which directly combines both sections into one ideological unity.

This unity is conditioned by the consciousness that Symbolism, properly understood and realized, is promoted in art by the same principle of properly understood cultural building, which is symbolic by its essence:

"everything transitory," in Goethe's words, being "only a likeness," it is justified by the faithfulness of the likeness, the correspondence of its symbolic image to the eternal realities of universal Truth.

NOTES

On the Reasons for the Decline, and the New Currents, in Contemporary Russian Literature

Page 17   The work translated here was written in 1892 and first published as part of a book in St. Petersburg in 1893. The excerpt is from the fourth chapter," The Beginnings of a New Idealism in the Works of Turgenev, Goncharov, Dostoevsky, and Tolstoy," pp. 37-43. The book deals with a broad range of topics, from Russian poetry and culture to critics, from major and minor writers to the press, honoraria, and editors and publishers, most of which is devoted to the Russian literary scene of the 19th century, with the exception of the pages translated.

Page 17   *Carlyle*—Thomas Carlyle (1785-1881). British historian and essayist.

Page 18   *Zola*—Emile Zola (1840-1902), leading French Naturalist author; the works mentioned by Merezhkovsky are the Rougon-Macquart series of novels (1871-93); *Nana* (1880), *Pot-Bouille* (*The Stockpot*, 1882), and *Débâcle* (1892).

Page 18   *Huret*—Jules Huret (1864-1915), author of *Enquête sur l'évolution littéraire* (*Inquiry into the Evolution of Literature*, 1891).

Page 19   *Insulted and humiliated*—a reference to a novel by Dostoevsky by the same name, *Unizhyonnye i oskorblyonnye*, 1861.

Page 19   *Loti*— Pierre Loti (1850-1923), French author.

Page 19   *Goethe*—Goethe's *Gespräche mit Eckermann* (*Conversations with Eckermann*) were published first in three parts from 1836 to 1848.

Page 20   *Alcestis*—wife of King Admetus of Thessaly.

Page 20   *Antigone*—daughter of King Oedipus of Thebes; cf. Sophocles' plays *Oedipus Rex* and *Antigone*.

Page 20   *Ibsen, Doll's House, Ghosts*—Ibsen's plays, *Et Dukkehjem* and *Gengangere*, 1879 and 1881, respectively.

Page 20   *Madame Bovary*—a novel by Gustave Flaubert (1821-1889), published in 1857.

Page 20   *"Any thought..."*—a quotation from a poem by F. I. Tyutchev (1803-1873), "Silentium!" ("Silence!" 1833), one of the Symbolists' favorite lines from Russian literature. Cf. the beginning of Ivanov's essay, page 143.

Page 20   *Schwankende Gestalten*—literally, vascillating figures or characters. Merezhkovsky is referring to the first line of Goethe's *Faust*, where he introduces the "wavering apparitions" of his tragedy.

Russian Symbolists

Page 22   All three of the introductions to the issues of *Russian Symbolists* were written by Bryusov, despite his attempts to convince the reader otherwise.

Page 22   *Maslov*—one of the pseudonyms Bryusov used.

Page 22   *Stranger*—in Russian the stranger, another of Bryusov's inventions, is female.

Page 23   *Sar Peladan*—J. E. Peladan, French Symbolist author (1859-1918).

Page 23   *Mallarmé*—Stéphan Mallarmé (1842-1898), French poet, precursor of Symbolism.

Page 23   *Maeterlinck*—Maurice Maeterlinck (1862-1949), Belgian Symbolist author.
Page 24   *Gautier*—Théophile Gautier (1811-1872), French poet and critic.
Page 26   *Zoilus and Aristarchus*—here, negative and positive critics; the former lived from around 400 to 320 B.C., the latter from around 217 to 145 B.C.
Page 26   *Miropolsky*—pseudonym of A. Lang (died 1917), Russian author, friend of Bryusov and co-author of parts of *Russian Symbolists.*
Page 26   *Romances without Words*—a book of poems by Paul Verlaine; the book was published in 1875 and could be translated as *Romances without Words* or *Songs without Words (Romances sans paroles).*
Page 26   *Mey, Apukhtin, Fofanov*—Lev Mey (1822-1862), Aleksei Apukhtin (1841-1893), Konstantin Fofanov (1862-1911), minor writers.
Page 27   *Fet*—Afanasy Fet (1820-1892), one of the most important Russian poets of the second half of the nineteenth century.

Reviews of "Russian Symbolists"

Page 28   These reviews were first published in *Vestnik Evropy (The Messenger of Europe)*, No. 8 (1894), No. 1 (1895), pp. 421-424, and No. 10 (1895), pp. 847-851.
Page 28   *Mallarmé*—the quotation is from an untitled sonnet by Mallarmé.
Page 30   *Maslov, Bronin, Darov, Martov, Novich, Sozontov, Fuchs*—Some of these names Bryusov made up or took from real people (Maslov, Darov, Fuchs), others were pseudonyms of real people (Martov for Bugon, Novich for Bakhtin). See N. Gudzii's article "Iz istorii rannego russkogo simvolizma" ("From the History of Early Russian Symbolism"), in *Iskusstvo (Art)*, Vol. 3, book 4, pp. 180-218, for more information on these names.
Page 30   *Generatio aequivoca*—Latin, ambiguous propagation.
Page 32   *Tambov*—a topical reference to a decision made by a council in Tambov to support corporal punishment.
Page 320   *In jene Sphären...*—I don't dare lay claim to every sphere, a quotation slightly distorted, from Goethe's *Faust,* line 767.
Page 32   *Les Cshefs...*—correct title, *Chefs d'oeuvre,* a book of poems by Bryusov (1895).
Page 34   *Moon*—in Russian, there are two forms, *mesyats,* which is masculine, and *luna,* which is feminine.
Page 34   *Carrara*—a marble quarry in Italy.

An Elementary Statement about Symbolist Poetry

Page 38   This piece was first delivered as a lecture in Paris in the spring of 1900, later it was published in 1904 in Balmont's book *Gornye vershiny (Mountain Heights);* the excerpt is taken from pp. 75-79 and 94-95.
Page 40   *Prière*—prayer; a very free translation of the end of a poem called "Les litanies de Satan" ("The Litanies of Satan," pub. in 1857) by Charles Baudelaire (1821-1867).
Page 41   *Ariadne's thread*—Ariadne helped Theseus to find his way out of the Minotaur's labyrinth with her thread.

A Review of "Let's Be Like the Sun"

Page 43   The review first appeared in *Mir iskusstva,* Nos. 7-8, 1903, pp. 29-36. This translation is taken from that initial publication.

Page 44   *Fortunate is the person...* —from Tyutchev's "Tsitseron" ("Cicero," 1830).

Page 44   *I want to...* —from A. Dobrolyubov's "Na vecherinku uedinennuyu" ("At a secluded party," pub. 1900).

Page 45   *You and I were drunk...* —from Balmont's "Cheryomukha" ("Bird Cherry Tree," 1902).

Page 46   *Sleep, half-dead...* —from Balmont's "Pridorozhnye travy" ("Roadside Grasses," 1900).

Page 46   *Tropical flower...* —from Balmont's "Arum" (Spring, 1902).

Page 47   *Ocean...* —from Balmont's "Vozzvanie k okeanu" ("Appeal to the Ocean," pub. 1903).

Page 48   *I have seen the sun...* —from Balmont's "S morskogo dna" ("From the Bottom of the Sea," 1902).

Page 49   *I am the refinement...* —the first line of Balmont's untitled poem (1901).

Page 49   *On an airy ocean*—from Lermontov's "Demon" ("Demon," 1841).

Page 50   *Dehmel, D'Annunzio*— Richard Dehmel (1863-1920), German author; Gabriele D'Annunzio (1863-1938), Italian author.

Keys to the Mysteries

Page 52   The essay was first published in the initial issue of *Vesy*, No. 1 (1904) and was considered a programmatic expression of Symbolist theory; it was delivered as a lecture in Moscow in March, and again in Paris in April, 1903.

Page 52   *Derzhavin*—Gavriil Derzhavin (1743-1816), Russian poet; the reference about "lemonade" is from his ode "Felitsa," pub. 1783.

Page 52   *Pushkin*—Aleksandr Pushkin (1799-1837), Russia's greatest poet; the "cooking pot" statement is from Pushkin's "Poet i tolpa" (The Poet and the Crowd), 1828; the two lines quoted are from his "Ya pamyatnik sebe vozdvig nerukotvornyi" ("I Built a Monument for Myself" = the monument is his poetry), 1836.

Page 52   *Zhukovsky*—Vasily Zhukovsky (1783-1852), Russian poet and translator; Zhukovsky was compelled to change certain lines in Pushkin's "Monument" poem, because of the censors, when he published the poem after Pushkin's death.

Page 52   *Pisarev*—Dmitry Pisarev (1840-1868), Russian writer and critic; Bryusov is referring to Pisarev's article about Pushkin's lyrics in the book *Pushkin i Belinsky* (1865).

Page 52   *Korolenko*—Vladimir Korolenko (1853-1921), Russian author who was popular at the time.

Page 53   *Ruskin*—John Ruskin; see his *Lectures on Art*, delivered at Oxford University in 1870, especially the lecture "The Relation of Art to Use."

Page 53   *Suderman* and *Bourget*—G. Suderman (1857-1928), German dramatist, and P. Bourget (1852-1935), French Naturalist writer; both were quite popular in Russia at the time.

Page 53   *come lo specchio è maestro de' pittori*—"how the mirror is the teacher of the artists."

Page 54   *Zeuxis*—Greek painter (420-380 B.C.), who according to the legend painted grapes so realistically that birds pecked at them.

Page 54   *Guyau*—Jean-Marie Guyau (1854-1888), French philosopher; much of what Bryusov says later in his essay about Schiller and Spencer is lifted directly from the first pages of Guyau's *Les Problèmes de l'esthétique contemporaine*, 1884.

Page 55   *Pushkin*—the quotation is from Pushkin's unfinished novel in verse, "Ezersky" (1833).

Page 55   *Krylov*—Ivan Krylov (1768-1844), author of numerous fables; the one Bryusov
             has in mind is Krylov's "Krestianin i topor" ("The Peasant and the Ax"), 1816.

Page 56   *Pushkin*—the quotation is from Pushkin's "To Dawe Esqr" (The title is in
             English in the original), 1828.

Page 56   *Maykov*—Apollon Maykov (1821-1897), Russian poet, librarian, and censor;
             the quotation is from Maykov's "O tsarstvo vechnoy yunosti" ("O Kingdom of
             Eternal Youth"), 1883.

Page 56   *Baudelaire*—The quotation is from Baudelaire's "La Beauté" in his *Les Fleurs
             de mal* (*The Flowers of Evil,* 1857).

Page 56   *Thersites*—Greek warrior, depicted in less than favorable light in the *Iliad.*

Page 57   *Plyushkin*—unpleasant character in Gogol's *Dead Souls* (1841-42).

Page 57   *ultima coelestum*—"the last of the celestial bodies" (more correctly: *ultima
             caelestium*)

Page 57   *Pergamon*—a city in Greece; the altar (second century B. C.) was dedicated to
             Zeus and depicted mythological themes.

Page 57   *Ugolino*—Count Ugolino, a character in Dante's *Inferno* (Canto XXXIII).

Page 58   *Le beau c'est rare*—"Beauty is rare."

Page 58   *Pushkin*—the quotation is taken from Pushkin's novel in verse *Evgeny Onegin*
             (4, VIII), pub. as a book first in 1833.

Page 59   *Brown*—Thomas Brown (1778-1820), Scotish philosopher; see his *Lectures on
             the Philisophy of the Human Mind,* especially lecture LVII.

Page 60   the Greek word for "poet" can mean either poet or creator.

Page 61   *Spencer*—Herbert Spencer (1820-1903). The sentence is from a letter from
             Spencer to Guyau, which Bryusov cites directly from Guyau's book mentioned
             above.

Page 63   *Fet*—The reference to a "blue prison" is from Fet's "Pamyati N. Danilevs-
             kogo" (To the Memory of N. Danilevsky), written in 1886; the line quoted is
             from Fet's "Lastochki" (Swallows), 1885.

The five lines from Baudelaire's poem on page 68 could be translated thus:

I am beautiful, o mortals, as a dream of stone,
And my breast, where each has bruised himself in turn,
Was created to inspire a love for the poet
Eternal and silent as matter
. . . .
And I never cry and I never laugh.

A Holy Sacrifice

Page 65   First published in the first issue of *Vesy* for 1905, and often considered a
             "manifesto" of Symbolism.

Page 65   The epigraph is from Pushkin's poem "Poet" ("The Poet"), 1827.

Page 65   *Gautier*—the lines are from his poem "L'Art."

Page 66   *Parnasse*—a group of French writers; their main journal was *Le Parnasse
             Contemporain* (1866-76); they favored pure art, "art for art's sake."

Page 66   *We, who chisel...*—the quotation is from Verlaine's *Poèmes Saturniens*
             (1866), more specifically from the last poem of that collection.

Page 67   *Rops*—Felicien Rops (1833-1898), Belgian painter.

Page 67   *Gavarni*—pseudonym of Sulpice G. Chevalier (1804-1866), French artist.

Page 67   *Trophées*—a book by José-Maria de Heredia (1893), in English *Trophies.*

Page 67   *Arno Holz*—(1863-1929), German critic and poet.

Page 67   *Rodenbach*—Georges Rodenbach (1855-1898), Belgian Symbolist poet and novelist.

Page 68   *Yazykov*—Nikolai Yazykov (1803-1846), a poet of Pushkin's time; the quotation is from his "Poetu" ("To the Poet").

Page 68   *Baratynsky*—Evgeny Baratynsky (1800-1844, his last name is sometimes spelled Boratynsky), Russian poet; the line quoted is from his "Bokal" ("The Goblet").

Page 69   *Poe*—"The Imp of the Perverse" is the title of a story by Poe.

Decadence and Society

Page 70   This essay was written in late 1905 as an answer to Bely's article "Lug zelenyi" ("The Green Meadow"). It first appeared in No. 5 of *Vesy* for 1906, under the name of her husband, a fact which later scholars (Any Barda and Georgette Donchin, and even Temira Pachmuss) have not noticed. The essay was included in Gippius' *Literaturnyi dnevnik (Literary Diary),* published in 1908. The translation of "Society" for *obshchestvennost'* is consistent with the *Oxford English Dictionary*'s second entry for "society."

Page 70   *Nadson*—Semyon Ya. Nadson, a popular poet of the nineteenth century (1862-1887).

Page 71   *Herzen*—Aleksandr Ivanovich Herzen (1812-1870), Russian revolutionary leader and author.

Page 73   *Eunuchs*—a reference from Matthew 19:12.

Page 74   *Blok*—Gippius is referring to several poems by Blok from 1901 through 1903.

Page 75   *Meadow*—She refers to Bely's essay "Lug zelenyi," first published in the eighth issue of *Vesy* for 1905 and quotes (or distorts) several lines from that essay.

Page 75   *Tragic and bloody absurdity*—the Revolution of 1905.

Page 76   *Kay*—a personage in H. C. Andersen's *Snow Queen* (1844).

Page 76   *Seek ye the final kingdom*—Matthew 6:33.

A Review of Gippius' "Literary Diary"

Page 77   First published in *Vesy,* No. 3, 1908, later included in his *Arabeski* (A-rabesques), Moscow, 1911.

Page 77   *Anton Krayny*—because Gippius' pseudonym is masculine, Bely creates potential confusion by referring to her as *him* in the review; the masculine gender is dictated by *Krayny,* and Anton, both masculine names.

Page 78   *Emelyanov-Kokhansky*—Aleksandr N. Emelyanov (pseud. Kokhansky) was a very minor writer who published a little from 1890 to 1895.

Page 78   *Machtet*—Grigory A. Machtet (1852-1901), Russian writer.

Page 78   The German philosophers and scientists Bely lists are H. L. F. von Helmholtz (1821-1894), G. T. Fechner (1801-1887), J. I. Volkelt (1848-1930), Theodor Lipps (1851-1914), and W. Ostwald (1853-1932).

Balmont as a Lyric Poet

Page 80   This essay was first published in Annensky's first collection of essays, *Kniga otrazhenii (Book of Reflections,* 1906); the excerpt is from pages 171, 176-178, 179-183, 187, 190, 213.

Page 80   Annensky refers to Balmont's collections of verse *Goryashchie zdaniya* (*Burning Buildings*, 1900), *Budem kak solntse* (*Let's Be Like the Sun*, 1903), and *Tolko lyubov* (*Only Love*, 1903).

Page 82   *Exegi monumentum*—a reference to Horace's "Ode to Melpomene" or Pushkin's poem "Ya pamyatnik...," 1836.

Page 82   *Quintillian*—(ca. 35-100), Roman rhetoretician.

Page 82   *Vladimir, Churilo, Zabava*—references to heroes of Russian *byliny*, folk epic songs.

Page 82   *Pushkin*—the line is from his poem "Zaklinaniya" ("Invocations"), 1830.

Page 83   *The Ukrainian night is calm...*—a line from Pushkin's *Poltava* (1828-29).

Page 830   *I go out...*—the first line from Lermontov's poem (1841).

Page 85   *Albert*—Henri Albert (1869-1921); the quote is from his 1903 biography of Nietzsche, *Frédéric Nietzsche*.

The Veil of Isis

Page 86   First published in *Zolotoe runo*, No. 5, 1908, pp. 66-72.

Page 86   *Mallarmé*—the French poet died in 1898.

Page 86   *Remy de Gourmont*—(1858-1915), French critic and novelist.

Page 87   *Demeter*—Greek goddess of the harvest and fertility.

Page 87   *Symbalon*—lit., token for identification.

Page 87   *Universalia ante rem*—generalities before the thing, general before specific.

Page 88   *Je suis belle...*—a line from Baudelaire's "Beauté."

Page 88   *Musique...*—from Verlaine's "Art poétique" (1874).

Page 89   *Jules LaForgue*—(1860-1887), French Symbolist poet.

Page 89   *Tyutchev*—the line is from his untitled poem "Den' vechereet, noch' blizka" ("The day is drawing toward evening, night is near"), 1851.

Page 89   *Divagations*—a book by Mallarmé published in 1897, selections of prose.

Page 89   *Huysmans*—Joris-Karl Huysmans (1848-1907), French writer; his novel *A rebours* (1894), could be translated as *Against the Grain*.

Page 91   The gods and goddesses mentioned by Chulkov are Egyptian (Isis and Osiris), Phrygian (Axierus, Axiocersa, Axiocersus), Greek (Demeter, Persephone, Dionysus), and Roman (Ceres, Proserpina, Bacchus).

Page 95   *Hofmannsthal*—Hugo von Hofmannsthal (1874-1929), Austrian dramatist and poet.

Page 95   *Wedekind*—Frank Wedekind (1864-1918), German dramatist.

Page 96   *Bergson*—Henri Bergson (1859-1941), French philosopher; his *L'Evolution créatrice (Creative Evolution)* was published in 1907.

Symbolism and Contemporary Russian Art

Page 97   The essay was first published in the tenth issue of *Vesy* for 1908, under a slightly different title; then it appeared in Bely's collection of critical essays, *Lug zelenyi* (*The Green Meadow*, 1910).

Page 97   *Sanin*—a novel by M.P. Artsybashev, often considered pornographic by readers of the time.

Page 97   *Sergeev-Tsensky*—real name Sergei N. Sergeev (1875-1958), Russian Soviet writer.

Page 97   *L. Andreev*—Leonid N. Andreev (1871-1919), popular Russian writer.

Page 97   *O. Dymov*—real name Osip I. Perelman (1878-1959), Russian writer.

Page 98   *Pisemsky*—Aleksei F. Pisemsky (1821-1881) and Vasily Sleptsov (1836-1872).

Russian realist authors.

Page 98   *Gorodetsky*—Sergei M. Gorodetsky (1884-1967), Russian Soviet poet.

Page 100   *Gorky*—real name Aleksei M. Peshkov (1868-1936), important writer and public figure before and after the Revolution. His *Confession* was published in 1908.

Page 100   writers—A. I. Kuprin (1870-1938), whose "Duel" was published in 1905; Boris Zaitsev (1881-1972); V. V. Kamensky (1884-1961); E. N. Chirikov (1864-1932); A. M. Remizov (1877-1957); S. A. Ausländer (1886-1943); M. A. Kuzmin (1875-1936); Ivan A. Bunin (1870-1953), all Russian authors. Bunin was awarded the Nobel Prize for Literature in 1933.

Page 100   philosophers—Shestov's real name was L. I. Schwartzman (1866-1938); Minsky's real name was N. M. Vilenkin (1855-1937); A. P. Volynsky (Flekser, 1863-1926); V. V. Rozanov (1856-1919).

Page 100   publicists—D. V. Filosofov (1872-1940); N. A. Berdyaev (1874-1948); E. V. Anichkov (1866-1937); A. V. Lunacharsky (1875-1933).

Page 100   *Kozhevnikov*—Vladimir A. Kozhevnikov (?—1917), friend of Russian philosopher N. F. Fyodorov (1828-1903).

Page 100   *Znanie*—publishing group in St. Petersburg, 1898-1913; one of the leaders of this group was Gorky.

Page 100   *Essays of a Realistic World View*—a volume published in 1904.

Page 100   *Shipovnik*—a publishing house (1906-1918) associated with Symbolists and other writers.

Page 100   *A. Meyer*—Aleksandr Al. Meyer (1875-?).

Page 100   *authors... religion*—A. S. Volzhsky (real name Glinka, 1878-?); S. N. Bulgakov (1871-1944); P. A. Florensky (1882-1943); V. P. Sventsitsky (?-?); V. F. Ern (1882-1917).

Page 100   *Minsky, meonism*—"meonism" is a term that Minsky derived from Plato's dialogue *Sophist* and used with a general meaning of "a religion of non-being"; the poem about the proletariat, "Hymn of the Workers" (first line "Workers of the world, unite!"), was published by Minsky in 1905.

Page 101   *Yushkevich*—S. S. Yushkevich (1868-1927); his work *Jews (Evrei)* was published in 1903.

Page 101   *Inspector General*—a play by N. V. Gogol, pub. in 1836.

Page 101   *Mehring*—Franz Mehring (1846-1919), German politician and writer, author of *Geschichte der deutschen Sozialdemokratie* (1897/8).

Page 101   *Boborykin*—P. D. Boborykin (1836-1921), popular Russian writer at the time.

Page 101   *Moleschott, Avenarius*—Jacob Moleschott (1822-1893), physiologist, adherent of Materialism; Richard Avenarius (1843-1896), Swiss philosopher.

Page 106   *Privat-Sache*—private matter, personal affair.

Theater of One Will

Page 107   First published in *Kniga o novom teatre (A Book about the New Theater)*, 1908; an anthology of essays about theater by Sologub, Bely, Chulkov, Bryusov, and others.

Page 107   *Only the children...* —the first lines of an untitled poem by Sologub (1897).

Page 108   *Reed*—a reference to B. Pascal's *Pensées* (1669/70).

Page 109   *Aisa, Ananke*—both are taken from Greek notions about fate; *aisa* means fate or allotment; Ananke is fate, especially necessity, personified.

Page 111   *Chaliapin*—the Russian bass F. I. Chaliapin (1873-1938).

Page 111   *As a rebuke*...—the last lines from Sologub's poem "Kogda ya v burnom more plaval" ("When I sailed on a stormy sea"), 1902.

Page 112   *Moira*—another Greek word for fate, similar to *aisa*.

Page 117   *Shuysky and Vorotynsky*—historical figures from the "Time of Troubles" (1598-1613), an interregnum period in Russian history; this period has been treated in Russian literature by Pushkin, A. K. Tolstoy, and others.

Page 119   *Isadora Duncan*— (1878-1927), American dancer and innovator.

Page 120   *Gift of the Wise Bees*—the name of a play by Sologub (1907).

Page 120   *Wedekind*—Frank Wedekind's play *Awakening of Spring (Frülings Erwachen)* was published in 1891.

Peredonov's Little Tear

Page 122   First published in the newspaper *Rech(Speech)* in St. Petersburg, No. 273, 1908, later in an anthology edited by Sologub's wife, A. Chebotarevskaya, called *O Fyodore Sologube (About F. Sologub)*, 1911.

Page 122   *Bryusov poem*—"Z. N. Gippius" ("To Z. N. Gippius"), written in 1901.

Page 122   *Peredonov*—Ardalion Peredonov, the hero of Sologub's major contribution to Russian Symbolist prose, his novel *Melkii bes (The Petty Demon*, also called *The Shabby Demon*), written in 1902, partially published in *Voprosy zhizni* in 1905, first full publication 1907, second edition 1908.

Page 122   *Nedotykomka*—(lit. "don't touch") an imaginary person in Sologub's novel, the product of Peredonov's fantasy.

Page 124   *Fiveysky*—The hero of L. Andreev's novella *Zhizn Vasiliya Fiveyskogo (The Life of Vasily Fiveysky)*, published in 1904.

On Contemporary Lyrism

Page 127   The essay was originally published in three parts in the first three issues of *Apollon*, 1909, Nos. 1, 2, and 3. Annensky died in 1909, before finishing the final installment of the essay. This excerpt adds only a little to the abruptness of the essay, which was in part caused by the serialized nature of its publication.

Page 127   *Céladon*—a character in Honoré d'Urfé's novel, *Astrée (Astrea)*, 1610.

Page 127   *Robert de Souza*—the reference is to his *La poésie populaire et le lyrisme sentimental* (1899).

Page 127   *Paul Bourde*—(1851-1914), French author; *Le Temps = The Time.*

Page 127   *Jean Moréas*—(1856-1910), French author; *XIX siècle = 19th Century.*

Page 128   *Arthur Rimbaud*—Annensky is referring to Rimbaud's sonnet "Voyelles" ("Vowels"), 1871, in which the French poet relates A to black, E to white, I to red, O to blue, and U to green.

Page 128   *Kuzmin*—Mikhail Kuzmin (1875-1936), Russian author, close to both Symbolist and Acmeist groups.

Page 129   *Voloshin*—Maksimilian A. Kirienko-Voloshin (1877-1932), Russian poet and artist.

Page 129   *Peplos*—title of a poem by Bryusov published in 1901.

Page 130   *Sabazius*—Thraco-Phrygian god associated with Dionysus and Jupiter.

Page 131   *Peter*—Peter the Great; Blok's poem is about the statue of Peter the Great in Leningrad.

Page 131   *Paeon*—a paeon is a foot with four syllables; a fourth paeon would have the stress on the last of the four syllables, a second would have it on the second syllable, and so forth.

Page 131   *Drawling, beck'ning*—the words have been changed to illustrate the metrics Annensky is describing.

Page 132   *Stecchetti*—Lorenzo Stecchetti (1845-1916), Italian poet.

Page 132   *Mälar*—a lake in Sweden.

Page 133   *Cheboksary*—a city on the Volga River.

Page 133   *Sully-Prudhomme*—René-François-Armand Prudhomme (1839-1907), French oet.

Page 133   *Light of Asia*—an epic poem about Buddha (1879) by Sir Edwin Arnold (1832-1904).

Page 134   *Francis Jammes*—(1868-1938), French author.

Page 134   *Tantalus*—a play by V. Ivanov (1905).

Page 134   *Henri de Régnier*—(1864-1936), French writer; *or* = gold, *mort* = death.

Page 135   *Pushkin*—the quotation is from his *Pikovaya dama (Queen of Spades)*, 1834.

Page 135   *Benois*—Alexander Benois (1870-1960), Russian painter, one of the founders of the *Mir iskusstva* group.

Page 135   *Corbière, Rollinat, Verhaeren*—Tristan Corbière (1845-1875), French poet, Maurice Rollinat (1846-1903), French poet, Emile Verhaeren (1855-1916), Belgian poet and critic.

Page 135   *Lutetia*—or Lutecia, Roman name for Paris.

Page 135   *Martial*—Roman poet (40-100 A. D.).

Page 136   *Balmont, Mexico*—Balmont traveled to Mexico in 1905.

Page 136   *Bryusov*—the two quotations are from two poems by him both titled "Fabrichanya" ("A Factory Song"), one written in 1900, the other in 1901.

Page 137   *Ilovaysky*—Dmitry I. Ilovaysky (1832-1920), Russian historian, wrote history texts for high school; Shipka refers to a battle between Russian and Turkish forces at Shipka Pass in Bulgaria, 1878.

Page 136   *Tolstoy*—*Vlast tmy* (The Power of Darkness), written in 1886.

Page 136   *Cyrano de Bergerac*—(1619-1655), French writer.

Page 136   *Gérard de Nerval*—(1808-1855), French writer.

Page 136   *Shevchenko*—Taras Shevchenko (1814-1861), Ukrainian poet and artist.

Page 139   *Heredia*—José-Maria de Heredia (1842-1905), French poet.

Page 140   *Pushkin*—the quotation is from his poem "K***" ("To*** [A. P. Kern]").

Page 140   *Kreutzer Sonata*—a short story by L. N. Tolstoy, pub. in 1891.

Page 140   *Anfisa*—a drama by Leonid Andreev, pub. in 1909.

Page 141   *Makovsky*—Sergei K. Makovsky (1878-1962), Russian poet and critic.

Page 141   *Poliksena Solovyova*—(1887-1924), Russian poet, pseudonym Allegro.

Page 142   *Charon*—the ferryman who took people to Hades.

Page 142   *Oní* and *oné*—at that time it was possible to distinguish masculine and feminine personal pronouns in the plural; *oní* as used by Annensky refers to male poets, *oné* to female poets. In contemporary Russian "they" is represented only by *oní*.

The Precepts of Symbolism

Page 143   The essay was first delivered as a lecture in Moscow and St. Petersburg during March, 1910; it was first published in *Apollon*, No. 8, 1910. The translation is taken from the first publication; the essay was later published in *Furrows and Boundaries (Borozdy i mezhi)* in a slightly different form.

Page 143   *Tyutchev*—"Any thought . . . ," "express . . . ," "Breaking out . . . ," all are from Tyutchev's poem "Silentium!" ("Silence!"), pub. 1833.

Page 144   *Quaternio terminorum*—here, four boundaries or four limits.

Page 144   *O my prophetic soul*—the first line of a poem by Tyutchev, untitled, pub. in 1857.

Page 144   *Novalis*—the reference here is to Novalis' *Hymnen an die Nacht (Hymns to the Night),* collected poems published in 1800.

Page 144   *"Are they not inimical?" "He tears away," "There is a certain . . . ,"*—quotations from Tyutchev's poems "Smotri kak zapad razgorelsya" ("Look how the west has caught on fire"; 1838), "O chem ty voesh, vetr nochnoy?" ("What are you howling about, night wind"; 1836), and "Videnie" ("Vision"; 1829), respectively.

Page 145   *Noumenal, phenomenal*—in Kant's view, something that is noumenal exists by itself, independent of human senses *(ding an sich);* something that is phenomenal is perceived or sensed.

Page 145   *"The gods agitate . . . ,"*—also from Tyutchev's "Videnie."

Page 145   *"Night falls . . . ," "The heavenly vault . . . "*—quotations from Tyutchev's "Kak okean obemlet shar zemnoy" ("How the ocean embraces the earthly sphere"; 1830).

Page 146   *Swan*—the quotation is from Tyutchev's "Lebed" ("Swan"; 1839).

Page 146   *"How can the heart express itself?"*—from Tyutchev's "Silentium!"

Page 146   *"The game . . . "*—from Tyutchev's poem "Vesna"("Spring"; 1839).

Page 147   *Asteria*—Asteria, according to Greek legend, was the sister of Leto and the mother of Hecate; she was supposed to have turned into a quail and eventually into the island of Delos.

Page 147   *Scamandrius*—also known as Astyanax, son of Hector.

Page 147   *Heraclitus, Eleatic School*—Heraclitus was a Greek philosopher who lived during the sixth century B. C.; the Eleatic school of philosophy flourished from the sixth to the fifth centuries B. C., primarily in Elea (a town in Italy).

Page 000   *doxa*—literally, opinion or judgment.

Page 147   *meon*—Ivanov seems to be using this term in a different sense than Minsky's meonism. See the earlier note about this term in Bely's 1908 article.

Page 147   *Rickert*—Heinrich Rickert (1863-1936), German philosopher.

Page 147   *Pater est bonus*—father is good.

Page 148   *Poet and Crowd*—a poem by Pushkin; see the note for the third Bryusov essay. The last lines of the essay are these by Pushkin again.

Page 149   *remata*—literally, words, something spoken.

Page 150   *Evening Lights*—a collection of poems by Afanasy Fet, published in four editions in 1883, 85, 88, and 91.

Page 150   *Zhukovsky*—see the note for the third Bryusov essay.

Page 151   *Nur ein Gleichnis*—a quotation from the second part of Goethe's *Faust,* lines 12104-05.

Page 152   *Correspondances*—a reference to Baudelaire's poem by the same name from *Les fleurs du mal,* 1857.

Page 152   *Argonauts*—a reference to a group of young Symbolists, headed by Andrei Bely, which thrived during the first few years of this century.

Page 152   *"Zum höchsten Dasein . . . "*—another quotation from the second part of *Faust,* line 4685.

Page 152   *Vrubel*—see the notes to the Blok essay.

Page 152   *War and liberation*—references to the Russo-Japanese war of 1904-05 and the unsuccessful revolution of 1905.

Page 152   *Golconda*—a symbol of riches, from a former city in India.

Page 152   *Ashes*—Bely's second volume of poetry, 1909.

Page 152   *Gorgon*—here a reference to Medusa.

Page 152   *Paladin*—Aleksandr Blok, who wrote numerous poems to and about the Beautiful Lady.

Page 152   *No, Yes*— from a poem by Ivanov, "Ognenostsy" ("Fire-bearers"; 1906).

Page 153   *Dobrolyubov*—see the notes for the second Bely essay.

Page 154   *Fiat*—literally, "let it be done."

Page 154   *Word, flesh*—cf. John 1:14.

Page 154   *Sun of the world*—the quotation is from Fet's poem "Izmuchen zhiznyu, kovarstvom nadezhdy" ("Tormented by life, by the cunning of hope"; 1883).

Page 155   *Maenad*—the paragraph relates to and contains a quotation from Ivanov's poem "Menada" ("Maenad," written in 1905, pub. in 1911).

Page 155   *Veniat*—"let it come."

Page 155   *"A wedding band fell"*—a quotation from Ivanov's "Ognenostsy."

Page 155   *"I wear a ring"*—a quotation from Ivanov's poem "Krasota" ("Beauty"; 1903).

Page 155   *Until now Symbolism has complicated life and complicated art*—Ivanov quotes the following passage from Blok's *Liricheskie dramy* (*Lyrical Dramas;* 1908) at this point: "In contemporary literature the lyrical element, it seems, is the most powerful... The most that lyric poetry can accomplish is to complicate experiences, encumbering the soul with unimaginable chaos and complexity."

On the Present Status of Russian Symbolism

Page 157   This essay was first presented as a lecture on April 8, 1910; it was later published in the journal *Apollon*, No. 8 (1910) and appeared as a book (brochure) in Petrograd in 1921.

Page 157   The lecture by V. Ivanov was delivered on March 26, 1910, and appeared in the same issue of *Apollon*.

Page 157   *Great Noon*—this is probably a reference to F. Nietzsche's *der grosse Mittag* in *Also sprach Zarathustra* (1883-84).

Page 157   *Fet*—the quotation is taken from his poem "Kak moshki zaryoyu" ("Like gnats at dawn"), 1844.

Page 158   *Bryusov*—the quotation is from Bryusov's poem "Tsaryu Severnogo polyusa" ("To the King of the North Pole"), 1900; the "king" is F. Nansen, Norwegian explorer.

Page 158   *Sologub*—the quotation is from Sologub's poem "Ya bog tainstvennogo mira" ("I am the god of the mysterious world"), 1902.

Page 158   *Blue flower*—the *Blaue Blume* of Novalis, a symbol of Romantic poetry.

Page 158   *Solovyov*—the quotation is from his "Tri svidaniya" ("Three Meetings"), 1898. The poetry quoted on page 159 is from Solovyov's "Iyunskaya noch na Sayme" ("June Night on Lake Saimaa"), 1896.

Page 159   *Vrubel*—Mikhail Vrubel (1856-1910), Russian painter; he painted a series of pictures for Lermontov's "Demon" from 1890 to 1902; the picture of the *Tsarevna-lebed* ("Swan-Princess") was done in 1900; Vrubel was plagued by madness (mentioned by Blok later in essay) in 1902, and by blindness in 1906; he died on April 1, 1910 (old style).

Page 160   *Puppet show*— in Russian *balagan*, cf. Blok's play *Balaganchik (The Puppet Show),* first performed in 1906.

Page 160   *Moment*—cf. *Faust:* "Werd ich zun Augenblicke sagen: / Verweile doch..." lines 1699-1700.

Page 160   *Stranger*—in Russian, *Neznakomka,* cf. Blok's poem by the same title, written in 1906.

Page 160   *The Earth in Snow* and *Unexpected Joy*—collections of Blok's poetry, published in 1908 and 1907, respectively.

Page 161   *Eros*—collection of poetry by V. Ivanov, published in 1907.

Page 161   *Russian revolution*—the reference is to the abortive revolution of 1905.

Page 161   *Nekrasov*—Nikolai Nekrasov (1821-1877), leading Russian "civic" poet of the last half of the nineteenth century.

Page 162   *The Song of Fate*—a play by Blok, written in 1908, later revised and published as a book.

Page 162   *Bryusov*—the quotation is from Bryusov's poem "Poetu" ("To the Poet"), 1908.

Page 163   *Solovyov*—the quotation is from Solovyov's poem "Poetu-otstupniku" ("To the Poet-Apostate"), 1885.

Page 163   *Lermontov, Gogol, Komissarzhevskaya*—Lermontov died in a duel ("submitted himself to the pistol"); the reference to N. V. Gogol (1809-1852) burning himself may relate to the burning of the second part of his major novel, *Dead Souls,* shortly before his death; V. F. Komissarzhevskaya (1864-1910) was a major Russian actress at the time; she set up her own theater, where Blok's *Balaganchik* was first performed, and died on February 10 (old style), two months before Blok delivered the lecture.

Page 163   *Carrière*—Eugene Carrière (1849-1906), French painter.

Page 164   *Verses about the Beautiful Lady*—a collection of Blok's poems, published in 1904 (October); the title page has 1905.

Page 164   The quotation in Greek that refers to Cleopatra can be translated as "Queen of queens."

Page 164

Reading Gaol—Oscar Wilde's "The Ballad of Reading Gaol" (1898); the quotation is the second stanza of the poem.

Page 165   *Lermontov*—the quotation is from Lermontov's poem, "Demon" (1829-41).

Page 165   *Santa conversazione*—there is no mistake in the singular (in Italian) and Blok's plural nouns; Blok is referring to a painting by Giovanni Bellini (1430?-1516) in the Uffizi.

Page 165   *Beato*—Beato Fra Angelico (1387-1455), Italian painter.

Page 165   *Signorelli*—Luca Signorelli (1441-1523), Italian painter; painted frescoes in the chapel of San Brizio in Orvieto (1499-1505), 'not exactly the twilight of Signorelli's years. Blok mentions these Italians because he had been in Italy in 1909 and had written poems about them (mostly from the summer of 1909).

About "Servile Speech," In Defense of Poetry

Page 166   This is a reply to the essays by V. Ivanov and A. Blok published in the eighth issue of *Apollon* (1910); Bryusov's essay appeared in the next (ninth) issue of *Apollon* that same year.

Page 166   *Krylov*—the reference is to a fable by Ivan Krylov entitled "The Musicians" ("Muzikanty," 1808).

Page 167   *F. Vielé-Griffin*—French Symbolist poet (1864-1937).

Page 167   *George*—Stefan George (1868-1933), German Symbolist poet.

Page 168   *Rossetti*—Dante G. Rossetti (1828-1882), English poet and painter.

Page 168   *Duma*—a Russian parliamentary body that existed from 1906 to 1917.

Page 168   *Alexander the Great*—the reference here is to a legend about Alexander the Great and the oracle at Delphi.

A Wreath or a Crown

Page 170   First published in *Apollon,* No. 11, 1910, as a reply to Bryusov's response to the essays by Ivanov and Blok.

Page 170   The first quotation in the epigraph is from Bryusov's article "A Holy Sacrifice," the second is from Bryusov's poem "Gimn" ("Hymn"), 1902.

Page 174   *Parisian Dialogue*—a piece by J. L. Charpentier that had appeared in *Apollon*,
No. 9, 1910.

Symbolism and the Future

Page 175   This work first appeared as the concluding chapter to Ellis' book *Russkie
simvolisty (Russian Symbolists)*, pp. 319-336; the excerpt is from pages 319-
327. Previous chapters in the book deal with the essence of Symbolism,
Balmont, Bryusov, and Bely.

Page 175   *Clarism*—alternate name for Acmeism, which was indeed in vogue in 1910 and
for a few years thereafter.

Page 176   *Res, realiora, Ens realissimum*—Thing, higher realities, and the existence or
entity of the most real.

Page 177   *Reappraisal of all values*—a reference to Nietzsche, in German *Umvertung
aller Werte*.

Page 180   *Ahasuerus*—King Ahasuerus in the Book of Esther.

Page 180   *Egypt, Canaan, burning pillar*—references from Genesis 12 and 13.

Thoughts about Symbolism

Page 181   This article first appeared in *Trudy i dni*, No. 1, 1912, pp. 3-10. The translation
here is taken from the original publication.

Page 181   *I met a shepherd . . .* —a poem from Ivanov's *Kormchie zvezdy (Guiding Stars)*,
1903.

Page 181   *Ut pictura poësis*—poetry is like painting.

Page 181   *Simonides*—Greek poet, ca. 556-467 B. C.

Page 181   *Horace*—Latin poet, ca. 65-8 B. C.

Page 182   *Jacob's Ladder*—a reference to a ladder seen by Jacob in Genesis 28:12.

Page 182   *Pur che il terzo . . .* —So that the third be present,
And that this third be Love.

Page 183   *Ictus*—in poetics, the place of the stress in a foot or syllable.

Page 184   *Ieros logos*—sacred word; *mythos*—myth.

Page 185   *Poëtae nascuntur*—poets are being born.

Page 185   *Lermontov*—The poems are the untitled "Iz-pod tainstvennoy kholodnoy
polumaski" ("From beneath the mysterious, cold demi-mask"), and the poem
"Est rechi—znachenie" ("There is a meaning for speech"), 1839.

Page 186   *Hesiod*—Greek poet of the eighth century B. C.

Page 187   *Mallarmé*—see the lines of his poetry quoted by Vl. Solovyov.

Page 187   *A realibus . . .* —From the real to the higher reality. Through the real to the
higher reality.

Page 187   *Tyutchev*—the poem is from the untitled "Yarkii sneg siyal v doline" ("Bright
snow shone in the valley"), 1836.

A Speech about Symbolism

Page 189   This essay was originally conceived as a lecture that was delivered in January,
1914, at a public "dispute" about contemporary literature. It was not really a
dispute but statements by Symbolists and other authors of their various points
of view. The stenographic recording of Sologub's speech was published in the
journal *Zavety (Precepts)*, 1914, No. 2, part 2.

Page 191   *Rukavishnikov*—Ivan Sergeevich Rukavishnikov (1877-1930), Russian writer. What Sologub has in mind when he speaks of Rukavishnikov's *Iron Family* is Rukavishnikov's novel *Accursed Family (Proklyatyi rod),* first published in 1911.

SELECTED BIBLIOGRAPHY

Books listed here which have extensive bibliographies devoted to individual authors and/or to Symbolism in general are marked with an asterisk.

I. General

English

*Donchin, Georgette. *The Influence of French Symbolism on Russian Poetry.* The Hague, 1958.

Mirsky, Dmitry. *Contemporary Russian Literature: 1881-1925.* New York, 1926.

Peterson, Ronald E. *A History of Russian Symbolism, 1892-1917* (forthcoming).

Poggioli, Renato. *The Poets of Russia: 1890-1930.* Cambridge, Mass., 1960.

Senelick, Laurence. *Russian Dramatic Theory from Pushkin to the Symbolists.* Austin, 1981 (contains seven essays by Symbolists, including Sologub's "The Theater of a Single Will").

Slonim, Marc. *From Chekhov to the Revolution: Russian Literature: 1900-1917.* New York, 1962.

West, T. G. *Symbolism: An Anthology.* London, 1980 (contains one essay each by Bely and Blok, including "On the Present State . . . ").

German

*Holthusen, Johannes. *Studien zur Ästhetik und Poetik des russischen Symbolismus.* Göttingen, 1957.

Stepun, Fedor. *Mystische Weltschau.* München, 1964.

*Wytrzens, Günther. *Bibliographie der russischen Autoren und anonymen Werke.* Frankfurt a/M, 1975. This bibliography provides a basic introduction to books by and about the Symbolists, among others.

Russian

Literaturnoe nasledstvo. Simvolizm. Nos. 27-28, Moskva, 1937.

Literaturnoe nasledstvo. Valery Bryusov. No. 85, Moskva, 1976.

Literaturnoe nasledstvo. Aleksandr Blok. No. 92, Moskva, 1980.

Brodsky, N. L. et al. *Literaturnye manifesty ot simvolizma do oktyabrya.* Moskva, 1929.

Byalik, B. A., gen. editor. *Russkaya literatura kontsa XIX—nachala XX veka.* Moskva, 1968-1972.

Mikhaylovsky, B. V. *Russkaya literatura XX veka: s devyanostykh godov XIX veka do 1917 g.* Moskva, 1939.

II. Individual Authors

(This listing is mainly limited to books in English of a general nature.)

Annensky

*Setchkarev, Vsevolod. *Studies in the Life and Work of Innokentij Annenskij.* The Hague, 1963.

Balmont

Markov, Vladimir. "Balmont: A Reappraisal," *Slavic Review.* 28 (1969) 221-264.
*Schneider, Hildegard. *Der frühe Bal'mont.* München, 1970.

Bely

Christa, Boris, ed. *Andrey Bely Centenary Papers.* Amsterdam, 1980.
Elsworth, J. D. *Andrey Bely.* Letchworth, Hertfordshire, 1972.
Elsworth, J. D. *Andrey Bely: A Critical Study of the Novels.* Cambridge, 1983.
Janeček, Gerald, ed. *Andrey Bely: A Critical Review.* Lexington, Ky., 1978.
*Maslenikov, Oleg. *The Frenzied Poets: Andrey Biely and the Russian Symbolists.* Berkeley and Los Angeles, 1952.
Mochulsky, Konstantin. *Andrei Bely: His Life and Work,* trans. N. Szalavitz. Ann Arbor, 1977.

Blok

*Hackel, Sergei. *The Poet and the Revolution: Aleksandr Blok's The Twelve.* Oxford, 1975.
*Kemball, Robin. *Alexander Blok: A Study in Rhythm and Metre.* The Hague, 1965.
Kisch, Sir Cecil. *Alexander Blok: Prophet of Revolution.* London, 1960.
Orlov, Vladimir. *Hamayun: The Life of Alexander Blok,* trans. O. Shartse. Moscow, 1980.
Pyman, Avril. *The Life of Aleksandr Blok.* Oxford, 1979-1980.
*Reeve, Franklin. *Aleksandr Blok: Between Image and Idea.* New York, 1962.
Vickery, Walter, ed. *Aleksandr Blok Conference.* Columbus, Ohio, 1984.

Bryusov

*Grossman, Joan, ed. *The Diary of Valery Bryusov.* Berkeley, 1980.
Grossman, Joan. *Valery Bryusov and the Riddle of Russian Decadence.* Berkeley, 1985.
*Rice, Martin. *Valery Briusov and the Rise of Russian Symbolism.* Ann Arbor, 1975.

Ellis

Grechishkin, S. S., and A. V. Lavrov. "Ellis—poet-simvolist, teoretik, i kritik." *XXV Gertsenovskie chteniia. Lit. otdel.* Leningrad, 1972, pp. 59-62.

Gippius

*Matich, Olga. *Paradox in the Religious Poetry of Zinaida Hippius.* München, 1972.
*Pachmuss, Temira. *Zinaida Hippius: An Intellectual Profile.* Carbondale, Ill., 1971.
*Zlobin, Vladimir. *A Difficult Soul: Zinaida Gippius,* ed. Simon Karlinsky. Berkeley, 1980.

Ivanov

Deschartes, Olga. Introduction to Ivanov's *Sobranie sochinenii,* Vol. I. Brussels, 1971, pp. 7-227 (in Russian).
*West, James. *Russian Symbolism: A Study of Vyacheslav Ivanov and the Russian Symbolist Aesthetic.* London, 1970.

Merezhkovsky

*Bedford, C. Harold. *The Seeker: D. S. Merezhkovsky.* Lawrence, Kansas, 1975.
Hippius, Zinaida. *Dmitry Merezhkovsky.* Paris, 1951 (in Russian).
*Rosenthal, Bernice. *D. S. Merezhkovsky and the Silver Age: The Development of a Revolutionary Mentality.* The Hague, 1975.

Sologub

*Hansson, Carola. *Fedor Sologub as a Short-Story Writer: Stylistic Analyses.* Stockholm, 1975.
*Rabinowitz, Stanley. *Sologub's Literary Children: Keys to a Symbolist's Prose.* Columbus, Ohio, 1980.

Solovyov

Cioran, Samuel. *Vladimir Solov'ev and the Knighthood of the Divine Sophia.* Waterloo, 1977.
*Knigge, Armand. *Die Lyrik Vl. Solov'evs und ihre Nachwirkung bei A. Belyj und A. Blok.* Amsterdam, 1973.